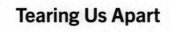

Tearing Us Apart

TEARING US APART

How **Abortion** Harms Everything and **Solves Nothing**

Ryan T. Anderson
Alexandra DeSanctis

Regnery Publishing
WASHINGTON, D.C.

Regnery® is a registered trademark and its colophon is a trademark of Salem Communications Holding Corporation

Cataloging-in-Publication data on file with the Library of Congress

ISBN: 978-1-68451-350-5
eISBN: 978-1-68451-354-3

Published in the United States by
Regnery Publishing
A Division of Salem Media Group
Washington, D.C.
www.Regnery.com

Manufactured in the United States of America

10 9 8 7 6 5 4 3 2 1

Books are available in quantity for promotional or premium use. For information on discounts and terms, please visit our website: www.Regnery.com.

For my children, my greatest joy

—Ryan T. Anderson

For my parents, who gave me the gift of life

—Alexandra DeSanctis

CONTENTS

Introduction

On June 23, 1984, abortionist Dr. Anthony Levatino experienced a tragedy: his five-year-old daughter Heather died after being hit by a car. Levatino took some time off work to grieve his daughter's death, and when he returned, something had changed. Here's how he described his experience of going back to work as an abortionist:

> One day it was my turn to perform a second trimester abortion. As I started the procedure, I inserted a clamp and ripped out the baby's arm. Then I paused for what seemed like forever, staring at the arm in the clamp. A procedure I had done over a hundred times before suddenly made me ill.
>
> At that moment, the only thing that mattered was the innocent child whose life I had just ended. I lost my child, someone who was very precious to us. And now I am taking somebody's child and I am tearing him right out of their womb. I am killing somebody's child. That day

marked the beginning of my journey from abortionist to pro-life advocate.[1]

"All of a sudden, I didn't see the patient's wonderful right to choose," Levatino said in a 2011 interview. "All I saw was somebody's son or daughter."[2] Within eight months of his daughter's death, Levatino quit performing abortions. "A change had come that I couldn't take back. Once you finally realize that killing a baby at 20 weeks is wrong, then it doesn't take too long to figure out that killing a baby of any size is wrong," he said.[3]

Levatino is far from the first abortionist to experience a wake-up call exposing abortion as a gravely unjust act that takes the life of an unborn human being. In the 1960s and 1970s, the late Dr. Bernard Nathanson presided over, by his own admission, more than sixty thousand abortions as director of the Center for Reproductive and Sexual Health. Prior to his pro-life conversion, Nathanson performed five thousand abortions himself, one of which took the life of his own child.[4] In addition to being an abortionist, Nathanson was an activist who led the movement to overturn laws protecting the unborn. He cofounded the National Association for the Repeal of Abortion Laws (NARAL), today known as NARAL Pro-Choice America. He assisted the legal team that challenged the Texas abortion law at stake in *Roe v. Wade*, the 1973 Supreme Court case that invented a constitutional right to abortion.

Thankfully, Nathanson experienced a profound change of heart, sparked by the realization that the creature in the womb is a human being. In 1974, he admitted the "increasing certainty that I had in fact presided over sixty thousand deaths."[5] Over the subsequent years, Nathanson performed fewer and fewer abortions, limiting himself only to abortions he considered necessary for "health" reasons. But with the advent of medical technology such as the ultrasound, he found that he could no longer deny the humanity of the unborn child.

By 1980, he quit performing abortions altogether. He went on to become one of the foremost leaders of the pro-life movement and produced a landmark documentary, *The Silent Scream*, which used ultrasound footage to depict the abortion of a twelve-week-old child in the womb.

The horrific reality of abortion has the power to change people's lives and transform even the most hardened hearts. But despite the irrefutable reality of human life in the womb and the indisputable violence of abortion, we live in a society that permits abortion until birth for virtually any reason. We live in a society where many people believe that abortion is unobjectionable or even good. Since the Supreme Court invented a constitutional right to abortion in *Roe v. Wade* in 1973, abortion has killed more than sixty-five million of our youngest neighbors, a staggering loss. As we write, the Supreme Court is considering *Dobbs v. Jackson Women's Health Organization*, a case that could lead to the reversal of *Roe* and subsequent cases that have made it nearly impossible to legally prohibit abortion. If the Court does reverse *Roe*, it would be a major victory for the pro-life movement in the United States, which has argued for decades that we must alter the legal, political, and cultural frameworks enabling abortion.

Pro-lifers insist that every human being has intrinsic worth and value, and that a just society would protect the unborn from the lethal violence of abortion. By the time this book is in your hands, we will all know how the Court has ruled. No matter what the justices do, the pro-life movement must continue its work to ensure that every life is protected by law and welcomed in life, and that every mother and family receives the assistance needed to bring children into the world and raise them to maturity. This book is meant to equip readers to defend life as the pro-life movement looks to the future.

While it's essential to focus on the unborn child—whose death is the gravest harm of abortion—there's much more that needs to be said, because abortion harms far more than the child in the womb. The case against abortion is far more comprehensive. Abortion harms every single one of us by perpetuating deeply rooted falsehoods about what it means to be human. Abortion attacks the humanity and value of the child in the womb. Abortion strikes at the bond between mother and child, turning it into a conflict between adversaries and a justification for violence, a relationship not of love but of antagonism and mutual destruction. Abortion corrupts the relationship between man and woman and rejects the responsibilities that mothers and fathers have to their children and to one another. Abortion cuts at the fabric of marriage and of entire families, harming mothers, fathers, siblings, and grandparents.

Abortion distorts science and corrupts medicine, pretending that the child in the womb isn't a human being at all and that tools meant for healing can rightly be turned to killing. Abortion perverts what it means to live in a justly ordered political community with laws that protect all of us—and in a society where our laws say that some human beings don't deserve to live, we are all at risk. Abortion leads to a particular devaluation of unborn children diagnosed with illnesses or disorders in the womb, as well as a devaluation of girls in parts of the world where sons are more highly prized. It undermines solidarity with the poor, the weak, the marginalized, people with disabilities, and anyone on the periphery of life. It allows those in power to deem certain lives expendable, allowing people to eliminate "populations that we don't want to have too many of," in the words of the late Supreme Court justice Ruth Bader Ginsburg. Abortion has been a disaster. As Mother Teresa once put it in an *amicus curiae* brief to the U.S. Supreme Court:

> America needs no words from me to see how your decision
> in *Roe v. Wade* has deformed a great nation. The so-called
> right to abortion has pitted mothers against their children

and women against men. It has sown violence and discord at the heart of the most intimate human relationships. It has aggravated the derogation of the father's role in an increasingly fatherless society. It has portrayed the greatest of gifts—a child—as a competitor, an intrusion, and an inconvenience. It has nominally accorded mothers unfettered dominion over the independent lives of their physically dependent sons and daughters. And, in granting this unconscionable power, it has exposed many women to unjust and selfish demands from their husbands or other sexual partners. Human rights are not a privilege conferred by government. They are every human being's entitlement by virtue of his humanity. The right to life does not depend, and must not be declared to be contingent, on the pleasure of anyone else, not even a parent or a sovereign.[6]

Mother Teresa is correct: the individual's right to life does not depend on our consent, but the brutality of abortion is possible today because enough citizens have agreed, either implicitly or explicitly, to close their eyes to the truth about what abortion is. That truth is almost too painful to acknowledge, and many have learned to look away instead. We talk about abortion with euphemisms such as "women's rights," "reproductive freedom," "bodily autonomy," and the "right to choose." But the right to choose *what*? Rarely in our public debates do we argue about what abortion *is*. No one who supports abortion wants to talk about what really happens in every abortion procedure, because that reality is grisly and horrifying. It can persist only when we refuse to acknowledge this violence and the many ways that it damages our society and our solidarity with one another.

For a typical American who doesn't spend much time thinking about abortion, consider what it would mean to admit that, for the past fifty years, our country has legally sanctioned the killing of more than sixty-five million human beings. Think of the millions of women who have had abortions, many of whom did so based on misguided conceptions of freedom and autonomy, but many of whom did so because they felt pressured or abandoned. Large numbers of both sets of women have suffered physical harm and psychological trauma as a result, and yet they struggle to give voice to those harms in a culture that claims abortion is either no big deal or a cause for celebration. Consider the relationships and marriages blighted by abortion, women used and abused by men, children who lost a sibling, grandparents who never got to meet a grandchild. No family has ever been better off because of abortion.

Think about the doctors who performed these abortions, who used their medical expertise to kill the vulnerable patient in the womb. It might be difficult to feel sympathy for them, but how can a person perform abortions and not be harmed by having committed such an evil? As Aristotle teaches, we become what we do. Those who kill become killers. Think of the countless politicians and activists who have enabled and promoted abortion, pretending it is a simple, harmless medical procedure, akin to having a tooth pulled. Think of those who have done nothing to stop this terror. Think of those—ourselves included—who haven't done enough.

These are the costs of admitting the truth about abortion, just a small part of why many prefer to turn away and pretend it isn't true at all. But acknowledge it we must, because ignoring it will only make the problem worse. All of us are affected by the lethal logic of abortion. A society that endorses abortion devalues the life of every single member, as it allows mothers to destroy their children and sanctions violence against the most vulnerable members of the human community. Each of us enters life dependent on our families, particularly on our mothers, and though our level of dependence fluctuates throughout the course of our lives, we remain dependent on one another. A healthy society doesn't deny or try to eliminate dependency; it helps people meet the needs of their neighbors and bear one another's burdens.

One of the most fundamental truths about what it means to be human is that *we belong to each other.*[7] Abortion is premised on an utter repudiation of this reality, using the dependence and vulnerability of the unborn child as a justification for lethal violence. And that denial has ramifications for all of us. Abortion has been declared a constitutional right in the United States for nearly fifty years. In that time, we have witnessed exactly how harmful abortion is, not only for the millions of babies who lost their lives, but for nearly every element of our society. In this book, we take stock of just how much has been lost.

In Chapter One, we make the case that the most fundamental harm of abortion is to the unborn child. We refute a number of justifications for abortion, including claims that the child in the womb is neither a human being nor a human person. We address the straightforward, biological case for the humanity of the unborn child, and we argue that every human being is a person with dignity and worth. As a result of these two truths, we make the case that a rightly ordered government must protect human beings from lethal violence. Finally, we address a well-known philosophical argument that justifies abortion as purportedly non-intentional killing, an argument now popularized by emphasizing the bodily autonomy of women. But, as we explain, all of our liberties have limits, and the unborn baby isn't an unjust intruder that can be fended off using lethal means.

Chapter Two addresses the argument that abortion is a boon to women, allowing them to participate in sex and the economy on equal footing with men. The real story is far more complicated. Abortion has injected violence into the sacred relationship between a mother and her child. Abortion has not solved the problems that supporters claimed it would, and even on its own terms it has not been the cause or even a condition of increased educational or workplace success for women.[8] Rather than freeing women from the burden of pregnancy as feminists claimed it would, abortion has intensified the ways in which our culture treats pregnancy as a "woman's problem."[9] Abortion has not increased support for pregnant mothers in need but has fed a culture that treats women who continue pregnancies as if they're on their own, because, after all, they could've chosen abortion. Abortion has made it easier for men to leave women and harder for women to refuse abortion, even when they would prefer to choose life. And, as we document in this chapter, it has put women at risk of immediate physical consequences from botched procedures, as well as long-term risks to both their physical and psychological health.

In Chapter Three, we document the ways in which abortion has exacerbated inequality, perpetuating racial division and social stratification. We explain the eugenic roots of the modern abortion-rights movement, which originated with birth-control advocates who wanted to limit the growth of supposedly undesirable populations such as non-white Americans, the poor, and people with disabilities. We show how today a disproportionate number of black and Hispanic babies are killed in the womb—an ominous trend that abortion supporters either ignore or celebrate—as well as discriminatory abortions, especially those that target unborn baby girls or children diagnosed with disabilities. Finally, we address the important work of pregnancy-resource centers in offering mothers alternatives to abortion, a mission that abortion supporters not only neglect but actively oppose—thus revealing them to be much more pro-abortion than "pro-choice," at least when that choice is anything other than abortion.

In Chapter Four, we consider the ways that legalized abortion has corrupted our medical system, leading medical organizations and a significant number of doctors to lie about the biology of human life and use their expertise to kill rather than cure. We explain how pro-abortion doctors influenced the Supreme Court decision inventing a right to abortion, and tell the story of how the American College of

Obstetricians and Gynecologists evolved from a non-partisan professional organization into a transparently political abortion advocacy group. We examine the brutal business of Planned Parenthood, the nation's largest abortion provider, and refute falsehoods that the group and its supporters promote. Lastly, we consider the risks that abortion poses to conscience rights and religious freedom.

In Chapter Five, we outline the history of the Supreme Court decisions that created the legal landscape perpetuating abortion. We explain the bad history, flawed reasoning, and political machinations that led the Court to manufacture a constitutional right to abortion in *Roe v. Wade*. We also consider the Supreme Court case *Planned Parenthood v. Casey*, which upheld the core of *Roe* while altering its reasoning, and we explain how abortion jurisprudence has created an unjust and unworkable status quo. Rightly understood, nothing in our Constitution protects lethal violence in the womb. Appeals to "privacy," "autonomy," and "equality" should not prevent lawmakers from protecting unborn children.

In Chapter Six, we examine the political ramifications of those judicial decisions and the subsequent decades of our permissive abortion regime. We explain that most Americans would prefer to protect unborn children far more than *Roe* and *Casey* allow, and we tell the story of how the Democratic Party slid in a radically pro-abortion direction over the span of a few decades, turning abortion into a politically polarizing issue, eventually excluding from the party anyone who does not support an increasingly extreme position. Finally, we discuss how abortion has turned judicial confirmations into toxic political battles. Our politics and our society would be better served if neither of our major political parties supported abortion, a blatant violation of fundamental human rights. Democratic politicians' excuses for embracing abortion require them to deny the proper role of morality and religion in our politics. As Martin Luther King Jr. wrote in his famous "Letter from Birmingham Jail," justice requires that our man-made laws comport with the natural and eternal law. The rhetoric of Democrats who support abortion urges us to sever our legal system from its natural and divine sources. Meanwhile, the party's embrace of abortion has made our political process hostage to abortion. It would be far better for pro-life citizens to have a meaningful political choice between two parties, neither of which was committed to gross injustice.

In Chapter Seven, we turn to culture. There we argue that the widespread acceptance of abortion has corrupted legacy media outlets, making it far less likely that the truth about abortion will reach many Americans and disrupt their settled views on the subject. We survey pro-abortion bias at major tech and social-media companies and the significant support for abortion in Hollywood, which shapes how users and viewers think about abortion. Censorship and bias limit the ability of pro-lifers to share the truth with those who need to hear it, while glamourous depictions of abortion spread the fundamental lie that abortion should be celebrated. We also consider the growing support for abortion among major corporations, which are increasingly using their social power to preserve legal abortion and block pro-life policies.

In our conclusion, we take stock of where fifty years of abortion have left our nation, and the work that still needs to be done. We suggest that pro-lifers remember that ending abortion will require a "both-and" approach on a number of levels, not an "either-or." We need plans for shifting our laws and our culture, efforts to care for babies and mothers, work from state and federal governments—and we must do all of this in service of ending the supply of and demand for abortion.

■   ■   ■

In a 2016 essay, Frederica Mathewes-Green explained her journey from being a progressive, pro-abortion feminist to a pro-life advocate, a change of heart that—like the conversions of Levatino and Nathanson—began when she realized the humanity of the child in the womb:

> There I was, anti-war, anti–capital punishment, even vegetarian, and a firm believer that social justice cannot be won at the cost of violence. Well, this sure looked like violence. How had I agreed to make this hideous act the centerpiece of my feminism? How could I think it was wrong to execute homicidal criminals, wrong to shoot enemies in wartime, but all right to kill our own sons and daughters?
>
> For that was another disturbing thought: Abortion means killing not strangers but our own children, our own flesh and blood.... Every child aborted is that woman's own son or daughter, just as much as any child she will ever bear.
>
> We had somehow bought the idea that abortion was necessary if women were going to rise in their professions and compete in the marketplace with men. But how had we come to agree that we will sacrifice our children, as the price of getting ahead? When does a man ever have to choose between his career and the life of his child? Once I recognized the inherent violence of abortion, none of the feminist arguments made sense....
>
> Abortion indisputably ends a human life. But this loss is usually set against the woman's need to have an abortion in order to freely direct her own life. It is a particular cruelty to present abortion as something women want, something they demand, they find liberating. Because *nobody* wants this. The procedure itself is painful, humiliating, expensive—no woman "wants" to go through it. But once

it's available, it appears to be the logical, reasonable choice. All the complexities can be shoved down that funnel. Yes, abortion solves all the problems; but it solves them inside the woman's body. And she is expected to keep that pain inside for a lifetime, and be grateful for the gift of abortion....

The pro-life cause is perennially unpopular, and pro-lifers get used to being misrepresented and wrongly accused. There are only a limited number of people who are going to be brave enough to stand up on the side of an unpopular cause. But sometimes a cause is so urgent, is so dramatically clear, that it's worth it. What cause could be more outrageous than violence—fatal violence—against the most helpless members of our human community? If that doesn't move us, how hard *are* our hearts? If that doesn't move us, what will ever move us?[10]

Because this book examines the many ways abortion has harmed our country and our culture, it is full of stories and facts that can be hard to stomach. But while it's difficult to acknowledge much of the suffering we chronicle, ultimately the case against the evil of abortion is a positive case, an affirmation of the beauty and goodness of every human life. That goodness is most evident within the context of families and communities where people serve and sacrifice for each other.

That truth was exemplified by the life of Michael Kniffin, the love he showed his family, and the way he taught his family how to love, even when it required tremendous sacrifice. We quote a portion of his obituary, written by his father:

Michael Patrick Kniffin left suffering behind on December 31, 2021, and entered eternal life in the Kingdom of the Lord.

He was a beloved son of Eric and Bonnie, and brother to his seven siblings. At three months old, Michael was diagnosed with lissencephaly, "smooth brain," a severe congenital neurological condition.

Through the love of his family and the generous care he received from scores of doctors, nurses, and therapists—affectionately called "Team Mo"—Michael defied the odds and nearly reached his tenth birthday.

Michael's condition left him non-verbal, non-mobile, and legally blind. But his heart was perfect. In his earliest years, Michael had a beaming smile and an infectious belly laugh. He used all his strength to wiggle just a little bit closer for a snuggle. Michael reserved his biggest laughs for the smallest things, which made his joy all the more wondrous: the way light sparkled off an iridescent poster board, the feeling of a string brushing across his forehead, or the sound of wind chimes.

Michael was prone to seizures, pneumonia, and scoliosis. He received medications ten times a day, and regular medical interventions to keep him healthy.

Despite Team Mo's best efforts, Michael's seizures continued to take their toll, and in recent years his smiles and laughter became less frequent.

Michael had profound limitations, but had a beautiful ability to draw the best out of other people.

His limits required us to quiet ourselves, and to look closely for the smallest indications that he was tired, happy, or that he had enough of the sun. Finding ways to make Michael laugh was like a puzzle that his siblings were always thrilled to solve.

Michael also drew together a beautiful community whose common thread was love for him and dedication to his wellbeing. His gentle spirit also created a safe space when his brothers and sisters were having a tough day. Cozying up next to Michael set the troubles of the world at bay, and no one was better than Michael at keeping secrets.

Michael's life and the extraordinary care he received stand as a witness to the dignity and worth of every human being, no matter how small, no matter how fragile. He also taught his family that love involves great sacrifice and carrying each other's burdens (Gal. 6:2). We thank God for entrusting this beautiful child to us, and for the countless gifts we and our children have received from and through him.[11]

Many families who receive a prenatal diagnosis of a condition similar to Michael's choose abortion, but his story reminds us that we find our deepest joy and fulfillment precisely when we choose to care for and love one another in the midst of suffering. Families, communities, and entire societies become better when they treat the most vulnerable among us with love and consideration. This is not to minimize the real challenges many families face, but whether in the case of a difficult prenatal diagnosis, a challenging financial situation, or pressure to abort, no form of suffering can erase the value of the unborn child, a child who is always worthy of love and protection. Families that rise to the occasion and love in the face of suffering are the best witnesses to this truth.

As we write this, we don't yet know what the Supreme Court will do in *Dobbs*. As you're reading this, you know. But regardless of when the Court finally undoes its jurisprudence that makes it nearly impossible to protect unborn children, we all have a responsibility to ameliorate the harms of abortion—a task that starts by remembering the profound and inherent goodness of life, even in the face of suffering.

It is our hope that this book will show those who haven't made up their minds on this issue how abortion has hurt our country, and that it will equip pro-life readers with the truth so they can offer it courageously to others.

CHAPTER ONE

Abortion Harms the Unborn Child

One of us (Ryan) vividly remembers the first time he saw an ultrasound of his son. Of course, he didn't yet know it was a son—the twelve-week ultrasound is too early to recognize the sex of the child, and Ryan and his wife Anna chose not to find out at a later ultrasound. But it was their son all the same. It was undeniable that this was a human being—a baby.

They breathed a huge sigh of relief when they first heard their baby's heartbeat, and though they first heard it at the twelve-week ultrasound, the heartbeat itself had developed around week six. The ultrasound technician never uttered the phrase "fetus" but repeatedly said things such as, "That's your baby's heartbeat" and "There's your baby's face."[1] At the twenty-week ultrasound, the technician made a point of identifying and taking pictures of every major organ and bodily structure.

After that first appointment, Ryan and Anna texted ultrasound photos to both sides of the family, shared the due date, and started to prepare for the baby's arrival. Eventually, they made a public announcement, and people offered congratulations and promised to pray for both mother and baby. (Ryan felt left out.)

There's no denying it. At least when people are happy about its existence, they will admit that the entity in the womb is a child. A human child. A human being. Though it is immature, it is not in any sense a "potential life." It already *is* a life, with potential, and with a potential future. That's why we instinctively mourn miscarriage. That's why parents feel relieved when they hear that heartbeat on the ultrasound and are comforted when the unborn baby kicks, both signs that the life is thriving and developing well.

Abortion cuts short this potential by ending the life of the child. That's the foundational harm in every abortion. Abortion harms the unborn child. Abortion *kills* the unborn child, a child who is as fully human and as fully valuable—as fully a person—as the person reading this book.

Some people try to deny this reality in order to justify abortion. They deny that the unborn child is really a human being. They try to dehumanize the child by using sterile terms outside the clinical context. (Has any expectant mother ever shared ultrasound pictures of her "fetus" with family and friends?) Some go further and refer to the child as a "clump of cells." (Organisms aren't clumps, but if we are going to speak this way, couldn't each of us be considered in some sense "a clump of cells," too?)

The first purpose of this chapter, then, is to outline the basic facts of embryology and developmental biology, exposing the foolishness— even in purely scientific terms—of attempts to dehumanize the unborn child. But we also need to respond to more sophisticated abortion advocates, who know better than to pretend that biology is on their side and who turn instead to philosophy.

These interlocutors argue that while the unborn child might technically be a human *being*, the child isn't a human *person*. That is, according to some of today's leading bioethicists, the unborn child is not morally equivalent to the rest of us. This argument can come in at least two forms—that of body–self dualism, which denies our embodiment, and that of moral dualism, which denies our intrinsic worth and dignity. We'll explain these arguments in more detail, as well as why they both fail. Every human being is a person because every human being is a rational animal, and that rational-animal nature is the foundation of our intrinsic worth and profound dignity. This is true of all human beings, even if they can't immediately exercise their rational, personal capacities; they're still of the same nature and thus of the same worth as those who can.

Some defenders of abortion acknowledge that the unborn child is, in fact, a human being and a human person, but they argue that it isn't the role of the state to impose any one view of morality on other people. These thinkers might describe themselves as "personally opposed" to abortion, but they are also politically in favor of giving women the choice to abort. We will show that this position is incoherent. Surely no one would say that he is personally opposed to slavery but in favor of his neighbor's right to choose to own a slave. There are plenty of debates about the proper role of the state, and subsequent chapters will say more about them. But even those who advocate the most limited government acknowledge that a rightly ordered government must, at the very least, play a role in protecting human beings from lethal violence. Even in that "night watchman" state, it would be an appropriate use of state authority to protect unborn children from harm.

The basic case for the right to life of the unborn child rests on three theses:

1. Biological: A new human being comes into existence at conception.
2. Moral: Human beings are created equal and possess intrinsic dignity and worth.

3. Political: Governments exist to, at the very least, protect innocent human beings from lethal violence.

Finally, we consider a last-ditch argument for abortion. Acknowledging for the sake of argument that the unborn child is a human being with equal moral worth and that governments should protect people from intentional lethal violence, some abortion supporters argue that none of those considerations override a woman's bodily autonomy. That while the unborn child might be fully human and fully our equal, and while government might rightly prohibit intentional killing, the unborn child is an unjust trespasser in a woman's womb, and she has no duty to allow the child to continue occupying it, and thus the government has no legitimacy in requiring "forced pregnancy." We'll explain why this line of argument is specious and that, far from being an intruder in his mother's womb, the unborn child is where he belongs. Furthermore, parents bear special obligations to their children, and a woman's bodily autonomy does not justify lethal violence against the unborn.

Abortion is a grave moral evil, an act of violence against the most vulnerable members of the human family. Every abortion ends the life of an innocent human being in the womb, a child who, because he is human, necessarily possesses intrinsic worth and dignity and thus deserves to have his life protected. Parents, in particular, bear special responsibilities to their children, and thus abortion strikes at one of the most profound human relationships.

The Biological Thesis: Human Beings Come into Existence at Conception

When Ryan and Anna first saw that twelve-week ultrasound, every one of their son's bones had already formed. His heart was beating. His blood was circulating. He was nourished through the umbilical cord. Yes, he lived inside of Anna. But unlike what many abortion proponents claim, he wasn't a "part" of her. Nor was he just a clump of cells. He was an organism, with all his developing organs working together to sustain his whole body. He was their son. He was the same little boy that he is today, four years later. In fact, his life didn't begin when his parents first saw him in an ultrasound. His life started some weeks earlier (but Anna won't let Ryan write about that).

Abstracted from the abortion debate, the biology of when the life of a new human being begins is neither complicated nor controversial. We all know it.[2] When a sperm fertilizes an egg, a new organism comes into existence. The basic facts of biology and embryology—which have become much clearer and are now indisputable thanks to technological advancements in the decades following *Roe v. Wade*—make it clear that, from the moment of conception, the unborn child is a distinct, living human being, just like each one of us.[3]

Here's how the authors of one prominent embryology textbook put it: "Human development begins at fertilization when a male gamete or sperm (spermatozoon) unites with a female gamete or oocyte (ovum) to form a single cell—a zygote. This highly specialized, totipotent cell marked the beginning of each of us as a unique individual."[4] With the exception of identical twins, each of us began life as a single cell.[5]

This single-celled organism, a zygote, forms after the sperm and egg fuse, and it rapidly develops into a blastocyst and then an embryo and then a fetus. But none of these are separate organisms. Rather, these words refer to the same human organism at different stages of development, at different ages. The zygote is the very same organism that exits the womb nine months later as a newborn child.

Abortion supporters continue to deny this scientific reality, ignoring the facts of basic biology in order to justify abortion on the grounds that the unborn child isn't a child at all.

Some of those who defend abortion claim, for instance, that the fetus isn't even a human being. In reality, the unborn child is from the moment of conception a living human being. The gametes—sperm in a man and egg in a woman—are genetically and functionally parts of the potential parents, but by the time fertilization is completed, a unique human being has come into existence. He or she has human genetic material entirely distinct from both mother and father—and indeed from every human being who has ever existed or ever will exist.[6]

Other times, abortion advocates argue that the unborn child is merely a part of his mother, and therefore that destroying it through abortion is akin to removing a bad tooth or a burst appendix. In a 2019 CNN interview, for example, former New York City Democratic politician Christine Quinn claimed that pro-life laws are wrong, arguing, "When a woman is pregnant, that is not a human being inside of her. It's part of her body."[7] But Ryan's son wasn't a part of Anna's body at all; he was a distinct human being dwelling inside her. Though the unborn child lives inside his or her mother's womb, that human being isn't a part of the mother's body in the way that, say, her lungs or her heart are.

The woman's lungs and heart are organs, organized and operating within her body and enabling it to function properly as a complete organismic whole. The unborn child, by contrast, is both genetically and functionally distinct from both mother and father. It is its own organism, organized with its own parts, its own organs such as the lungs and heart, or the cells that will later develop into these organs. The structure and function of the unborn child's organs are parts of a distinct, complete organism dwelling inside the mother, not parts of the distinct whole that comprises the mother.

The clearest way to see this is to note that the unborn child has its own fundamentally distinct trajectory. The mother's various organs serve the purpose of the mother's organismic life. But the unborn child doesn't do that. It's not a part at the service of the mother's body. It is its own whole, with its own pathway for growth and maturation. The various parts of that child—the organs of the fetus—are at the service of the child's life. Looking at the different ends the parts serve, whether mother or child—or in the case of the placenta, both—helps clarify that the child is its own whole.

The unborn child is an entirely new organism—a *whole* human being. Yes, it is young and immature. Yes, it has yet to develop into something that looks like an adult. But the one-celled zygote is exactly what a one-day-old human being looks like, and it does exactly what a one-day-old human being does. So, too, with the eight-day-old blastocyst—that's what a human being of that age looks like, and it does exactly what it's supposed to do. So, too, with the twenty-week fetus. These are all complete, whole organisms, even though they are rapidly developing to reach the next stage of life.

The child in the womb needs the same things that we all need outside of the womb: nurture, care, protection, and a hospitable environment. The rapid growth that commences at conception, working to develop a full set of capacities, is a process that continues well after birth. The capacity for locomotion normally develops in the early years first as crawling, then walking, then running. The capacity for speech develops first as babbling, then as discrete words, eventually full sentences, and even foreign languages. The human brain doesn't even finish fully developing until a human being reaches his mid-twenties. Likewise, the unborn child is no different than the newborn (or, for that matter, the adult) in its dependence on others, though the form of dependence in the womb is more radical.

This is simply to say that human development is a dynamic process, one that extends far beyond the months before birth. We come into existence as organisms who develop over time to be able to exercise more and more of our capacities. That's what we mean when we say the newly conceived child is a human life with potential, rather than a potential life. The one-celled zygote, multi-celled embryo, fetus, newborn, toddler, teen, and adult are all various stages of a single organism's growth and development; these stages don't each represent different organisms but rather periods in the life of one and the same human being. Birth may be an extraordinary event, but it is not a magical dividing line. Each of us (unless we're an identical twin) started out as a one-celled zygote and have been developing as continuous, unique biological entities ever since.

The Moral Thesis: Human Beings Have Intrinsic Value

When Ryan's son was born, he was entirely helpless. He relied on his mother to feed him and on his father to change his diapers. And his parents joyfully fulfilled the obligations they had to care for their son. For those first few weeks, all he seemed to do was eat, sleep, and poop. Many non-human animals do the same. Yet there is a fundamental difference in terms of moral value between that newborn human being and all other forms of life. The newborn baby possesses profound intrinsic value and worth, even at that early and undeveloped stage, an intrinsic value that non-human animals don't possess.

Nearly everything around us is valuable for its instrumental worth. We keep chickens in the coop for the eggs they lay; we value trees in the field for their shade. When the chickens stop laying eggs, off they go. When the trees are more valuable as timber or firewood, down they come. But that's not how we value other human beings. Or at least not how we *should* value them. We shouldn't value them based on how useful or productive or instrumentally beneficial they are—to us or to society.

Rather, we should value human beings as subjects who possess immeasurable intrinsic worth, who are valuable simply because of who they are, not because of what they can do for us. That is, we should value them because they are valuable for their own sake; they don't have mere instrumental value that fluctuates based on what they can offer us at any given time.

What was true of Ryan's son when he first came home from the hospital was true several weeks earlier at his first ultrasound. He couldn't do much at all that was different from other animals, but his value was different in kind even then—because *he* was different in kind. The value he has today, and the value he had when he was born and when he was in utero, all stem from the fact that he is a *person*.

Because human beings are animal organisms of a special sort, we're valuable by virtue of who we are, not by virtue of what we can do for others or what other people believe about our worth. Some give a theological explanation for this: We are made in the image and likeness of God. As his image-bearers, we have profound, inherent worth, as he created us to be with him for eternity. Others offer a philosophical explanation: We possess a rational and free nature, and any creature with such a nature is the subject of intrinsic value. Others appeal to a purported self-evident truth of philosophical theology, that all men are created equal and endowed by their creator with inalienable rights.

All three of these arguments converge on one central point: Human beings are creatures of a certain personal nature, so that the only proper response is one of gratitude, appreciation, cherishing, protecting, and valuing.

Supporters of abortion have to get around this in order to argue that abortion is a morally acceptable choice. Some concede the biological thesis that the unborn child is a unique, living human being, but they deny that all human beings have a right to life, because they believe that not all human beings have intrinsic worth. In order to do this, abortion advocates rely on personhood arguments, which attempt to distinguish between human beings and human *persons*, defined as individuals who have moral worth and basic rights we must respect.

Rather than denying the humanity of the unborn—which they know is a losing argument—they deny the personhood of the unborn. While some will claim the unborn child is only a "potential life," these more sophisticated (and in some cases sophistical) supporters of abortion claim the unborn child is only a "potential person." That is, while they concede that this is a human being, they argue that it isn't yet a person because it can't yet engage in personal actions.

As philosopher Christopher Kaczor has summarized it, "Several authors such as [Michael] Tooley, [Peter] Singer, David Boonin, Mary Anne Warren, and many others affirm precisely that the fetus is a biological human being but not a moral person."[8] Singer in particular defines a person as "a being with awareness of his or her own existence, and the capacity to have wants and plans for the future."[9] Mary Anne Warren, meanwhile, offers these criteria for personhood: "consciousness of objects and events external and/or internal to themselves, in particular the capacity to feel pain"; "developed capacity to solve new and relatively complex problems"; "activity which is relatively independent of either genetic or direct external control"; "the capacity to communicate, by whatever means, messages of an indefinite variety of types, that is, not just with an indefinite number of possible contents, but on indefinitely many topics"; and "the presence of self-concepts, and self-awareness, either individual or racial, or both."[10] In her essay on the subject, Warren put it this way:

> Thus it is clear that even though a seven- or eight-month
> fetus has features which make it apt to arouse in us almost

the same powerful protective instinct as is commonly aroused by a small infant, nevertheless it is not significantly more personlike than is a very small embryo. It is somewhat more personlike; it can apparently feel and respond to pain, and it may even have a rudimentary form of consciousness, insofar as its brain is quite active. Nevertheless, it seems safe to say that it is not fully conscious, in the way that an infant of a few months is, and that it cannot reason, or communicate messages of indefinitely many sorts, does not engage in self-motivated activity; and has no self-awareness. Thus, in the relevant respects, a fetus, even a fully developed one, is considerably less personlike than is the average mature mammal, indeed the average fish. And I think that a rational person must conclude that if the right to life of a fetus is to be based upon its resemblance to a person, then it cannot be said to have any more right to life then, let us say, a newborn guppy (which also seems to be capable of feeling pain), and that a right of that magnitude could never override a woman's right to obtain an abortion, at any stage of her pregnancy.[11]

Some defenders of abortion make a slightly different argument. They say that what matters for moral status is the capacity to suffer. We should treat equally all creatures who can suffer, they say, whether equally well or equally poorly. They go so far as to argue that it is "speciest"—a species-based prejudice, akin to racism or sexism—to say that one species is more valuable as such than another. The unborn baby, they argue, is no more valuable than any other animal organism that can perform similar functions. At certain stages, the unborn baby cannot even experience suffering, so he ranks lower than various other animals. Moral worth is determined by what any given organism can do here and now. The greater your capacity to feel pain, experience pleasure, or engage in higher "personal" actions, the greater your moral worth—or so the argument goes.

If you don't balk at eating chicken, they'd say, you have no grounds to believe that an unborn child, with no greater mental or personal life than a chicken, has moral worth. This is why the philosophically robust argument for abortion ends up justifying infanticide as well, a reality that honest abortion defenders such as Tooley and Singer acknowledge, and which they deal with by arguing that infanticide is morally acceptable, too. After all, what can the newborn baby do in terms of personal actions that it couldn't do the day before birth?

What all of these arguments miss is that the unborn child—and the newborn, for that matter—is a creature of a rational and therefore personal nature. To have a rational nature means that you are capable of reason, when fully matured, in good health, and in a hospitable environment. Chickens don't have this capacity, no matter how mature or healthy, no matter their environment. Humans do. While Ryan's son couldn't yet talk as a newborn, no one was surprised when he started babbling later on, because it was the natural unfolding of his basic nature. It's why we all expect that the unborn baby will one day speak, but we'd all be shocked if the chicken one day bargained with us to spare its life. One is a rational, personal animal; the other is not.[12]

Personhood and Body–Self Dualism

Personhood arguments come in two main flavors. The body–self dualism version holds that human beings and human persons are two radically different substances. Human beings are physical bodily substances, while human persons are spiritual or mental substances, or brains. The end result is that the person is something other than the organism. The person is a part of the organism (the brain) or some non-physical substance, a center of consciousness or the seat of higher, personal actions. The bottom line, then, is that all "persons" have moral value, but not all human beings do.

On this view, not all human beings overlap with a human person; at the beginning of life the unborn and even newborns, and at the end of life the severely demented or those in a so-called persistent vegetative state, are all non-persons. Why are these human beings not persons? Because there is no personal substance associated with such bodily beings who can engage in personal actions. On this argument, persons are centers of consciousness somehow associated with bodies, not bodily organisms as such. Persons are those who can engage in immediately exercisable personal acts, such as self-consciousness and self-awareness.

The end result is that the entity reading this book is a person, because you are self-aware and capable of "higher" mental actions such as reading and speaking. But the entity reading this book, on this view, isn't a bodily being, even though you make use of a body. The entity reading this book, the "person," is a non-bodily center of consciousness somehow associated with a body. But you aren't the bodily being, and thus you were never an embryo or a fetus. On this strong version of body–self dualism, it is false even to say, "I was once in a womb" or "I was once a fetus," for there was no "I" associated with the body at those times. Dualism of this sort has been associated with Plato, René Descartes, and John Locke, and some philosophers have ridiculed it as the "ghost in the machine."[13] There are at least three good reasons to reject it.

First, we have a basic common sense and common experience of ourselves as bodily beings. The burden of proof—and it's a high burden—falls on the philosophers trying to convince us that their arguments are stronger than a more basic form of knowing: our direct embodied experience of ourselves.

This immediate, embodied, experiential form of knowledge works in conjunction with the second basic reason to reject body–self dualism: it can't account for the unity of action among physical acts and mental acts. Consider yourself reading this book. Perception and understanding are actions of the same agent, but one is bodily and the other is mental. That is, you are seeing the words on the page with your eyes, bodily organs. You're also interpreting those markings on the page as words and grasping the meaning of the words, sentences, and paragraphs—the argument of the book—with your mind. But it's a single agent, a single person—you—who both sees and reads, looks and understands. It's not two agents, a body who sees and looks and a mind who reads and understands.

This leads to the third reason to reject body–self dualism: it can't explain how the non-physical "self" interacts with the physical body. Descartes famously, or perhaps infamously, posited the brain's pineal gland as the way that mind and body are connected and the way they interact. A simpler solution is to say that there is no interaction problem, because there are not two substances interacting but rather a single substance, a single nature, a single organism, a single person, who is a bodily person and a personal body, a rational animal.[14]

Personhood and Moral Dualism

Another form of dualism recognizes that body–self dualism is metaphysically implausible. Human beings are an integrated whole of body and soul, mind and matter, personal bodies and embodied persons. The bodily self and the "personal" self aren't two substances that somehow interact, but are one and the same dynamic organism. These thinkers realize it's absurd to say, "I was never a fetus." Instead, they argue that while each one of us once was a fetus, we weren't valuable at that stage of development. Each of us is valuable now because we are able to engage in personal actions, but as fetuses we couldn't do so. Not all human beings are moral persons, because to be valuable as a person for moral purposes, a human being must have certain immediately exercisable capacities or abilities.

The views are similar, and to normal people it can seem like the logic-chopping that philosophers are notorious for. The distinction between the positions is fairly straightforward, though. One set of thinkers claims: "I am not a bodily being, and therefore I never was a fetus. If you had killed the fetus in my mother's womb that developed into the body I'm now associated with, you wouldn't have killed *me*." The other claims: "I am a bodily being. I was once a fetus, but when I was a fetus I wasn't valuable, though I am valuable now. Killing that fetus would have been killing me but it wouldn't have been morally wrong." Both hinge on the ability to engage in personal acts, but one argues about *who* I am while the other makes a claim about *when* I'm *valuable*.

For the latter sort of moral dualist, moral personhood is evaluative, an accidental property, rather than a property that's essential to every human being. These thinkers argue that just as not every human being has the right to vote, not every human being has the right to life. The violence of abortion against the unborn child is not morally significant to these thinkers because while the unborn child is the same entity as the adult, the child isn't of moral value. They argue that the unborn child doesn't have the moral status of a person because we are persons only when we can immediately exercise the ability to engage in personal acts, such as self-awareness, self-consciousness, memory, future planning, and so on. Remember how Warren put it: "In the relevant respects, a fetus, even a fully developed one, is considerably less person-like than is the average mature mammal, indeed the average fish."[15]

But think about what this moral argument would entail. It's not just unborn babies who would be denied the moral status of personhood;

this would also include anyone who could not immediately engage in personal acts. The same view would render an elderly man suffering from dementia, a woman in a temporary coma, or even a newborn baby all as non-persons. After all, a newborn can no more immediately engage in self-conscious acts than can an unborn baby.

This leads to some rather unappealing and untenable immediate moral implications. But it also has deeper philosophical problems. It is fundamentally arbitrary to allow a mere difference in the degree of development of a trait to serve as the basis for treating creatures in radically different ways. In matters of basic justice, hinging such a determination on an arbitrary characteristic is itself a gross injustice. That is, if all human beings have the same basic traits but some have developed them to a greater extent, making that difference of developmental degree the basis for treating those human beings in radically different ways is itself unjust, for those human beings aren't different in kind. Albert Einstein doesn't have greater moral worth than Joe the plumber.

All humans are fundamentally the same when it comes to their human nature. This explains why we treat humans, rational animals, in radically different ways than we do non-rational animals. It also explains why we treat—or at least should treat—all humans equally. For all humans share the same rational nature, regardless of how well developed that nature is at any given moment in time, and no non-rational animal has a rational nature.

Indeed, the view of moral personhood put forward by these thinkers would render it utterly impossible to defend equality as a moral principle. If what matters morally are our developed capacities, then those who develop their capacities the furthest should matter most. Why believe in moral equality if it isn't somehow connected to a common nature? Absent a coherent view of personhood based on intrinsic value and root capacities, a human being conceivably could gain and lose moral worth several times throughout the course of his life subject to fluctuations in his abilities.

In reality, every human being is a person with equal moral worth because we are all organisms of a certain kind, with a certain nature and a certain structure. We are rational organisms, and regardless of whether we are able to exercise any given capacity at a particular moment in time, the embryo, newborn, and adult share the same rational, personal nature, with basic root capacities for rational, personal actions. Theologically, we can express this truth as all being made in the image and likeness of God, a rational and free being, created for eternity with God. So, too, we have a rational and free nature, a personal nature—even if we can't immediately exercise all of our capacities, including our most personal ones.

We must therefore look to basic, root capacities, not immediately exercisable ones, when we determine natures and personhood. Ryan's son and a farm animal might have similar abilities in terms of what they can do immediately here and now, but a human child is now and always has been a person, because he has a personal nature.

Denials of personhood to categories of human beings have been used throughout history to subjugate, oppress, and extinguish groups of people that those in power wanted to eliminate. History gives us little reason to believe that denying personhood to some human beings has ever been used to further justice or equality—instead, in every such instance, it has been used in precisely the opposite way.

Political Thesis: Government Exists to (at the Very Least) Protect against Lethal Violence

The denial of personhood undergirding the defense of abortion entails another ugly position, with grave political consequences: the belief that might makes right. If we accept the framework of moral dualists, someone or some group must be able to decide which human beings count as persons. This belief means that stronger people, by virtue of their capabilities, can rule over the weaker—or the wiser over the dumber, the older over the younger, the prettier over the uglier, and so on. This view rejects a fundamental truth about human nature that government exists to defend, the truth that all human beings are created equal.

Yet many supporters of abortion argue that protecting babies from the violence of abortion is an illegitimate use of government power. They argue that the state may not impose morality on other people, or that it can't legislate based on "religious" values. They insist that a state that enacts laws protecting unborn babies has somehow exceeded its rightful authority.

None of these arguments withstands scrutiny. We don't even need to consider abstract academic debates about the role of the state. On even the most minimalist conception of the state, protecting innocent persons from lethal violence is a legitimate and necessary government function. Therefore, the state should protect all human beings. If we accept that the unborn child is a human being and that all human beings have intrinsic worth and are persons in that sense, then the government's role is indisputable: any government worthy of its name is obligated to protect the lives of unborn human beings, too. However expansive or limited your conception of the role of the state in promoting human flourishing, it must, at the very least, shield innocent human beings, including the unborn child, from lethal violence.

Indeed, the proper role of government runs counter to what abortion proponents normally argue. Laws that protect innocent life are a functioning government's default position, and the burden of proof is on those who would demand exceptions. In fact, a state that does *not* aim to protect innocent life from lethal violence should be considered illegitimate. If each of us enjoys the same natural dignity by virtue of our humanity, then there is no sound basis on which a government could arbitrarily deprive certain individuals of their lives, rights, or freedoms.

That protection begins by, at minimum, preventing people from harming one another. This is the first step that any legitimate government must take to safeguard its citizens and their freedoms. In order to promote human flourishing, government must, at the very least, secure the right to life, the right upon which all others depend. Securing this right is consistent with the equal and natural dignity of each person. We are glad the law protects Ryan's three-year-old son today. No one has the legal freedom to harm him. If someone did, he would be held accountable in ways commensurate to the harm caused. Because he is a walking, talking, and laughing little boy, it is easy to make the case that he deserves this protection, and most people would agree with us, including people who support abortion.

But while most abortion supporters would agree that it is right to legally protect Ryan's son now, they would have opposed any attempt to legally protect him while he was still in the womb. Often, those who favor legal abortion dismiss pro-life policy as a religiously motivated effort to impose one particular view of morality on the rest of society. But this critique is not quite right.

What the opposition means to say is that pro-life laws impose a morality with which they disagree—in other words, a *bad* morality. All laws, after all, have to do with morality, at least on some level. This defense of abortion suffers from the misguided notion that we should separate law from morality, an effort that even abortion supporters would not promote in most other areas. And there's nothing more or less "religious" about our abortion laws than our homicide laws, or laws against theft, tax evasion, or running a stop sign. What matters isn't whether a proposition coincides with secular or religious values but rather whether the proposition is true. If it is true that killing an innocent person is unjust, then it is appropriate for the state to prohibit such injustices. Whether we give a Kantian, utilitarian, Aristotelian, or biblical explanation for *why* homicide is unjust is ultimately beside the point. The public square should be open to all citizens working from their deepest convictions to dispute issues of public policy and law.

Challenges to pro-life legislation, especially in public commentary and legal scholarship, often rely on arguments about "imposing" morality or warning of a looming theocracy.[16] Ronald Dworkin, perhaps the most influential legal philosopher of the twentieth century, argued in his 1994 book *Life's Dominion* that "freedom of choice about abortion is a necessary implication of the religious freedom guaranteed by the First Amendment."[17] *New York Times* columnist Linda Greenhouse has likewise insisted for years that restricting abortion would constitute a formal establishment of religion: "If the First Amendment's Establishment Clause means anything, it has to mean that God's will cannot be a constitutional justification for a law that erases an individual right."[18] Of course, the same could be said about God's will when it comes to laws prohibiting homicide, which erase the individual right of the murderer. After all, it is only with the advent of Christianity that Western societies embraced the truth that every human life matters and deserves equal protection under the law. What's true outside of the womb is true inside as well. There are both religious and non-religious arguments against adult homicide—and against fetal homicide. Both are legitimate sources for public policy and law, and while theology can tell us that every human life matters, it doesn't tell us when the life of a human being begins. As we saw above, we need science for that.

A law protecting children from the violence of abortion will surely be considered burdensome by those who would prefer to allow women to kill their unborn children. But dismissing pro-life laws because they "impose morality" is a deflection; it doesn't explain why the law should permit abortion. This is the same deflection attempted by abortion supporters who attempt to sidestep the issue by declaring, "If you don't like abortion, don't have one." This misunderstands, or misrepresents, what we all recognize about law.

Consider an obvious parallel case. No one today would applaud the proposal, "If you don't like slavery, don't own a slave." Notwithstanding our nation's disgraceful history on this score, thankfully today we recognize that slavery is a grave moral evil, one that the government has justly abolished and prohibited. Telling those who disagree with slavery merely to avoid participating in it, and using this argument to justify continued government protection of slavery, would be a non-starter with reasonable people, because we know that slavery degrades and violates the personhood of the enslaved human being and of the enslaver. The same is true of the unborn child killed in an abortion, his mother, and the abortionist—and the government has the same responsibility to step in and prohibit this injustice.

In order to be consistent, abortion proponents either must advocate abolishing all of our laws because they are wrongful impositions of morality, or they must acknowledge that the real disagreement when it comes to abortion law is about which particular moral vision our laws should codify. Rather than condemning pro-life laws as an imposition of morality, abortion supporters must make a substantive case for whatever moral vision they believe justifies killing unborn children, an effort they avoid because it's an impossible case to make.

We propose that a society and government properly ordered toward promoting human dignity and human flourishing must protect the lives of all human beings, including the unborn. While persuasion and cultural change can help change hearts, so too can legal reform, which must play an important part in protecting unborn children.

Law is as much a teacher as it is a rulebook and a remedy. Eventually, in a just society, both federal and state law would explicitly protect the unborn child's life.

Abortion and Women's Rights: The "Bodily Autonomy" and "Forced Birth" Arguments for Abortion

Some abortion supporters sense the truth of what we've argued so far—that the unborn child is a human being and a person with moral value, and that the state has a legitimate role in protecting the lives of all people—so they make a different case. Conceding for the sake of argument all that we've said above, they argue that the state's protection of innocent life cannot come at the expense of women's bodily autonomy. That is, there are two goods—and two state interests—at play when it comes to abortion, and the state needs to balance them.

As a result, one significant set of arguments, often used by feminists, is that abortion is first and foremost a matter of female autonomy. These thinkers say that, without abortion, women cannot control their bodies and their reproductive choices. Even if the unborn child is a human being and a moral person, that doesn't give him a right to trespass in a woman's body. Women have authority over their own bodies and need the right to abortion in order to be free and equal. We say more about the social equality argument in the next chapter. Here we focus on the bodily autonomy argument.

This basic bodily autonomy argument for abortion was first fully articulated in 1971 by moral philosopher Judith Jarvis Thomson.[19] Thomson stipulated for the sake of argument that the unborn child is a human being—and even that it is a human *person*. But she nonetheless justified abortion as non-intentional killing. Her famous analogy compared a pregnant woman to a hypothetical individual who, without his consent, has been hooked up to a famous violinist who is sick and requires this connection to remain alive. Imagine someone with kidney or liver failure who needs to be plugged into your body so he can rely on your kidney or your liver for, say, nine months, until a transplant could be found.

In Thomson's analogy, just as it would be morally acceptable for you to choose to detach from the violinist, even if you know he will die as a result, so too would it be acceptable for a pregnant woman to have the unborn child detached. In neither case did you consent to having the violinist plugged in or the child exist in the womb. And in neither case are you seeking the person's death. You don't want it for its own sake, nor do you want it for the sake of something else it will bring. Death is neither your means nor your end, in the jargon of philosophers. It isn't intended, only foreseen. You cut someone off from invasive access to your body, while knowing this will result in death. With this argument, Thomson portrayed pregnancy as an act of violence against women. Just as the violinist was secretly hooked up without your knowledge or consent, violating your bodily integrity, so too the child conceived and growing in the womb does so without permission.

Thomson's argument fails spectacularly.[20] First, the bodily autonomy argument for abortion could only get off the ground if abortion entailed unintentional killing. But unlike the case of the violinist, where the intention truly is just to detach—with his death a foreseen but unintended side effect—in the case of abortion, the intended outcome is a dead child. Thomson's hypothetical is wrong about what people want when they seek abortion. An abortion where the child survives is a failed abortion.[21] By contrast, a detachment from the violinist where the violinist survives would be considered a success. In performing an abortion, the abortionist doesn't seek only to remove an "invading" child from a womb but also to ensure that the child no longer exists. (As we'll see in subsequent chapters, this is why the pro-abortion movement opposes even the Born-Alive Abortion Survivors Protection Act, which would legally protect newborns who survive an attempted abortion.)

To better illustrate the difference, consider situations in which the death of an unborn child is foreseen but not intended, such as when a pregnant woman has a cancerous uterus. In treating a woman in such a case, the death of the child is neither a means to the desired outcome nor the intended end itself. In fact, the death of the child in such situations is almost always lamented. The mother with the cancerous uterus doesn't intend to kill her child but rather to remove a cancerous organ. So, too, a woman with an ectopic pregnancy—in which the embryo implants and develops in the fallopian tube— doesn't intend to kill her child but to remove it from developing in a place inhospitable to continued life for both baby and mother. She foresees but does not intend that the child will inevitably die as a result. Women seeking abortion, however, don't just seek to be "unpregnant." They seek not to have a living child.[22]

Second, the analogy between abortion and the violinist is a non-starter in any case other than when the pregnancy itself was the result of a violation of bodily integrity—as it would be if the violinist were hooked up to you. The analogy doesn't apply to *nearly all* pregnancies, the vast majority of which result from consensual sex. In fact, the pro-abortion Guttmacher Institute's research has shown that only 1 percent of abortions are obtained in cases of rape—a percentage that holds steady across decades of data.[23]

In consensual sex, even in the case of failed contraception, the man and woman voluntarily engage in the act that brings a new life into existence. The unborn child is not an intruder who uses force and violence to attach himself to the mother, the way a parasite attaches to a host. Rather, the unborn child is right where he is supposed to be, doing what he's supposed to be doing. Conception is the natural fruit of sex, and a child developing in the womb is a sign of reproductive health. Conception and gestation are natural results of sex. People—parents especially—bear responsibilities for the natural consequences of their acts. A man and a woman who voluntarily engage in the act that can create new life, a life that comes into existence in the condition of radical dependency, owe duties in justice to care for that new life. This is the heart of parental obligation.

Pregnancy for many women can be a burden, and for some it can entail grave physical costs, but that doesn't justify the intentional killing of another innocent person—and not just any innocent person, but the woman's *child*. Missing from bodily autonomy arguments for abortion is any recognition that a moral relationship between mother and child already exists by the time a woman is contemplating an abortion. Both mother and father have natural duties to protect and care for their children, regardless of whether they are "wanted" or "unwanted," "planned" or a "surprise," "perfect" or "defective."

Thomson's analogy, then, fails as applied to nearly all pregnancies. The analogy seems apt only when the pregnancy in question was the result of rape. Even in the case of rape—a horrible violation of a woman's dignity, bodily integrity, personal autonomy, and rightful liberty—justice still requires respecting the unborn child's life. The child, after all, wasn't the rapist, did nothing wrong, and is still the mother's child. The burden of persisting in even a difficult pregnancy is not proportionate to losing one's life. That is, there exists a profound asymmetry between existence or non-existence on the one hand, and the burdens and costs of pregnancy, even one that comes with profound psychological challenges, as in cases of rape. And, of course, as a moral matter nothing justifies intentional killing of the innocent, let alone one's own child.[24]

But we shouldn't fall captive to this pro-abortion rhetorical red herring. Abortion supporters most often point to pregnancies resulting from rape not because they believe that abortion should be limited to these truly hard cases but to use these difficult examples to justify abortion on demand throughout all nine months of pregnancy. If the Thomson argument succeeded, it would justify abortion only in rare cases when the mother did not consent to sex and thus is not responsible for the fact that a new life came into existence inside of her. Even so, it still wouldn't justify intentional killing. What's important to remember is that the overwhelming majority of children are conceived as the natural result of consensual sex. Unlike Thomson's hypothetical individual, who suddenly woke up and found himself attached to the violinist, parents bear responsibility for the fact that they've conceived a child.

The first three steps of our argument—a new human being comes into existence at conception, human beings possess intrinsic dignity and worth, and government exists to protect innocent human beings from lethal violence—explain the long moral and legal tradition against murder. Examining the bodily autonomy for abortion highlights another pro-life point: Abortion is wrong not only because strangers shouldn't kill each other but also and especially because parents have special obligations to their children, and it isn't governmental overreach to require parents to fulfill those obligations. The unborn child in the womb isn't an intruder or parasite. He is exactly where he is supposed to be, doing exactly what he's supposed to be doing, and his parents are supposed to be nurturing, protecting, and loving him. Though some parents cannot care for their child after birth, they have a responsibility at least to bring their child into the world and find someone who can care for him. Carrying a baby to term and placing him for adoption is one way in which parents can fulfill their obligations to a child for whom they are unable to care after birth.

In public debate today, abortion proponents often echo Thomson's argument, describing the right to abortion with euphemisms focused on women's right to self-determination: bodily autonomy, the "right to choose," reproductive rights, or reproductive freedom. Other times, they claim that pro-lifers favor "forced pregnancy" or "forced birth." By this, abortion supporters mean that, if you oppose legal abortion, you favor forcing women to be pregnant and to give birth against their will, a denial of bodily autonomy.

This line of argument is so popular among abortion supporters that it even appeared during oral arguments at the U.S. Supreme Court in the 2021 case *Dobbs v. Jackson Women's Health Organization*. In her opening statement against Mississippi's fifteen-week ban on abortion, attorney Julie Rikelman said, "For a state to take control of a woman's body and demand that she go through pregnancy and childbirth, with all the physical risks and life-altering consequences that brings, is a fundamental deprivation of her liberty."[25]

Like most supporters of abortion, Rikelman is speaking as though she has no idea where babies come from. But we all know that sex naturally leads to children. As Erika Bachiochi (whose work we'll discuss in more detail in the next chapter) has noted, the original feminist movement was staunchly anti-abortion and in favor of voluntary motherhood. These feminists knew that bodily autonomy meant that women must consent to sex if it is to be just, including in the context of marriage, but that no one could rightly "consent" to killing an unborn child. That is, "reproductive freedom" applies prior to conception, when reproduction takes place. After conception, the issue is no longer "reproductive freedom" but rather ending a life that has already been produced. No one is in favor of "forced pregnancy" or "forced childbirth"—women should be free to decide whether or not to have children. But the way in which they exercise their freedom not to have children cannot entail killing the children they have already conceived.

But those who use Thomson's philosophy to justify abortion today have repurposed it and pushed it in an even more insidious direction. During the *Dobbs* oral arguments, for instance, both attorneys arguing against Mississippi's fifteen-week abortion ban were asked about "safe haven" laws, which shield women from prosecution if they terminate their parental rights and surrender an unwanted child to a safe haven. Justice Amy Coney Barrett asked both attorneys why safe haven laws are an insufficient solution to the supposed burden of parenthood, such that a right to abortion is still necessary.

In response, Julie Rikelman emphasized the burdens of pregnancy, echoing Thomson by arguing that continuing an unwanted pregnancy remains too burdensome on a woman's rights even if she can legally relinquish her child after birth. But the second attorney made an even more revealing admission. U.S. solicitor general Elizabeth Prelogar told Barrett that reliance on safe haven laws overlooks "the consequences of forcing [on a woman] the choice of having to decide whether to give a child up for adoption. That itself is its own monumental decision for her."[26]

The implication of Prelogar's argument was that the right to abortion is more than a right to "terminate pregnancy" or reject parenthood. As she herself said in the argument, part of the goal is to allow the woman not "to have a child in the world." The intention in abortion, then, isn't to remove a child from the womb but to make the child no longer exist. In the view of many abortion supporters, the right to abortion is the right to a dead baby. A *National Review* editorial put a fine point on it: "Abortion is valuable—it has constitutional status—because it lets mothers and fathers come as close as scalpel and poison can bring them to pretending they were never parents at all."[27]

For many abortion supporters, that is the aim: allowing mothers and fathers to choose abortion not to avoid the burden of pregnancy or the sacrifices of parenthood but as a means of eliminating their unwanted child from the world. The bodily autonomy arguments for abortion fail to acknowledge that all our liberties have limits. One standard limit on our liberty is that we aren't allowed to intentionally kill innocent people. Whether those other people are in utero or ex utero, the same basic principle applies.

Conclusion

Today, Ryan's son is a happy three-year-old, running around, playing with his sister and brother. He talks in sentences. He counts as a "person" according to the bioethicists. And he's protected under the law. As this chapter has shown, he was just as fully human, just as fully a person, and just as fully deserving of legal protection when he was still in Anna's womb. Ryan and Anna have obligations to care for, protect, and nurture him today—just as they had when he was in the womb.

The attempts to dehumanize the unborn baby fail spectacularly. There is simply no plausible scientific case that the unborn child is anything other than a human being at a certain early stage of development—an early age of life.

Likewise, the attempts to acknowledge the humanity of the unborn child but deny his moral worth and value—the various "personhood" debates—lack a firm philosophical foundation. They rely on implausible philosophical theories and lead to morally abhorrent conclusions that we'd never embrace in other circumstances.

The pro-life position alone is coherent: all human beings are moral persons because human nature is a rational nature that grounds our personal worth. That's why the law must protect all persons, born and unborn. Just as past societies once classified some human beings as non-persons based on race or religion, so today we classify a segment of humanity as non-persons based on age, size, location, or stage of development. The law should refuse to endorse such arbitrary standards of personhood and, in so doing, protect us all.

CHAPTER TWO

Abortion Harms Women and the Family

"**I** am one of sixteen million women who has had an abortion since 1973," writes Nancyjo Mann in the foreword to the 1987 book *Aborted Women, Silent No More*. Today, millions more women have joined her in seeking abortions.

"I exercised my 'right to choose,' and I became a victim of this Pandora's box," Mann continues. "It was a pretty tempting treasure. It promised to solve all of my problems and restore full control over my life. But instead, this 'right,' this 'gift,' was filled with sufferings and regret which I could never have anticipated or imagined."[1]

Mann had an abortion shortly after the Supreme Court's 1973 decision in *Roe v. Wade* invented a constitutional right to abortion. For nearly a decade thereafter, she suffered from physical side effects and severe psychological pain. By 1981, she had found peace despite her deep regret, and in 1982 she founded Women Exploited by Abortion, which ministers to women who suffer after undergoing an abortion.

Mann is one of millions of American women who have had an abortion, and she's one of countless women who suffered physically as a result of that decision and struggled with debilitating regret and shame. She, like most of those other women, was promised liberty, control, and security if she chose abortion, the best solution to a difficult situation. But rather than finding freedom or peace, she paid a steep price.

Feminists market abortion as a boon to women. In reality, it has harmed not only the unborn child but also the pregnant woman herself. In the process, it has corrupted our culture, making it a less hospitable place for both mothers and children. A mother's womb should be the safest place in the world, a sanctuary where the unborn child can grow and develop for nine months before emerging into the community of his or her family. Abortion injects violence into that sacred relationship. It tells women that, at least in some cases, her child is her enemy. By striking at the heart of that most foundational human relationship, a society that allows abortion risks compromising the solidarity that binds us all together.

It should come as no surprise, then, that in the decades since the Court decided *Roe*, legal abortion has proven itself an unmitigated disaster for American women, contrary to what feminists promised at the time. In 1992, the Supreme Court in *Planned Parenthood v. Casey* affirmed the central holding in *Roe* and declared that it could not overturn that ruling because, in the intervening two decades, women had come to rely on abortion for ordering their lives and achieving equality.

But the past fifty years since *Roe* have shown us that women are not better off when abortion is legal and widely available. We now know that women who undergo an abortion face the possibility of immediate physical and psychological harm, as well as devastating long-term ramifications. In this chapter, we outline data illustrating that, far from being safe and uncomplicated, abortion procedures expose women to significant health risks, including difficulty in future pregnancies. Some women wrestle with negative mental-health consequences for the rest of their lives.

Abortion, acting as the ultimate backstop that renders sex intentionally recreational and sterile rather than relational and fruitful, has poisoned the relationship between men and women. Its logic pits mothers and fathers against one another instead of preserving love and solidarity between them. The ready availability of abortion enables men to more easily justify abandoning their children and their children's mother.

The result has been five decades of broken hearts and broken homes, dissolution, destruction, and despair. Rather than climbing the social ladder and witnessing the gains promised by pro-abortion women's rights activists, women are more embittered than they were decades ago. To be sure, there have been some notable positive changes—such as women being able to work outside the home, have greater employment flexibility, and have more help at home from their husbands—but none of these are thanks to legal abortion. Even in spite of these developments, women on the whole aren't flourishing, and, by some accounts, say they are unhappier than ever.

A landmark study on the "paradox of declining female happiness" found that, over a period of thirty-five years starting in the early 1970s, women's subjective happiness and well-being has declined both absolutely and relative to men, a trend that holds consistent across industrialized countries. The study's authors, Wharton School researchers Betsey Stevenson and Justin Wolfers, question whether modern social constructs have done what they promised for women or whether perhaps they've caused some problems of their own.[2]

While supporters of *Roe* promised women that legal abortion would set them free and place them on equal footing with men, in reality it has accelerated the ongoing decay of relationships and families. It has brought with it a host of new problems for women to solve—including, in many cases, significant physical complications and long-lasting psychological consequences. In this chapter, we sketch the origins of the modern feminist crusade for legalized abortion. We detail the immediate physical risks of abortion to women, as well as the long-term physical and psychological ramifications. Finally, we explain how the abortion industry denies and tries to hide these realities, preferring instead to promote abortion as an easy, risk-free solution.

Second-Wave Feminists: The Original Cheerleaders for Legal Abortion

In the 1960s and 1970s, prominent liberal women's rights advocates, leading a movement known as second-wave feminism, made legal abortion the lynchpin of their case for female equality and empowerment. Whereas first-wave feminists such as Susan B. Anthony and Elizabeth Cady Stanton argued for full legal equality for women, and Clare Boothe Luce, Frances Willard, and Hannah More emphasized the equal dignity of women's distinctively feminine attributes, leading second-wave feminists argued that equality is sameness.

For women to be equal to men, second-wave feminists argued, they would need more than legal equality. They would also need to reject distinctively feminine attributes in order to achieve similar outcomes and ways of living as men. These thinkers argued that, without abortion, women could not fully control their bodies, their reproduction, and their future. In other words, women needed legal abortion in order to be sexually liberated and participate in society as free and equal citizens. If men could enjoy sexual activity and professional success without the burden of pregnancy and children, then so too must women.

Their commitment to abortion was so uncompromising that it caused a significant fracture within the feminist movement in the United States, as leaders of the women's rights movement ousted allies from their ranks for being insufficiently supportive of legal abortion.[3] Before long, the women's rights movement in the U.S. had become synonymous with the campaign for unlimited abortion on demand. Those pink p***y hats have a historical pedigree.

Some prominent second-wave feminist theorists, such as Shulamith Firestone, took the argument a step further, claiming that abortion was an essential step in liberating women from the "tyranny of biology."[4] Not only would abortion allow women to eliminate the physical burden of pregnancy and avoid the sacrifice of childrearing, but it would aid in dissolving marriage and the nuclear family, which many feminists believe are inherently harmful to women. Here's how Firestone put it in her landmark work *The Dialectic of Sex*:

> Just as to assure elimination of economic classes requires the revolt of the underclass (the proletariat) and...their seizure of the means of *production*, so as to assure the elimination of sexual classes requires the revolt of the underclass (women) and the seizure of control of *reproduction*: not only the full restoration to women of ownership of their own bodies, but also their (temporary) seizure of control of human fertility—the new population biology as well as the social institutions of childbearing and childrearing. And just as the end goal of socialist revolution was not only the elimination of the economic class *privilege* but of the economic class *distinction* itself, so the end goal of the feminist revolution must be, unlike that of the first feminist movement, not just the elimination of male *privilege* but of the sex *distinction* itself: genital differences

between human beings would no longer matter culturally.... The reproduction of the species by one sex for the
benefit of both would be replaced by (at least the option of)
artificial reproduction: children would be born to both
sexes equally, or independently of either, however one
chooses to look at it; the dependence of the child on the
mother (and vice versa) would give way to a greatly short-
ened dependence on a small group of others in general and
any remaining inferiority to adults in physical strength
would be compensated for culturally.... The tyranny of the
biological family would be broken.[5]

In this vision, the most distinctive characteristic of female
biology—nurturing a child in the womb—is something from which
women must be liberated. Biology is recast as slavery.

Today, most who consider themselves progressive women's rights
advocates remain dedicated to legal abortion, but they are even more
extreme in their support for it than were their foremothers in the
second-wave feminist movement. Modern feminists agree that women
are disadvantaged relative to men, and they continue to demand legal
abortion as a solution, but now they also demand that the federal
government fund all contraception and abortion. Anything less, they
say, won't allow women to achieve liberation and equal rights.[6]

No longer do *Roe*'s defenders lament abortion as a sad and difficult choice that women sometimes must make in challenging
circumstances. Instead, they insist that society must endorse every
abortion as an affirmative good. Activist groups such as Shout Your
Abortion maintain that, if women are ever unhappy after obtaining
an abortion, it is only because society perpetuates an unnecessary
stigma that women should work to erase by publicly celebrating
their abortions.[7]

But if legal, readily available abortion were really the solution to the problems of American women, why do prominent feminist advocates seem to remain so unhappy with what they've achieved? In her recent book *The H-Spot*, progressive writer and attorney Jill Filipovic argues that modern feminism has failed women. She acknowledges that American women are still unhappy despite getting what feminists demanded, a reality she accounts for by arguing that our society and government weren't founded to guarantee female pleasure.

Achieving feminist goals hasn't been enough, she admits, and her solution is to demand *more*. "For so many American women, contraception and abortion are nearly unparalleled social goods," Filipovic argues. "They make sex better. They make life better."[8] If women remain unhappy, it is only because—in her view—society has yet to be reshaped around the needs of women, down to government funding for contraception and abortion. "Contraception, abortion, and the ability to parent when we choose are unassailable social goods," Filipovic writes, "necessary not just for the rights of women but for our happiness, too. They should be easily available and affordable for every woman, regardless of income or location."[9]

Even though millions upon millions of women in the United States have obtained abortions in the decades since *Roe*, activists such as Filipovic aren't satisfied with the progress made toward female empowerment some fifty years later. Why are the feminists who got exactly what they wanted still clamoring for *more*?

Perhaps it's because abortion has done significant damage to women and society, even if they don't realize it, starting with how it encourages mothers to view their children as antagonists, how it allows men to view women as always sexually available without any marital commitment or promise of stability required, and how it allows employers and society as a whole to treat the male body as the norm and female fertility as a problem to be solved—rather than a reality to structure social relations around.

But even on its own terms, the promise of abortion as women's liberation is an illusion, a Band-Aid on a bigger wound, an act that can only compound any problem that already exists. Turning the most foundational and vulnerable human relationship into one of violence can only harm both mother and child—and that's exactly what it's done. Even though many women experience abortion as a solution—such as when abortion appears to alleviate financial or relationship concerns—and even though many women have abortions without suffering obvious physical or psychological consequences, no woman is better off for having participated in lethal violence against her child. Violence against innocent human beings is never a real solution.

Women Don't Need Abortion: *Casey*'s "Reliance Interest" Argument

Supporters of abortion argue that, while you might decide that abortion isn't the right choice for you, it has to remain an option so that women can live as full, equal citizens on par with men. Abortion, on this argument, enables women to participate in sex and the economy in the way that men can—rejecting the unchosen obligations of pregnancy and children.

On this view, consent to sex does not entail consent to a child. If your theory of morality grounds all duties in consent and rejects unchosen obligations, then consent to sex doesn't entail any obligations to the child who might result. Indeed, many men live out this theory on a daily basis when they abandon the women with whom they've conceived a child. Pro-abortion feminists simply ask for that same freedom to walk away from unwanted pregnancy—by killing the child.

But why should we treat walking away from obligations as the ideal? Why encourage or enable women to follow the path of the deadbeat dad, rather than insisting that men take responsibility for their actions? Reproduction is asymmetrical with respect to males and females throughout the animal kingdom, and this reality is particularly pronounced among humans. The male role in reproduction is relatively brief and enjoyable compared with the long, arduous role that women play in gestating a child. The question is: How should society respond to this reality? How do we structure a society to take the reality of asymmetrical reproduction seriously?

For pro-choice activists, abortion solves the dilemma of reproductive asymmetry by enabling women to erase the natural procreative result of sex when contraception fails to prevent an unwanted pregnancy. Their solution is to eliminate the asymmetry by eliminating the unborn child, the fruit of reproduction—in other words, to reject the bodily nature of women and use abortion to pretend that their bodies can function like those of men.[10]

This logic has reached the Supreme Court. Consider the 1992 decision in *Planned Parenthood v. Casey*, which upheld the heart of *Roe* and preserved the right to abortion. Some readers will remember the sophomoric passage in the plurality opinion: "At the heart of liberty is the right to define one's own concept of existence, of meaning, of the universe, and of the mystery of human life."[11] That was at the core of *Casey*. But so too was the argument that women needed abortion precisely to define for themselves the meaning of life. Part of the justices' rationale was that American women had come to depend on access to abortion. In legal parlance, this is known as a "reliance interest," and it is one criterion the Court uses to determine whether a case should be upheld.

As the plurality opinion put it in *Casey*, in the decades since *Roe*, women had become used to being able to access abortion, and they would suffer inordinately if that right were taken away:

> For two decades of economic and social developments, people have organized intimate relationships and made choices that define their views of themselves and their places in society, in reliance on the availability of abortion in the event that contraception should fail. The ability of women to participate equally in the economic and social life of the Nation has been facilitated by their ability to control their reproductive lives.[12]

In other words, the *Casey* plurality—led by Justice Anthony Kennedy—argued that American women need abortion to participate in society as men's equals. Rather than structuring "the economic and social life of the Nation" to respect the asymmetry of reproduction, abortion allows women to "participate equally" without requiring the nation to take female bodily nature seriously.

On this rationale, if the Court reversed *Roe* in *Casey* and allowed states to legislate on abortion as they saw fit, women would sink back to where they were before 1973. Justice Harry Blackmun, the author of *Roe* and a concurring justice in *Casey*, argued that this was a disadvantaged position relative to American men: "Because motherhood has a dramatic impact on a woman's educational prospects, employment opportunities, and self-determination, restrictive abortion laws deprive her of basic control over her life."[13]

But in reality, the fifty years since *Roe* have demonstrated the exact opposite of what the *Casey* plurality decided. At the very least, abortion has not solved the problems its supporters claimed it would, and even on its own terms it has not been the cause of increased educational or workplace success for women. An analysis of labor, education, and poverty statistics, for instance, reveals that while abortion rates have steadily decreased since they peaked shortly after *Roe*, women's college-graduation rates and workforce participation have continued to increase.[14] Between 1980 and 2017, the U.S. abortion rate dropped by more than 50 percent, but during that same time frame, women have made major advancements judging from key economic, professional, and academic metrics.[15] Since 1980, even as the abortion rate has been plummeting, women's per capita earnings have increased, and the income gap between men and women has decreased.[16] Today, women earn a higher percentage than men of bachelor's, master's, and doctoral degrees.[17] In 2019, women out-paced men 53 percent to 47 percent in doctoral degrees and 59 percent to 41 percent in master's degrees—they've maintained a bigger share of these degrees for over a decade, and today outnumber men in graduate programs 141 to 100.[18]

It seems unlikely that abortion, in other words, has been a major component of women's achieving greater and greater educational and career success.

Below we explain how abortion has fostered an anti-woman and anti-natal culture, how it harms the physical and psychological well-being of women who have abortions, and how it poses risks to women that the abortion industry doesn't take seriously.

Legal Abortion Enables an Anti-Woman Society

Women are much worse off for living in a society that has embraced abortion. Because abortion is so readily available and widely accepted, it has increasingly become a choice that women are expected to make, especially when they find themselves in less than ideal circumstances. Perhaps the most significant detriment to women of such a culture is that widespread acceptance of abortion has undermined healthy relationships between men and women and severed the natural connection between sex and reproduction.

"Abortion restrictions do not deny sexual and reproductive autonomy to women; reality does," writes legal scholar Erika Bachiochi. "While pregnant, a woman is carrying a new and vulnerable human being within her. Unlike a biological father, a pregnant woman cannot just walk away; to approach the desired autonomy of the child-abandoning man, a pregnant woman must engage in a life-destroying act."[19] This disparity imposes natural obligations on men and women to care for each other and for the children they conceive together.

Rather than neutralizing the disparities between men and women to free women from the burden of pregnancy—as feminists claimed it would—abortion has intensified the ways in which our culture treats pregnancy as a "woman's problem."[20] Abortion has not increased support for pregnant mothers in need but has fed a culture that treats women who continue pregnancies as if they're on their own, because, after all, they could've chosen abortion.[21]

"Under the guise of women's rights, equality arguments for abortion suggest that females are intrinsically blighted by their reproductive capacity to bear children," wrote pro-life female scholars in an amicus brief in the 2021 Supreme Court case *Dobbs v. Jackson Women's Health Organization*. "These arguments tend, unwittingly perhaps, to promote the male childless norm in educational and employment settings."[22]

Abortion has made it easier for men to leave women and harder for women to say no to abortion, even when they would prefer to choose life. Abortion fuels male abandonment, making it easier for cowardly or irresponsible fathers to justify leaving the mother of their child if she refuses to seek an abortion for an unexpected pregnancy. As Nobel prize–winning economist George Akerlof and his wife, Janet Yellen—who served as chair of the Federal Reserve and is currently President Joe Biden's treasury secretary—noted in a 1996 article in the *Quarterly Journal of Economics*, abortion and contraception have led to a decline in "shotgun" marriages, which in turn has led to increases in child poverty, as well as a trend they deemed the "feminization of poverty." "By making the birth of the child the physical choice of the mother, the sexual revolution has made marriage and child support a social choice of the father," they wrote.[23]

Some women choose abortion based on a selfish ideology of autonomy. But some women obtain an abortion under significant duress from their partner, whether literal force or coercion, including financial pressure or threats to leave the relationship.[24] One study out of Norway found that about a quarter of women said "pressure from male partner" was part of why they had an abortion: "Women in this study gave examples of what they experienced as pressure from the male partner—one man said that if the woman did not have an abortion, she would ruin his future and his whole life. Another man threatened to break up the relationship and let the woman become a single mother. Thus, lack of important social support, sympathizing with the male partner, a broken heart and fear of standing alone may be components of the reason 'pressure from the male partner' to have an induced abortion."[25]

According to some surveys, a majority of women in the United States who seek abortion do so because of lack of support from a partner.[26] As we'll discuss in Chapter Three, the easy availability of abortion has done much to exacerbate racial disparities rather than promote greater equality. The breakdown of families, fueled in part by abortion, has intensified inequality especially among black Americans. A 1996 study in *Economica* found that, while changes in family structure and marriage patterns increased poverty for all Americans, they harmed black children the most: "Had 1971 black marriage patterns prevailed in 1989, one-third of poor black children would have escaped poverty. The overall poverty rate would have declined from about 14% to 13% instead of increasing to 17%. Income inequality among black and white children would have increased in the absence of family structure changes, but only by half as much as the actual increase."[27]

Abortion treats pregnancy as a disease and treats the male body as the norm, disadvantaging women because of their natural role in the reproductive process. In the workplace, such a mindset lends itself to a corporate culture within which women must behave like men to succeed. Instead of accommodating women's natural capacity for childbearing and, often, natural desire for childrearing, a culture that permits abortion encourages women to behave like career-focused men: delaying marriage and childbearing and minimizing the negative effects of childbearing and parenthood on workplace performance.[28]

A society that treats abortion as an acceptable solution to an unplanned pregnancy is less likely to prioritize positive goals such as community and spousal support for women who are raising children, and greater workplace opportunity that's compatible with family life, including more flexibility in employment. In Chapter Seven, we will discuss how major companies, including the abortion business called Planned Parenthood, have discriminated against pregnant employees, refusing to accommodate their physical needs and disadvantaging them for promotions as a result of their choice to become mothers.

The alternative is to enable men and women to flourish in their roles as husbands and wives, fathers and mothers, to encourage men and women to share the hard work of making a home, building a marriage and family, and offering a witness of self-sacrificial love to a world longing for meaning. Law and policy, grounded in an anthropology that takes seriously the realities of human embodiment, would view both pregnant mothers and their unborn children as vulnerable, dependent members of society who are entitled to the protection of the law. Not only that, but they, like all of us, are entitled to our support, to rely on the networks of giving and receiving that all human beings need to survive and flourish.[29]

Abortion Poses Both Short- and Long-Term Physical Consequences for Women's Health

Though abortion-rights advocates bill themselves as supporters of women's health, the sad reality is that both chemical and surgical abortions pose significant physical risks to women, even under the safest medical conditions. While the unborn child is always a victim of abortion, all too often the conditions under which doctors perform abortions are risky for women, too. The data on such complications and side effects are spotty at best, as abortionists aren't always required to report such occurrences, and regulators have been known to ignore or even cover up violations.

Consider, for instance, the shocking story of Kermit Gosnell and his house of horrors.[30] Gosnell is a former abortionist who operated a filthy clinic outside Philadelphia and is now spending the rest of his life in prison, in part for the involuntary manslaughter of Karnamaya Mongar, who obtained an abortion at his clinic.[31]

In Gosnell's clinic, the surgical-procedure rooms were unsanitary. Medical equipment was unsterilized and rusty. The emergency exit was blocked by furniture and padlocked with a lock to which no one had a key. The recliners where women rested after an abortion were dirty and equipped with bloodstained blankets. Investigators found jars containing the severed feet of babies, and testimony indicated that, at one point, Gosnell had saved at least twenty such jars. All told, the clinic contained the fetal remains of forty-seven babies, stored throughout the clinic in freezers, empty water and milk jugs, juice bottles, and cat-food containers.[32]

An especially concerning element of Gosnell's story is how he evaded notice and avoided legal consequences for as long as he did, operating his clinic in squalid conditions for decades. When Mongar died after an abortion at Gosnell's clinic, the abortionist informed the state health department, as per legal requirements. What happened next defies any reasonable explanation.

Gosnell's fax, received by health quality administrator Darlene Augustine, was passed up the chain at the Pennsylvania Department of Health (DOH). It went first to Cynthia Boyne, director of Home Health, and next to Janice Staloski, head of the Bureau of Community Licensure and Certification. Boyne and Staloski were the two state employees charged with regulating all of Pennsylvania's abortion facilities. Faced with the report of Mongar's death as a result of her abortion at Gosnell's clinic, they decided to do nothing.[33]

As Gosnell documentarians Ann McElhinney and Phelim McAleer report, Boyne and Staloski "did not follow up with the medical examiner's office, or the Hospital of the University of Pennsylvania where Mongar was taken by ambulance and later died. They did not call the responding paramedics or the Philadelphia police department.... No one from the Department of Health bothered to visit [the clinic] to speak with Gosnell or anyone else about Mongar's death."[34]

In fact, not only did no one at the Pennsylvania DOH follow up with Gosnell, but they actively suppressed the information. Department of Health attorneys told Augustine, the administrator who received the initial fax about Gosnell, not to speak with anyone about Mongar's death. Even when law enforcement raided Gosnell's clinic in a drug bust several months later, Augustine likewise instructed a clinic nurse to stay similarly silent.

But the extent of the attempted cover-up was even worse. As it turns out, Staloski had visited Gosnell's decrepit clinic as early as 1992, then as state health inspector, and despite the fact that she observed "multiple violations of the law and threats to patient safety," her report on the facility said she had found "no deficiencies."[35] This lack of oversight and enforcement wasn't confined to the state health department. The grand jury report in Gosnell's eventual trial found that the National Abortion Federation (NAF) inspected his abortion clinic after he applied for NAF membership, but despite finding conditions so poor that they refused to certify him, they neglected to report any of what they had found to the requisite authorities.[36]

Gosnell was brought to justice not by anyone tasked with regulating the abortion industry or overseeing its standards but because of what began as a drug bust, operated by local Philadelphia law enforcement. When the drug raid turned up overwhelming evidence of filthy conditions and unsafe procedures—conditions that someone other than state health officials had finally witnessed—the state had no choice but to take the problem seriously.

While most abortion facilities in the United States operate far more cleanly than Gosnell's, his story is illustrative. He was able to violate multiple state and federal laws for years, performing dangerous abortion procedures in unsafe conditions, under the eye of regulators explicitly tasked with monitoring abortion providers. That reality is of great concern to pro-lifers, who want to protect the unborn child, to be sure, but who also care about the health of the mothers seeking abortions.

The reality is that the abortion industry in the United States remains largely unregulated, and often enough, rules that apply to regular medical providers go unenforced or are explicitly rejected when it comes to abortion. Even worse, the abortion industry seeks to protect this status quo, routinely opposing efforts to impose safety standards or reporting requirements on clinics for the benefit of women's health. This state of affairs obscures the costs of abortion to women, which range from immediate complications and long-term physical risks to psychological distress long after the fact.

The Risks of Abortion for Women's Short-Term Physical Health

Even when abortion is legal and mainstream, and even when it takes place in clinics with higher standards of care than Gosnell's, women suffer complications from abortion. Take as just one small example "The Abortion Profiteers," an investigative series published by the *Chicago Sun-Times* in the mid-1970s, which found that a dozen women had died in the Chicago area after legal abortions, and their deaths hadn't been reported. The investigators found that these abortions had been performed by "incompetent, unlicensed or unqualified physicians under unsterile conditions, without the benefit of anesthesia, and sometimes on women who were not even pregnant." The report continued: "Because of unsanitary conditions and haphazard clinic care, many women suffered debilitating cramps, massive infections and such severe internal damage that all of their reproductive organs were removed, investigators said."[37]

These sorts of complications didn't end in the 1970s. Indeed, even if we assume that physicians are generally licensed and competent, and operating environments sterile, serious complications still occur. According to a recent study from Drexel University, of the roughly one million abortions in the United States each year, about 2 percent result in complications—ranging from bleeding and infection to uterine atony and hemorrhaging, disseminated intravascular coagulation (a life-threatening condition that leads to massive hemorrhage), and injuries to adjacent organs.[38]

Two percent might not sound like much, but this means that somewhere in the realm of twenty thousand American women will suffer each year from significant medical problems as a result of undergoing an abortion—and given how underreported abortion and related complications are, twenty thousand is likely the lowest number of women who experience these consequences. That risk is all the more troubling when we consider that it comes as the result of a procedure that is medically unnecessary.[39] Modern medicine can treat the mother without intentionally harming the child. While it might be necessary to deliver an unborn child early or give a pregnant mother a treatment that's risky or even known to be lethal for her baby—as in treatments for ectopic pregnancies or a cancerous uterus, as we saw in the last chapter—intentionally killing an unborn child is never medically necessary.

While many abortion defenders are quick to argue that women suffer from complications only when they undergo illegal "unsafe" abortions, this isn't true. Women experience complications even in well-developed and medically advanced countries.[40] This is well documented, despite the fact that our record-keeping on such events is shoddy, reporting requirements are minimal, and abortionists often fail to admit their mistakes.

For the past several years, Americans United for Life (AUL) has produced a report called *Unsafe*, a comprehensive research project compiling statistics on the nation's abortion clinics, gathered from Freedom of Information Act requests in states that require abortion-related reporting. Its reports exclude California, New York, and several other states that decline to report abortion statistics—several of which are states with the most permissive abortion laws in the country. Even without those large states, the AUL report still finds egregious violations, and the absence of that reporting data suggests that the information we do have represents only a small part of a larger problem.

The most recent iteration of *Unsafe* documented more than 2,400 health and safety violations in about 300 abortion facilities between 2008 and 2020.[41] Among other violations, these clinics were found to have employed unlicensed, untrained, or otherwise unqualified abortionists and staff, operated without the requisite licensing, faced fines for failing to maintain clean conditions, and mishandled narcotics, sometimes with severe consequences.

An illustrative and tragic example is that of twenty-four-year-old Tonya Reaves, who in 2012 bled to death after obtaining a surgical abortion at a Planned Parenthood clinic in Cook County, Illinois.[42] After she experienced severe hemorrhaging during the procedure, Reaves was taken to a nearby emergency room, where staff completed the abortion and discovered that her uterus had been severely perforated and about a third of her total blood volume was located in her abdomen. The Cook County medical examiner later determined via autopsy that Reaves's cause of death was "hemorrhage resulting from cervical dilation and evacuation [second-trimester abortion]."[43]

Shockingly, pro-abortion activists often minimize tragedies such as the death of Reaves, emphasizing the rarity of such occurrences and arguing that abortion must remain legal so it can be "safe," insisting without evidence that abortion regulations cause more deaths among pregnant women. The best evidence actually suggests that the opposite is true, as we'll explain later in this chapter.[44]

Planned Parenthood was quick to defend abortion in the wake of Reaves's death, even before offering condolences: "While legal abortion services in the United States have a very high safety record, a tragedy such as this is devastating to loved ones and we offer our deepest sympathies," said Carole Brite, president and CEO of Planned Parenthood of Illinois.[45]

Tragic deaths such as this one are relatively rare, but even the supposedly safer option of chemical abortions—FDA-approved for use only up to ten weeks' gestation, but often recommended by abortion providers beyond that point—poses more risks than abortion supporters are willing to admit.[46] Indeed, it's actually more dangerous than surgical abortion. Chemical abortions, or the abortion pill, now account for more than half of all abortions in the United States, and by some analyses an uptick in chemical abortion was the reason for an overall increase in the U.S. abortion rate in 2018 and 2019.[47] According to the most recent data from the Centers for Disease Control (CDC), 43.7 percent of all abortions in the United States are chemical abortions.[48] Statistics from the pro-choice Guttmacher Institute, meanwhile, show that the share of all U.S. abortions that are chemical abortions rose from 5 percent in 2001 to 54 percent in 2020.[49]

The two pills used in a chemical abortion work in concert: first, the mother takes mifepristone, which cuts off the nutrients to the unborn child and begins to make the mother's womb inhospitable. Next, the mother takes misoprostol, which induces early labor and triggers her body to expel the unborn child, who has likely already perished due to lack of nutrients. According to providers, abortion pills don't pose the same risks as surgical abortion, and they're perfectly safe. "It's kind of like having a really heavy period," Planned Parenthood's website promises of the abortion pill.[50]

Abortion businesses and their supporters, including media reporters, typically refer to chemical abortion as "medication abortion." This phrase suggests that pregnant mothers are somehow being "medicated" or receiving health-care treatment for a pathology, when in fact the chemical-abortion drugs treat no disease; they do quite the opposite, blocking nutrients from the unborn child so that he gradually starves and dies.

And chemical abortion isn't risk-free for mothers, either. According to information collected by the Food and Drug Administration, prescribers of mifepristone have reported 24 deaths, 4,195 adverse events, 1,042 hospitalizations, 599 incidents of blood loss requiring transfusions, 412 infections, and 69 severe infections—and this accounts only for what was voluntarily reported, as adverse-event reporting for mifepristone is not mandatory.[51]

Most significant, women administer chemical abortions to themselves at home. If they require follow-up care for complications, it can be hard to come by, especially if they don't know when they need to seek it. Sometimes, women don't know what to expect or what side effects are normal, because abortionists decline to inform them of possible risks. Later in this chapter, we'll address the particular types of psychological consequences that women face as a result of self-administering a chemical abortion.

One major risk of prescribing chemical abortions via telemedicine— a policy abortion supporters advocate—rather than in a doctor's office is that a woman will misidentify how far along she is or take abortion pills when she has an ectopic pregnancy: "At-home abortion means that the gestational age is simply the woman's best guess and the timeline extends as she waits for the pills to arrive by mail. For the one to two percent of pregnancies that are ectopic, telemedicine abortion is going to be both ineffective and dangerous to the mother's health, a tradeoff that activists seem to have calculated is worth accepting to ensure access to at-home abortion on demand."[52]

The World Health Organization has acknowledged "that it is more difficult to diagnose an ectopic pregnancy during and after medical methods of abortion, due to the similarity of symptoms. Additionally, neither mifepristone nor misoprostol are treatments for ectopic pregnancy, which, if present, will continue to grow. Therefore, health-care staff must be particularly alert to clinical signs of ectopic pregnancy.... Women should be told to seek medical advice promptly if they experience symptoms that may indicate ectopic pregnancy, such as severe and intensifying abdominal pain, particularly if it is one-sided."[53] These risks are, of course, impossible to mitigate in the absence of in-person medical examination prior to prescribing a chemical abortion.

The United Kingdom's experience with shifting its policy on telemedicine abortions suggests that these concerns are not unfounded. In early 2020, Britain began allowing women to obtain chemical abortions via telemedicine. In the first six months of 2020, the overall number of abortions in the United Kingdom increased by about 4 percent. One researcher found that from 2019 to 2020, emergency calls related to chemical-abortion complications increased by 54 percent across England and Wales, and ambulance responses for such calls rose by 19 percent. The U.K.'s Care Quality Commission identified eleven cases in which women were admitted to the hospital after taking the chemical-abortion drug that had been prescribed via telemedicine beyond the gestational age limit for the pills.[54] Though officials announced in February 2022 that the United Kingdom would abolish the telemedicine policy out of concern for women's safety, the Parliament decided in a narrow vote to leave telemedicine chemical abortions in place.[55]

Another risk of chemical abortions via telemedicine is that it will enable sex trafficking. Criminals trafficking women are less likely to be caught if they can receive abortion-inducing drugs without ever having to bring a woman they are trafficking to an in-person clinic. If a woman trapped in trafficking or abuse visits a clinic in person, she might be identified as a victim and could receive assistance. Moving the chemical-abortion process to telemedicine will make it easier to traffic women without discovery.

Even so, there is no guarantee that a victim of trafficking or abuse will receive help at an abortion clinic. A 2014 review found that, in the United States, trafficking victims are highly likely to visit Planned Parenthood; about 30 percent of the victims surveyed said they had visited a Planned Parenthood clinic while being trafficked.[56] Unfortunately, undercover pro-life investigations suggest that not all Planned Parenthood employees are prepared to assist such victims. In 2011, an undercover investigation by pro-life group Live Action found that Planned Parenthood staffers at seven abortion clinics in Arizona, New Jersey, New York, Virginia, and Washington, D.C., appeared willing to aid and abet the trafficking or abuse of minors.[57] Though Planned Parenthood subsequently pledged to train all of its employees to detect and disclose suspected sexual abuse of minors, a follow-up investigation suggests that Planned Parenthood executives didn't take the problem all that seriously.

In an interview with Live Action, former Planned Parenthood clinic manager Ramona Treviño said that instead of training employees to assist victims, the organization taught employees to discern when they were being secretly recorded. Treviño says that Planned Parenthood officials played Live Action's undercover footage for staffers, demonstrating how managers could better identify undercover journalists.

"I said, 'I'm confused. When are we going to actually begin the retraining? What can I do as a manager to take this information back to my staff and enforce policies and procedures that would help protect women who are experiencing either sex trafficking or sexual abuse in any way?'" Treviño recalled. She says she was told in response, "We're not here to talk about that, Ramona. We are here to teach you to identify if you're being videotaped or recorded or entrapped in any way."[58]

Meanwhile, a recent paper in *Issues in Law and Medicine* cataloguing FDA reports of adverse events after chemical abortion found that, over the last two decades, "significant morbidity and mortality have occurred following the use of mifepristone as an abortifacient."[59] This conclusion tracks with other studies. One study using data from women in California's Medicaid program found that chemical abortions had four times the complication rate of surgical abortions.[60] Another study, this one from Australia, found that more than 3 percent of women who took mifepristone required ER admission to manage complications—not an insignificant figure, if the rate holds true across populations, considering that somewhere between 300,000 and 450,000 women obtain chemical abortions each year.[61] The pro-abortion group Marie Stopes Australia reported a 6.37 percent complication rate for chemical abortions, including complications such as incomplete abortion, continuation of pregnancy, or infection, but seemingly not including common complications such as hemorrhage.[62] By contrast, the same Marie Stopes report found a complication rate for surgical abortions of 1.82 percent.

A study out of Finland, meanwhile, found that chemical abortions have a four times higher complication rate than surgical abortions—and that about 6 percent of women who undergo a chemical abortion will require follow-up surgery.[63] And a groundbreaking new study published in *Health Services Research and Managerial Epidemiology* found that the hospitalization rate for complications from chemical abortion is twice that of the complications related to surgical abortions. The study also found that hospital visits for follow-up treatment after a chemical abortion are often misreported as treatment for a miscarriage, making it even more difficult to ascertain the true complication rate.[64]

Across the pond, Philippa Stroud, member of the House of Lords, called attention to the reporting gaps in complications from at-home abortions. While official government forms reveal only one complication for more than twenty-three thousand at-home abortions between April 2020 and June 2020, Stroud noted, Freedom of Information requests "to just six hospitals during the same period suggested that women were presenting due to complications at a rate *five times higher* than that reported by the Department of Health and Social Care."[65] In response, Britain's under secretary for health and social care acknowledged the problem, saying that Stroud "alludes to exactly the kind of data gaps that we wish to address."[66] Those knowledge gaps are strikingly similar here in the United States, and efforts to improve reporting requirements for abortion and related medical complications have not been successful, stymied at every turn by supporters of abortion.[67]

While the complication rates for abortion in the United States may appear low, it's essential to remember that these side effects and complications are almost certainly underreported, a problem that supporters of abortion strenuously oppose fixing. In 2016, the FDA reviewed its mifepristone regulations and removed the requirement to report any complications other than death.[68] When the FDA decided in December 2021 to approve chemical abortion prescribed via telemedicine, it cited this subsequent lack of reported complications as proof that the drugs cause no major problems.[69] The reporting and complication rates appeared low, in other words, precisely because the FDA essentially asked not to be told about any issues that arose, a politically motivated decision aimed at making it easier to authorize at-home abortion.

Thankfully, even as the rate of chemical abortions in the United States has increased dramatically, doctors have pioneered abortion-pill reversal, a safe and effective method of halting and reversing an in-progress chemical abortion if a pregnant mother regrets her decision. Abortion-pill reversal can be attempted only for women who have taken the first of the two chemical-abortion drugs but not the second, and she must start the reversal process within seventy-two hours of taking the abortion pill. The method entails prescribing a sustained regimen of progesterone, which competes with the abortion drug in the woman's body and, best-case scenario, prevents the drug from cutting off nutrition and support to the unborn child.

Though abortion supporters have attempted to argue that abortion-pill reversal is unscientific and even harmful to women—going so far as to sue states that require abortionists to inform women about the method prior to prescribing a chemical abortion—the largest case series studying abortion-pill reversal found that nearly 70 percent of the 754 women studied were able to undo the effects of mifepristone and carry healthy babies to term.[70] Since doctors first began prescribing it, the method has helped somewhere in the realm of 2,500 women save their unborn children.

The Risks of Abortion for Women's Long-Term Physical Health

Even if a woman manages to avoid a dangerous or unsanitary clinic, an incompetent doctor, and immediate complications following an abortion procedure, she remains at risk for long-term health consequences. There is a substantial and growing body of evidence from multiple studies showing that women who have an abortion, especially in their first pregnancy, are at an increased risk of developing pre-menopausal breast cancer. This results from the way that a woman's first pregnancy causes growth in immature breast tissue, growth that is halted if the pregnancy ends before the woman gives birth, leaving her with a large amount of cancer-susceptible tissue.[71] From 1957 to 2018, seventy-six studies differentiated between induced abortion and spontaneous abortion (the technical term for miscarriage), sixty of which found an association between induced abortion and increased breast cancer risk.[72]

Substantial public-health research has also found a significant link between abortions later in pregnancy and the likelihood of being diagnosed with breast cancer later in life.[73] Abortion providers and proponents deny this connection, often promoting a single study that they argue disproves the abortion–breast cancer link.[74] What they ignore is that the very study they cite demonstrates an increased risk of breast cancer among women who obtained an abortion after eighteen weeks' gestation.[75] Many of the most reliable studies on the topic have found a statistically significant increase in risk of breast cancer after elective abortion.[76] This risk is one major concern; the way abortion supporters downplay or deny it is another. An understanding of breast physiology, common sense, and unbiased research demonstrate that having an abortion before ever carrying a pregnancy to term increases a woman's lifetime risk of breast cancer, while carrying one's first baby to term decreases that risk. As Dr. Donna Harrison told us:

> The single most important factor in a woman's risk for breast cancer is her age at the time that she brings her first pregnancy to term. Why? When a girl goes through puberty, her breast tissue grows. But that breast tissue is mostly what is called "Type 1 and Type 2" tissue. This kind of breast tissue cannot produce milk, because the tissue has to change into Type 4 tissue in order to produce milk. And that change requires pregnancy.
>
> When a woman becomes pregnant for the first time, her breasts begin to grow, and she feels breast tenderness from this rapid growth. But the growing breast tissue is still Type 1 and 2 tissue until she reaches about eight months of pregnancy, at which point a little more than half of her breast tissue has turned into Type 4 tissue.
>
> Why is this important? Ninety-nine percent of breast cancers arise from Type 1 and 2 breast tissue. Type 4

(milk-producing) breast tissue is permanently cancer resistant.

Once a woman has taken a pregnancy past thirty-two weeks, she has significantly decreased her chances of ever developing breast cancer. That is why age at first pregnancy is the single most important determinant of breast-cancer risk. The earlier she brings a first pregnancy to term, the lower her risk. The older she is when she brings a first pregnancy to term, the higher her risk. This fact is universally recognized and undisputed. That is why nuns tend to develop breast cancer. In fact, almost all breast-cancer risk factors boil down to two questions: 1) How much immature Type 1 and 2 breast tissue do I have? and 2) How long have I had immature Type 1 and 2 tissue before maturing that tissue to milk production?

Once we understand the basic physiology of the breast, the connection between abortion and breast cancer is intuitively obvious. When a woman becomes pregnant for the first time, she experiences growth in immature breast tissue. If she then ends this pregnancy prior to carrying her pregnancy to term, she has just arrested her breasts in a state where there is a large amount of cancer-susceptible tissue. In fact, this risk holds true if her pregnancy ends from a later miscarriage or a car accident or any other reason why her pregnancy would end before thirty-two weeks. But the single most common reason for a woman ending a pregnancy before thirty-two weeks is elective abortion.[77]

Another significant long-term consequence of abortion is an increased risk of preterm birth in future pregnancies. Even the pro-abortion National Academy of Medicine (formerly the Institute of Medicine) considers induced abortion a risk factor for preterm birth.[78] This increased risk of preterm birth is especially noticeable among black women, who are already three to four times as likely as white women to obtain an abortion and twice as likely to experience preterm birth.[79]

The pro-abortion Royal College of Obstetricians and Gynaecologists likewise acknowledges that this is the case, relying on a 2009 systematic review suggesting that a history of induced abortion can lead to infants born with low birthweight or delivered preterm. The review found that "infection, mechanical trauma to the cervix leading to cervical incompetence and scarred tissue following curettage are suspected mechanisms."[80]

The American Association of Pro-Life OBGYNs, meanwhile, reports that at least 160 studies over the past fifty years have demonstrated a link between abortion and preterm birth.[81] A survey of several reliable studies on the subject found that surgical abortion increases risk of preterm birth by approximately 35 percent after one abortion and up to 90 percent after two abortions. Chemical abortions that require a follow-up surgery—which occurs in about 6 percent of cases—increase the odds of preterm birth by as much as 300 percent.[82] Giving birth prematurely, UNC Department of Obstetrics and Gynecology professor Tracy Manuck has demonstrated, poses risks not only to the newborn but also increases a woman's chances of future medical complications such as cardiovascular disease and stroke.[83] These long-term risks are the price women pay for a procedure that, again, is never medically necessary. And these risks receive little to no attention from those who support the right to abortion.

Abortion has been legal in the United States—and supposedly safe—for almost fifty years. But the past few decades have shown us that women are in fact the second victim of abortion, a reality that at least some of the time results in significant problems for women's health. And while many who work in abortion facilities might be well-intentioned, if severely misguided, the sad truth is that the abortion industry demonstrates little concern about the risks of abortion, especially when acknowledging those risks would damage their political cause. Rather than seriously addressing women's safety concerns, unclean clinic conditions, and underreporting of complications, abortion businesses and their defenders resist every effort to more closely regulate them, preferring instead to evade notice and downplay the severity of what abortion does to women.

Refuting the Myth of "Back-Alley" Abortions

Some argue that if we ban abortion, or even limit when it's available, it will create black markets for abortion, the so-called back-alley abortions, leading to more Kermit Gosnells. If abortion became illegal once more, this thinking goes, women would continue to seek abortions at the same rate that they do today, but they would be forced into the "back alleys," where they would suffer enormous health hazards. Abortion supporters often use the imagery of coat hangers, a reference to a time when abortion was illegal and, supposedly, women resorted to all sorts of dangerous homemade methods for performing their own abortions.[84]

A *USA Today* opinion piece from November 2021 recounted how the author's great-grandmother died after obtaining an illegal abortion, asserting, "Such will be the fate of millions of American women if the Supreme Court dares to backtrack on women's reproductive rights—because women always have, and always will, seek ways to end unwanted pregnancy."[85]

But there's no reason to think that a Court decision reversing *Roe* would create the dire landscape the author references. For one thing, a variety of public health research, including from those who favor legal abortion, has shown that protecting unborn children under the law effectively reduces the incidence of abortion, in many cases quite substantially.[86]

Meanwhile, consider what happened in Texas in 2021 after the state enacted a law protecting unborn children from the time a fetal heartbeat can be detected, at around six weeks' gestation. Following the law's enactment, pro-life organizations stepped up their efforts to help pregnant mothers in need. Texas has more than two hundred pregnancy-resource centers, the most of any state in the country.[87] In September 2021, reporting suggested that pregnancy-resource centers in the state had seen an increase in call volume between 30 percent and 40 percent, and a more than 100 percent increase in ultrasounds provided since the law took effect.[88] The legislature increased funding for their Alternatives to Abortion program to $100 million, and early reporting suggests that women who chose not to travel to a nearby state to obtain an abortion have availed themselves of that assistance in bringing their babies into the world.[89] There has been no evidence, at least not yet, that the law led to negative maternal-health outcomes. Nationally, pregnancy-resource centers outnumber abortion businesses by three to one, and in some states by as many as eleven to one, suggesting that these centers have expanded their reach to meet women's needs, making so-called back-alley abortions less attractive.[90]

Nor is it the case that American women died by the thousands in illegal abortions prior to *Roe*, even though most states had laws criminalizing abortion. Abortion supporters often assert that the United States had high maternal-mortality rates due to "back-alley" abortions before *Roe* legalized abortion. Lawyers advocating legal abortion in *Roe* even presented statistics before the Court arguing to this effect. Much later, the doctors who lobbied against the pro-life Texas law at stake in *Roe* admitted that they had fabricated those maternal-mortality statistics in order to convince the Court to legalize abortion.[91] Nevertheless, abortion providers such as Planned Parenthood continue to insist that thousands of women died in unsafe abortions every year before *Roe*, a falsehood so egregious that even the *Washington Post* has debunked it as a myth deserving of four Pinocchios.[92]

As the *Williams Obstetrics* textbook has noted, five thousand maternal deaths from abortion annually would amount to five times the total number of maternal deaths from all causes in 1966.[93] According to Americans United for Life senior counsel Clarke D. Forsythe, the five thousand deaths statistic likely originated with gynecologist Frederick Taussig, who later repudiated it and acknowledged it was too high. Far more reliable statistics from the five years before *Roe* suggest that the abortion-related maternal deaths each year were fewer than 150.[94]

Meanwhile, a significant amount of recent international evidence suggests that, rather than experiencing worse maternal-health outcomes, jurisdictions with abortion regulations actually tend to see improvements in women's health. A study in Mexico, for example, found that laws restricting abortion did not lead to an increase in maternal mortality—in fact, quite the opposite. The study found that states with more restrictive abortion legislation actually exhibited lower maternal-mortality ratios overall, lower maternal-mortality ratios related to abortion, and lower induced-abortion mortality ratios than in more permissive states.[95]

Countries such as El Salvador, Chile, Poland, and Nicaragua passed laws prohibiting abortion after having allowed it, and each country subsequently saw improvements in maternal-mortality rates, not increased rates of maternal deaths as abortion supporters claimed would occur. Maternal-mortality rates in South Africa, on the other hand, have worsened after the country legalized abortion.[96] In countries such as Rwanda, the Netherlands, and Ethiopia, the liberalization of abortion also seems to have negatively affected women's health.[97]

The best data suggest that regulating or restricting abortion in the United States would be an overall improvement for women's health. Especially if the pro-life movement and pro-life lawmakers continue helping women in need find alternatives to abortion, laws protecting unborn children would not only lower the supply of abortion but also lower the demand for abortion and increase access to options enabling women to choose life. Far from driving women into "back alleys" to obtain unsafe abortions, such laws would create a climate far friendlier to women's health.

The Abortion Industry Doesn't Care

Another concerning element of this problem is that abortion providers appear unworried about the significant physical risks of abortion to women. In fact, large abortion providers and advocacy groups such as Planned Parenthood regularly sue state governments to preserve their ability to operate abortion clinics without disclosing risks to women or reporting adverse reactions after they occur. Defenders of legal abortion claim to support "women's health," but their resistance to laws protecting women's safety as it relates to abortion suggests otherwise.

Abortion providers treated the COVID-19 pandemic as an opportunity to fight to relax the FDA's long-time safety regulations for chemical-abortion drugs. Despite several losses in court, abortion advocates got their way, as the Biden administration eventually directed the FDA to undo the safety regulations, which had required doctors to meet with women in person before prescribing chemical-abortion drugs. This was an odd strategy from supposed "women's health" advocates, considering that, as we documented above, chemical abortion poses significant risks to women's health, and it makes little sense to remove them further from the care of a physician, especially during a time when access to follow-up care and hospital access was imperiled by COVID-19.

Two of the most recent Supreme Court cases involving abortion—*Whole Woman's Health v. Hellerstedt* and *June Medical Services v. Russo*—dealt with state laws requiring abortion clinics to take measures protecting women's health. At stake in *June Medical* was a Louisiana statute requiring abortionists to maintain admitting privileges at a nearby hospital so that women could more quickly obtain follow-up emergency care in the event of complications during a surgical abortion. Far from targeting abortion providers, the law would've brought Louisiana's abortion clinics into compliance with the same regulations that apply to every other ambulatory surgical center in the state.

The Supreme Court ultimately struck down that provision after June Medical Services, a major Louisiana abortion business, sued the state—allegedly representing the interests of women—in order to avoid having to comply with a law aimed at protecting the health of women seeking abortions.[98] While abortion proponents argued that the law was aimed at making abortion less accessible, the reality is that it isn't difficult at all for doctors to secure admitting privileges—that is, as long as they're properly licensed to perform their medical work. That was exactly what the Louisiana abortion providers' opposition turned on: they were worried not about women's health, but about their inability to attain proper licensing for their facilities. Consider that the state had documented two abortion clinics in the state that employed a radiologist and an ophthalmologist to perform abortions.[99] As Steven Aden, chief legal officer of Americans United for Life, has observed, what June Medical Services was permitted to do in this case was the equivalent of permitting a dentist to sue on behalf of his patient, not himself, and make the argument that patients don't need his dental work to be regulated.[100]

Major abortion advocacy organizations such as the American College of Obstetricians and Gynecologists (ACOG), which we'll study in detail in Chapter Four, routinely oppose regulations aimed at protecting women's health and ensuring informed consent. These organizations argue that such provisions are thinly veiled attempts to limit abortion, not to protect women's health. But it's telling that the country's most prominent medical associations oppose informed consent and admitting privileges, basic tenets of good medical practice, only in the context of abortion.

Abortion providers regularly bring legal challenges against laws requiring them to inform women about the side effects and risks of abortion, laws that have nothing to do with restricting access to abortion—unless the pro-choice side fears that giving women accurate information might lead them to make a different "choice." To take just one example, in August 2021, Planned Parenthood sued Montana over several new laws, including one that required abortionists to share with women the possible risks and complications of an abortion procedure.[101] In the suit, Planned Parenthood alleged that the informed-consent requirement constituted "biased counseling [that] attempts to scare women out of having" an abortion. But informed consent, including the disclosure of risks, is a basic demand of medical ethics—except, apparently, when it comes to abortion.

The potential for physical risks from an elective procedure like abortion is bad enough. But what makes the problem especially concerning is how little abortion providers seem to care. Rather than responding to the squalor of Kermit Gosnell's clinic or the death of Tonya Reaves by embracing greater oversight of abortion clinics to prevent similar tragedies, abortion providers and their cheerleaders do everything in their power to resist regulation. They reject proposals to more carefully document incidents of abortion complications or to make their clinics safer for women. They even oppose informed-consent requirements such as informing women of possible side effects and complications. These realities do not suggest that the abortion industry has the best interests of women at heart. They suggest, rather, that abortionists care first and foremost about profiting from abortion and maintaining their political power, and that they treat caring for women as, at best, an afterthought.

Abortion Puts Women's Mental and Spiritual Health at Risk

Abortion facilitates an inhospitable culture. In addition to posing serious physical risks to women, it threatens their long-term mental and spiritual health. But if you talk to most pro-choice activists, they're likely to reject the idea that women ever suffer from regret, guilt, or other negative emotional consequences after undergoing an abortion. If they acknowledge post-abortion regret at all, they dismiss it as the result of the supposed stigma surrounding abortion, which activists claim causes women to feel guilty when they would otherwise be relieved.

"Telling our [abortion] stories at full volume chips away at stigma, at lies, at the climate of shame that destroys the lives (sometimes literally) of women and girls and anyone anywhere on the gender spectrum who can become pregnant," wrote pro-abortion feminist Lindy West in a 2015 column.[102] West is one of the founders of Shout Your Abortion, a group that encourages women to publicly celebrate their abortions as a way of eroding stigma. In reality, a significant number of women end up suffering from significant psychological repercussions after abortion, ranging from decreased self-esteem to severe guilt, depression, and even suicide.

These regrets appear to be particularly intense in cases of chemical abortion, likely because women self-administer the abortion pill and feel especially responsible for the outcome. Heartbeats, a group of regional Ohio women's centers, posts the stories of women who have had abortions describing their regret. In early 2020, a young, recently engaged girl reflected on her heartbreaking experience with chemical abortion:

> I took the medication as prescribed. I remember the excruciating pain during the termination process. I was doubled over on the floor of the living room, biting a washcloth because the pain was so intense. Eventually, I passed out on the floor falling asleep for several hours. I would wake up and it would all start again. This went on for a few days but with each day, I started feeling more myself.
>
> Several days had gone by and I still hadn't miscarried. Until one evening at work, I started to feel what would be menstrual cycle pains and excused myself to the restroom. I sat down on the toilet and blood began pouring out of my body. I stood up and gazed down at the small sack that had exited my womb. Everything felt very surreal at that moment as if I were in a dream. When I fully realized that my baby was lying on the bottom of the commode, I began to cry. The loss that I had felt was very real at that moment . . . recognizing what I had done and that I had ended my own child's life.[103]

This story captures the pain and anguish not only of making the decision to abort but also of administering the abortion oneself. This is particularly tragic because chemical abortions are on the rise, and are likely to continue increasing after states are permitted to regulate abortion.

Some of women's regret likely stems from the fact that women aren't aware of alternatives prior to choosing abortion—in other words, they don't feel like they actually had a choice. One 2004 study of women who had an abortion suggests that there's a link between that lack of information, alternative options, and support, and the negative mental-health outcomes. About two-thirds of the women surveyed said they received no counseling prior to abortion, and only 11 percent said the counseling they received was adequate. Just 17 percent said they were counseled on abortion alternatives, and about two-thirds reported feeling pressured to choose abortion. A majority said they weren't sure of their decision at the time they received an abortion.[104] The survey went on to show that many of these women suffered mental-health consequences after their abortion, perhaps as a result of that lack of information and certainty leading up to the procedure. About a third of women said they experienced suicidal ideations, and a mere 4 percent said they felt more in control of their life after their abortion. These statistics suggest that abortion is far from an easy solution to the problems facing pregnant women.

Dr. Aaron Kheriaty, most recently professor of psychiatry and human behavior at University of California Irvine School of Medicine and director of medical education in the UCI Department of Psychiatry, has explained in testimony, "Abortion often touches on three features of a woman's self-identity and self-understanding: her sexuality, her morality, and her maternal identity. It invariably involves loss, and therefore it often leads to complex forms of grief that accompany loss."[105] His testimony offered this example of a woman who suffered following an abortion:

> I recall also a minor that I treated in therapy for several years. I first met her when she was hospitalized on our adolescent inpatient psychiatric unit after a suicide attempt.

The year prior she had undergone an abortion. As is the case for many teenage girls who have abortions, she was pressured by her parents—in this case her father—who argued that abortion was her only option. This patient described to me her experiences with her unintended pregnancy in detail. She recalled lying in bed with her hand on her belly, feeling a deep bond and connection with her unborn child. When I asked her about her decision to have an abortion, she stated in cold and clear language: "I killed my baby."

This was a young woman who was raised in a pro-choice household. Religious instruction was not a part of her upbringing, and she did not consider herself a religious or pro-life person. There seemed to be no reason for her, given the culture and her family upbringing, to adopt an anti-abortion attitude. Her shame and regret over her abortion stemmed neither from religious values, nor from others accusing her of wrongdoing. It stemmed from her own experience of the maternal bond she had formed with the unborn life inside her during her unintended pregnancy.[106]

Rarely do abortion supporters show themselves willing to seriously consider stories such as this one. Instead, abortion advocates often cite one particular study, the Turnaway study, to claim that women who obtain abortions don't suffer from subsequent mental-health challenges. The study reported that women who have an abortion are not more likely than those denied the procedure to experience depression, anxiety, or suicidal ideation. But the Turnaway study has faced substantial criticism, including for the fact that it had poor participation rates and an 83 percent attrition rate, or a high rate of women dropping out of the study before its completion.[107]

Indeed, the best studies come to a rather different conclusion. The largest existing quantitative analysis of mental-health risks associated with abortion found that post-abortive women had an 81 percent higher risk of mental-health problems when compared with women who had not had an abortion.

The meta-study, published in the *British Journal of Psychiatry* in 2011 by Priscilla Coleman of Bowling Green State University, surveyed data from twenty-two existing studies on women who had abortions and their mental-health outcomes. The studies included in Coleman's review had surveyed a total of 877,181 women, 163,831 of whom had undergone an abortion.[108] All five negative outcomes Coleman measured rose steeply after women had an abortion: anxiety disorders increased by 34 percent, depression increased by 37 percent, alcohol abuse and suicidal behaviors increased by more than 100 percent, and marijuana abuse increased by more than 200 percent. These results remained the same even after controlling for prior psychiatric health problems.

In her more recent work, Coleman surveyed seventy-five studies conducted between 1993 and 2018 examining the link between abortion and subsequent mental-health problems and found that two-thirds of the studies demonstrated an increased risk of mental-health complications after abortion. A majority of the studies deemed highly reliable by Coleman's scoring rubric—including factors such as sample size and attrition rate—found an association between abortion and later mental-health problems.[109]

Coleman's research has even been replicated by pro-abortion scholars such as David Fergusson, whose 2013 meta-analysis with John Horwood and Joseph Boden found that "abortion was associated with small to moderate increases in risks of anxiety, alcohol misuse, illicit drug use/misuse, and suicidal behavior."[110] The researchers set out to disprove Coleman's findings—hypothesizing that abortion might actually reduce the mental-health risks of pregnancy—but found instead, as Coleman did, that there is a significant link between abortion and negative mental-health outcomes.

The problem of debilitating abortion regret is so pervasive that the pro-life movement has dedicated a large amount of its resources to operating ministries that help women heal after abortion. Most pregnancy-resource centers dedicate part of their work to caring for women who are suffering after having had an abortion. The Sisters of Life, an order of Catholic nuns, devote a significant part of their ministry to caring for these women, in addition to helping women in difficult pregnancies choose life. Catholic churches operate chapters of Project Rachel, a ministry that cares for anyone who has been involved in abortion, not only women but also their partners and anyone who has worked in the abortion industry. Campaigns such as Silent No More assist women who regret their abortions and who wish to share their stories so that women similarly suffering know they are not alone.

Solidarity with these women is especially important considering that, more often than not, women who experience regret or other negative mental-health outcomes after having an abortion are dismissed or attacked by abortion-rights activists. It is easier to defend abortion when you pretend that women who choose abortion are always happy with their decision. For the abortion activist, women who feel otherwise are just collateral damage.

Conclusion

Abortion in the United States is marketed primarily as a boon to women, the best solution for unwanted or inconvenient pregnancies.

Second-wave feminists demanded legal abortion as a means of putting women on equal footing with men. In 1992, Supreme Court justices in *Casey* preserved the core of *Roe v. Wade* in part on the rationale that women rely on abortion to order their lives and participate meaningfully in society. Abortion supporters today defend abortion chiefly in terms of women's rights and autonomy, arguing that abortion is merely another form of health care.

But as we have seen, nothing could be further from the truth. Abortion pits women against their children, telling pregnant mothers that violence against their unborn child might be necessary for them to flourish. Abortion fosters a culture within which it is easier for a man to abandon the mother of his children and easier for a mother to reject the child in her womb. Abortion attempts to resolve the disparities between men and women not by empowering women but by enabling them to behave like irresponsible men who walk away from their unborn child.

Abortion is not without health risks to women, sometimes resulting in immediate physical harm or long-term ramifications to their physical and emotional health. These significant problems are all too often brushed aside or covered up by abortion businesses and advocates, who appear more concerned with keeping their doors open than with keeping women safe. Fifty years later, and it appears that the dream of abortion for American women has been much more like a nightmare.

CHAPTER THREE

Abortion Harms Equality and Choice

R yan Bomberger is a husband, a father, and a pro-life activist—and his life is a particular witness to the reality that every human life has value, no matter the circumstances. Ryan's mother became pregnant with him after being the victim of rape, but she courageously chose to carry him in her womb and give birth to her son. Sensing that she couldn't give him the gift of an upbringing, she worked to find a family that could do so through adoption. Ryan was adopted when he was six weeks old and raised in a multi-racial family with twelve siblings, nine of whom were, like him, adopted. Today, in addition to raising his children—two of whom were adopted—he and his wife Bethany lead the Radiance Foundation, a pro-life group that seeks to inform the public about the reality of abortion, and in particular the disproportionate devastation of abortion in black communities.

Ryan's mother chose life. Not every woman does. "In 2001, when I was nineteen years old and a sophomore in college in Georgia, I found out I was pregnant," explains Catherine Glenn Foster.[1] She tells the rest of her story this way:

I didn't know what to do or where to turn. I was embarrassed and scared. I searched "pregnant and need help" online and called the second-cheapest abortion clinic in the results, thinking it was sure to be safer than the absolute cheapest. I didn't know for sure what I would do, but I knew that if I did end up getting an abortion, it would have to be fast because I could tell I was already bonding with my child.

I remember that week vividly. I was wearing my boyfriend's oversize sweatshirt and tried to comfort my baby—and myself—as I walked around campus. I named her. And then walking through the doors of that abortion business, nothing felt right.

No information, no care, no compassion. I was still making up my mind, and I asked to view the ultrasound they performed to see how far along I was. The technician refused. It was against their policy. Nothing about that day restored my choice, my autonomy or my sense of empowerment. They were just stripped from me over and over. I aborted my first child that day. And that decision has been with me every day since.[2]

Foster goes on to describe her experience while pregnant with her third child, when she was told at a doctor's appointment that her daughter "was at a significantly elevated risk of a trisomy disorder, the most well-known of these being Down syndrome." Her doctor told her to consider abortion. Foster refused, and after giving birth, it turned out the test had been wrong: "My curly-haired little girl was born healthy as could be, with no trisomy conditions. Fetal diagnoses and prognoses are not a guarantee, but many women may be directed towards abortion based on those results."[3] Today, Foster is the president and CEO of Americans United for Life.

Sadly, it is becoming far more common for women to have an abortion after their unborn child is diagnosed with Down syndrome or another disorder, even though, as in Foster's case, those tests can be wrong. And unborn children diagnosed in the womb aren't the only ones being targeted for discriminatory reasons; in many parts of the world where sons are highly desired, unborn girls are selectively aborted at high rates. These eugenic impulses aren't surprising considering that Planned Parenthood, our nation's largest abortion business, was founded by Margaret Sanger, one of the foremost leaders of the eugenics movement of the early twentieth century. Though early eugenicists focused especially on contraception and sterilization, it is undeniable that abortion has furthered their goals, disproportionately reducing populations they wanted to eliminate, including non-white Americans, the poor, and the disabled.

In this chapter, we outline the racist history of the eugenics movement and explain how black and Hispanic women today have much higher abortion rates than white women, exacerbating racial inequality. We also discuss the prevalence of discriminatory sex- and disability-based abortion, horrible realities that the abortion industry continues to defend. And we survey the work of pregnancy-resource centers, which help pregnant mothers in need choose life for their unborn children despite the fact that the abortion industry and its supporters oppose them at every turn.

Though all unborn children are at risk when abortion is legal, racial minorities, girls, and babies with disabilities are at heightened risk. Abortion harms these groups at elevated rates, as they experience lethal discrimination in the womb. Meanwhile, women who need help carrying their babies to term get little help from the abortion industry, and abortion activists do everything in their power to oppose groups that actually assist pregnant mothers. Every abortion harms a baby and a mother, but today's abortion-rights crusade places some babies and mothers at increased risk.

The Eugenics Movement and Disparate Racial Impact of Abortion

In 1916, Margaret Sanger opened a birth-control clinic in Brooklyn, New York, marking the first major endeavor of her career in social activism, which culminated in 1942 when she founded Planned Parenthood.[4] Contrary to what many might assume from witnessing Planned Parenthood operate today as the nation's largest abortion business, Sanger wasn't an abortion activist.[5]

Instead, she founded Planned Parenthood as part of a crusade for contraception, which she believed would be an important element of social progress. Unlike feminists later in the twentieth century who demanded birth control as a means of liberating women from the supposed tyranny of the female body, Sanger and her allies had a more nefarious angle. It was the Progressive Era, and elite progressive leaders were advocating a frightening campaign: Anglo-Saxon–oriented eugenic policy as a means of reshaping the U.S. population to look, in their view, more ideally American.[6]

In her 1919 essay "Birth Control and Racial Betterment," Sanger couched her argument for birth control in the context and aims of the eugenics movement. "Elimination of the unfit," Sanger argued, could not be fully achieved without widespread access to birth control.[7] Sanger later elaborated on what she meant by "unfit," describing the link as she saw it between birth control and progress:

If we are to develop in America a new race with a racial soul, we must keep the birth rate within the scope of our ability to understand as well as to educate. We must not encourage reproduction beyond our capacity to assimilate our numbers so as to make the coming generation into such physically fit, mentally capable, socially alert individuals as are the ideal of a democracy.[8]

As Kevin D. Williamson put it, "The birth-control movement of the Progressive era is where crude racism met its genteel intellectual cousin."[9] While Sanger and her fellow twentieth-century eugenicists were not abortion advocates themselves, they no doubt would be pleased by the way in which the widespread acceptance of abortion has furthered their goal of reducing "undesirable" parts of the population.

The eugenics movement of the early twentieth century was full of elite thinkers who advocated contraception and sterilization as a means of minimizing the reproduction of unwanted minorities: non-white Americans, the poor, and those deemed mentally disabled or otherwise unfit. Clarence Little—a university president and renowned genetic researcher—served on Planned Parenthood's founding board and believed increased availability of birth control would help protect "Yankee stock," or what Sanger would call those of "unmixed native white parentage."[10] "The feebleminded are notoriously prolific in reproduction," is how Sanger described the problem as she saw it in *Woman and the New Race*.

In an essay on Planned Parenthood's connection to the early eugenics movement, Williamson summarized how entangled these elites' views about race and population control were with their promotion of birth control:

Birth Control Review, the in-house journal of Planned Parenthood's predecessor organization, published a review, by the socialist intellectual Havelock Ellis, of Lothrop Stoddard's *The Rising Tide of Color against White World Supremacy*. Ellis was an important figure in Sanger's intellectual development and wrote the introduction to her *Woman and the New Race*; Stoddard was a popular birth-control advocate whose intellectual contributions included lending to the Nazi racial theorists the term "untermensch" as well as developing a great deal of their theoretical framework: He fretted about "imperfectly Nordicized Alpines" and such. Like the other eugenics-minded progressives of his time, he saw birth control and immigration as inescapably linked issues.[11]

Activists such as Sanger, Little, Stoddard, and Ellis focused their crusade on widespread contraception—some supported sterilization, too—which they hoped would reduce the birth rate among populations they viewed as undesirable. These thinkers weren't seizing eugenics as a helpful rhetorical tool for promoting birth control; it was the other way around. Birth control and sterilization—and subsequently abortion—were the means by which they wanted to achieve their eugenic goals, which were their priority. This disturbing mindset proved to be highly influential with some of our foremost institutions.

In 1927, the Supreme Court upheld a Virginia law allowing the forced sterilization of the institutionalized, supposedly to protect the "health of the patient and the welfare of society."[12] Ruling that the state was within its rights to forcibly sterilize Carrie Buck—a patient at a mental hospital whom Justice Oliver Wendell Holmes referred to as a "feeble minded woman"—Holmes famously wrote that laws such as Virginia's prevented the nation from "being swamped with incompetence." "Three generations of imbeciles are enough," Holmes added.[13] In a letter to his friend Harold Laski that same year, Holmes wrote that he had "delivered an opinion upholding the constitutionality of a state law for sterilizing imbeciles the other day—and felt that I was getting near the first principle of real reform."[14]

Though the formal eugenics movement in the United States began to die out by the 1940s, its goals are still being achieved today, propelled in large part by the way in which legal abortion has led to the disproportionate extermination of non-white and disabled children. In a 2009 interview with the *New York Times Magazine*, Justice Ruth Bader Ginsburg described *Roe* as having been a decision about population control, "particularly growth in populations that we don't want to have too many of."[15] It is unclear whether Ginsburg was endorsing this eugenic motivation or merely describing it—though in 2014 Ginsburg told *Elle* in the context of abortion that "it makes no sense as a national policy to promote birth only among poor people."[16] Either way, Ginsburg correctly realized that, at least for some, the legalization of abortion would function as the next tool in a larger campaign to reduce the population, particularly the population of undesirables.

This is evident in how today's white supremacists embrace abortion, cheering that it eliminates non-white children at a disproportionate rate, thus limiting the growth of the non-white population. White supremacist Richard Spencer has argued that abortion is essential in bringing about his ideal, racially homogenous American people. He supports abortion because, as he puts it, "the people who are having abortions are generally very often black or Hispanic or from very poor circumstances."[17] White women, Spencer notes, avail themselves of abortion "when you have a situation like Down Syndrome"— an acceptable use of abortion, in his view. Meanwhile, Spencer says, "the unintelligent and blacks and Hispanics...use abortion as birth control," something that in his view ought to be celebrated.[18]

In the view of modern-day racists, the pro-life position is "dysgenic," by which they mean that protecting babies from the lethal violence of abortion will harm later generations by allowing supposedly undesirable characteristics to continue to be passed on. In Spencer's white-supremacist *Radix Journal*, Aylmer Fisher wrote: "The only ones who can't [avoid unwanted pregnancy] are the least intelligent and responsible members of society: women who are disproportionately Black, Hispanic, and poor."[19] Spencer and his racist ilk make this hateful argument because non-white and low-income women are indeed the ones who most often have abortions today.

■   ■   ■

Margaret Sanger's disgusting views on race and eugenics are impossible to deny. So much so that in 2021, amid broader racial tensions in the United States, Planned Parenthood finally attempted to distance itself from its founder. In a *New York Times* op-ed, Planned Parenthood president Alexis McGill Johnson wrote that the group was "done making excuses for [its] founder" and that it was prepared to "reckon with Margaret Sanger's association with white supremacist groups and eugenics."[20]

This move came nearly a year after Planned Parenthood of Greater New York, one of the group's largest affiliates, denounced Sanger's racism and removed her name from its flagship clinic. "The removal of Margaret Sanger's name from our building is both a necessary and overdue step to reckon with our legacy and acknowledge Planned Parenthood's contributions to historical reproductive harm within communities of color," Karen Seltzer, the chair of the New York affiliate's board, said in a statement.[21] It would have been better had they dissolved the whole organization. Today's Planned Parenthood perpetuates Sanger's racially discriminatory beliefs, wittingly or not.

"We are committed to confronting any white supremacy in our own organization, and across the movement for reproductive freedom," Johnson wrote in her op-ed. But Planned Parenthood's move was too little, too late. For one thing, pro-lifers have been pointing out Sanger's racist views for quite some time, greeted with radio silence from Planned Parenthood. From 1966 until 2015, the group gave out its highest honor, the annual "Margaret Sanger Award," to "recognize leadership, excellence, and outstanding contributions to the reproductive health and rights movement."[22] Both Hillary Clinton and Nancy Pelosi have been recipients.

Meanwhile, Planned Parenthood—and the abortion industry at large—continues to operate in a way that would thrill the eugenicist proponents of contraception. Due in large part to Planned Parenthood's abortion business, the past half-century of abortion has deepened the effects of racial inequality in the United States, and Planned Parenthood profits from that reality. As former NFL tight end Benjamin Watson has put it: "The same Sanger they [Planned Parenthood leaders] claim to disavow would applaud their efforts and results, as a disproportionate percentage of Black children have been killed in Planned Parenthood's abortion clinics."[23]

According to research from Ryan Bomberger's Radiance Foundation, nearly 80 percent of Planned Parenthood's clinics are located within walking distance of neighborhoods occupied predominantly by black and Hispanic residents.[24] While abortion providers and advocates insist that this is a service to lower-income and minority women who need access to affordable health care, abortion statistics tell a different story. Despite constituting only 13 percent of the female population, black women represent well over one-third of all abortions in the United States each year.[25] Black women are five times more likely than white women to obtain abortions, Hispanic women are twice as likely, and abortions are highly concentrated among low-income women.[26] Shockingly, according to vital statistics data, in recent years more black babies were aborted than were born alive in New York City.[27] Between the years 2012 and 2016, black mothers in New York City had 136,426 abortions and gave birth to only 118,127 babies.[28] Among white, Asian, and Hispanic women, births far surpassed abortions.

According to data from the Centers for Disease Control (CDC), in 2019 black women accounted for the largest percentage of all abortions in the United States, at 38.4 percent. White women had the lowest abortion rate, with 6.6 abortions per 1,000 women, while black women had the highest, with 23.8 abortions per 1,000 women. For every 1,000 live births to black women, there were 386 abortions, whereas for every 1,000 births to white women, there were 117 abortions.[29] And the true disparities are likely even greater, considering that a number of states refuse to report demographic breakdowns in their abortion data to the CDC, including abortion-friendly ones such as California and New York.

These disparities can't be chalked up to merely a matter of unfortunate differences in financial status that lead to greater reliance on abortion. As the pro-abortion Guttmacher Institute reports, "At every income level, black women have higher abortion rates than whites or Hispanics, except for women below the poverty line, where Hispanic women have slightly higher rates than black women."[30]

The problem is so severe that black pro-life leaders have founded groups to put particular focus on reducing abortion rates among black women. Christina Bennett, a pro-life activist who works with pregnant women in need, told one of us (Alexandra) in a 2020 interview that black women in her community don't think about abortion the way the national abortion-rights movement does: "Abortion supporters talk about things like 'reproductive justice' or 'reproductive freedom,' but this language doesn't trickle down. The women having the abortions aren't thinking in this language. It's really the elite, privileged women who push this message that abortion is health care."[31]

Bennett told the story of a pro-choice group that created candles decorated to say "Abortions are magical" to hand out to volunteers. "If I was to take those to the inner-city abortion clinic in Hartford and try to hand them out, the girls actually getting abortions wouldn't want those candles. That's not their reality. They're getting an abortion because they have to feed their kids. They already have another child at home or they're thinking about how their man is going to leave if they have that kid," Bennett said.[32] Abortion among black and Hispanic women isn't driven by female empowerment and the celebration of "choice" but by the crushing limitations of poverty and lack of meaningful options or alternatives. But, as we'll see in the last section of this chapter, rather than provide tangible assistance to help these women choose life, pro-abortion activists actively oppose groups that do provide that assistance, further fueling a skewed race ratio when it comes to abortion.

This reality is why racists embrace abortion: whether or not Planned Parenthood and its supporters notice or admit it, abortion has led to a disproportionate reduction of non-white populations in the United States. Perhaps in an effort to distract from this reality, abortion-rights supporters have begun to argue that the modern pro-life movement is nothing more than a smokescreen for racism.

"White Supremacists oppose abortion because they fear it'll reduce the number of white infants and thus contribute to what they fear as non-white 'replacement,'" tweeted Harvard Law professor Laurence Tribe in 2019. "Never underestimate the way these issues and agendas are linked. This turns 'intersectionality' on its head," Tribe added. In a 2020 *GQ* article titled "The Anti-Abortion Movement Was Always Built on Lies," journalist Laura Bassett advanced the incoherent thesis that Republicans before Ronald Reagan were pro-abortion because they were racist and that Republicans after Reagan became pro-life also because they were racist.[33]

Just after the Supreme Court oral arguments in *Dobbs*, columnist and professor Noah Smith tweeted, "Who's going to be the first to let conservatives know that since people of color are disproportionately high users of abortion, banning abortion will hasten the 'Great Replacement,'" insinuating that, if pro-lifers realized this, they'd cease opposing abortion.[34] But pro-lifers have been decrying the disproportionate abortion rate for decades.[35] New York University law professor Melissa Murray repeated a similar error in an interview with Slate: "Abortion restrictions were fueled by the fear that white women were using abortion and, as a consequence, were not having as many children, and the white race was about to be overwhelmed by African Americans and immigrants."[36]

But the link between abortion and white supremacists' concerns about "non-white replacement" works in precisely the opposite way. The connection between abortion and "replacement" is why white supremacists have long supported abortion, applauding the sad reality that minority women tend to abort their children at disproportionate rates.

The womb is one of the most dangerous places for a black American. White supremacists celebrate this tragic reality while progressive elites cheer on the laws that perpetuate it—and both groups attack the pro-lifers who seek to ameliorate it.

Lethal Discrimination on the Basis of Sex and Disability

In addition to the racial aspect of eugenic abortion, there is discrimination on the basis of sex and disability. But the pro-abortion movement doesn't want to acknowledge this reality, let alone do anything to stop

it. Today's abortion-rights activists typically defend abortion by emphasizing the primacy of female autonomy, saying that no matter her reason,
a woman must have access to abortion—and, moreover, that we can't
so much as ask a woman why she's choosing it.

This unflinching logic takes abortion defenders to some especially
unfortunate places. While every abortion is an unjust act of lethal
violence against the unborn child, regardless of the mother's reasons,
there is something startling about the reality that some women choose
abortion precisely because of a specific unwanted characteristic of
their unborn child. Yet many of the loudest progressive voices who
decry sex discrimination and disability discrimination when it comes
to adults remain silent when it comes to discrimination against unborn
children based on their sex or disability—or worse, they actively support these types of abortions.

In some parts of the world, abortions chosen because the child is
of an unwanted sex—usually a girl—are common. A 2019 study in
the *Proceedings of the National Academy of Sciences* estimated that
over a span of about fifty years, more than twenty-three million girls
are now missing as the result of discriminatory abortion. Researchers
from the National University of Singapore, the United Nation's
Department of Economic and Social Affairs, and UMass Amherst's
School of Public Health found that China (11.9 million) and India
(10.6 million) account for more than 90 percent of these missing girls.

Especially when the Chinese government was enforcing a
"one-child policy"—now expanded to a three-child allowance—there
was an incentive for families to abort their unborn daughters to leave
room for highly prized sons. These two countries have the most
imbalanced sex ratios at birth, which, the authors argue, is "a direct
consequence of sex-selective abortion, driven by the coexistence of
son preference, readily available technology of prenatal sex determination, and fertility decline."[37]

Despite public outcry, it appears that these troubling trends will persist. In a 2021 study, the same researchers predicted that there will be between 5.7 million and 22.1 million girls missing through the end of the century.[38] While we don't have much data on this practice in the United States—in part because abortion supporters oppose requiring women to disclose the reasons for their abortions—political economist Nicholas Eberstadt argues that there have been alarming developments in this regard in the Western world. In his 2011 article "The Global War against Baby Girls," Eberstadt wrote:

> In both the United States and the United Kingdom, these gender disparities were due largely to sharp increases in higher-parity SRBs [sex ratios at birth], strongly suggesting that sex-selective abortions were the driver. The American and British cases also point to the possibility that sex-selective abortion may be common to other subpopulations in developed or less developed societies, even if these do not affect the overall SRB for each country as a whole.[39]

Meanwhile, there is abundant evidence that women often choose abortion when their unborn child is diagnosed via prenatal testing with a disorder or sickness. Parents and doctors tend to promote abortion in these circumstances, claiming that it is more compassionate to end a child's life than condemn him to a life of suffering.

Indeed, abortion supporters often portray abortion as a solution in cases when unborn children are diagnosed with genetic disorders such as Down syndrome. In 2017, CBS News reported that Iceland was leading the world in "eradicating Down syndrome births."[40] The article made it sound as though the country had pioneered a cure for the chromosomal disorder, when in fact the "solution" was far simpler: using prenatal testing and abortion to all but exterminate children diagnosed with Down syndrome. About 85 percent of expectant mothers in Iceland choose to receive the prenatal test, and virtually 100 percent of women who receive a Down syndrome diagnosis choose abortion. Just two children with Down syndrome are born in Iceland each year, often as the result of faulty testing.[41] Rather than eradicating Down syndrome, Iceland has eradicated *people* with Down syndrome.

No one would think doctors had cured cancer if they began killing every person diagnosed with the disease, but abortion is fast becoming the norm for children diagnosed with disabilities in the womb. Denmark is much like Iceland, with a 98 percent abortion rate for babies diagnosed with Down syndrome.[42] In the United Kingdom, 90 percent of pregnant mothers who receive a Down syndrome diagnosis choose to abort.[43] In Europe as a whole, somewhere in the realm of 92 percent of babies diagnosed with Down syndrome are aborted. In the United States, it's somewhere between 61 percent and 93 percent—a range researchers narrowed to a "weighted mean" of 67 percent—according to one meta-study of Down syndrome abortion rates between 1995 and 2011.[44]

This practice is publicly supported by abortion proponents, many of whom become even more supportive of abortion in cases when parents have received an unfortunate fetal diagnosis. In 2018, *Washington Post* columnist Ruth Marcus penned a piece announcing that she "would've aborted a fetus with Down syndrome" and defending the right of women to do so. "I can say without hesitation that, tragic as it would have felt and ghastly as a second-trimester abortion would have been, I would have terminated [my] pregnancies had the testing come back positive," she wrote. "That was not the child I wanted."[45] This provides further confirmation of our argument in Chapter One that women seek abortion not merely to avoid the burden of pregnancy but to ensure the death of the child.

But condemning a child to death is not acceptable, no matter the reason. It's neither an acceptable means of ensuring that parents get the child they want nor of preventing a particular type of suffering. No parent gets the child she wants. Every child is a unique, unrepeatable gift, and all children deserve to be welcomed and cherished for who they are regardless of whether they are "perfect" or "disabled." In reality, no child is "perfect," and children with disabilities aren't any less valuable or lovable than children without them. Likewise, every human life entails some suffering. Intentionally killing a person who suffers or who might suffer doesn't solve that unfortunate reality. Parents have obligations to love and care for their children, not to decide for their children that their suffering might be too great to allow them to live.

Jerome Lejeune, the French geneticist who discovered the chromosomal basis for Down syndrome, once offered this perspective: "It cannot be denied that the price of these diseases is high—in suffering for the individual and in burdens for society. Not to mention what parents suffer! But we can assign a value to that price: It is precisely what a society must pay to remain fully human."[46] The truly human response to suffering is compassion—to suffer with another—not to eliminate suffering by eliminating the one who suffers.

But we shouldn't overstate the amount of "suffering" experienced by people with Down syndrome. While they face a different set of challenges than those who do not have trisomy, by all accounts they can lead fulfilling, happy lives. According to one study, nearly 99 percent of individuals with Down syndrome reported being happy with their lives, 97 percent said they liked who they are, and 96 percent said they like how they look.[47] They also bring tremendous joy to their families, friends, and neighbors.

Here's how George Will, the parent of a child with Down syndrome, put it in a column marking his son's fortieth birthday:

Jon was born just 19 years after James Watson and Francis Crick published their discoveries concerning the structure of DNA, discoveries that would enhance understanding of the structure of Jon, whose every cell is imprinted with Down syndrome. Jon was born just as prenatal genetic testing, which can detect Down syndrome, was becoming common. And Jon was born eight months before *Roe v. Wade* inaugurated this era of the casual destruction of pre-born babies.

This era has coincided, not just coincidentally, with the full, garish flowering of the baby boomers' vast sense of entitlement, which encompasses an entitlement to exemption from nature's mishaps, and to a perfect baby. So today science enables what the ethos ratifies, the choice of killing children with Down syndrome before birth. That is what happens to 90 percent of those whose parents receive a Down syndrome diagnosis through prenatal testing.

Which is unfortunate, and not just for them. Judging by Jon, the world would be improved by more people with Down syndrome, who are quite nice, as humans go. It is said we are all born brave, trusting and greedy, and remain greedy. People with Down syndrome must remain brave in order to navigate society's complexities. They have no choice but to be trusting because, with limited understanding, and limited abilities to communicate misunderstanding, they, like Blanche DuBois in "A Streetcar Named Desire," always depend on the kindness of strangers. Judging by Jon's experience, they almost always receive it.

Two things that have enhanced Jon's life are the Washington subway system, which opened in 1976, and the Washington Nationals baseball team, which arrived in

2005. He navigates the subway expertly, riding it to the Nationals ballpark, where he enters the clubhouse a few hours before game time and does a chore or two. The players, who have climbed to the pinnacle of a steep athletic pyramid, know that although hard work got them there, they have extraordinary aptitudes because they are winners of life's lottery. Major leaguers, all of whom understand what it is to be gifted, have been uniformly and extraordinarily welcoming to Jon, who is not.

Except he is, in a way. He has the gift of serenity, in this sense:

The eldest of four siblings, he has seen two brothers and a sister surpass him in size, and acquire cars and college educations. He, however, with an underdeveloped entitlement mentality, has been equable about life's sometimes careless allocation of equity. Perhaps this is partly because, given the nature of Down syndrome, neither he nor his parents have any tormenting sense of what might have been. Down syndrome did not alter the trajectory of his life; Jon was Jon from conception on.

This year Jon will spend his birthday where every year he spends 81 spring, summer and autumn days and evenings, at Nationals Park, in his seat behind the home team's dugout. The Phillies will be in town, and Jon will be wishing them ruination, just another man, beer in hand, among equals in the republic of baseball.[48]

People with disabilities are our equals, and we should treat them that way, not just in the republic of baseball but in the American republic as well.

Not only do people with disabilities lead happy, fulfilling lives, but the best evidence suggests that at least some of the time, prenatal tests diagnosing disorders can be wrong. In the case of testing for rare and serious genetic disorders, those tests can be wrong in as many as 90 percent of cases, according to a January 2022 *New York Times* report.[49] How many mothers have killed perfectly healthy children because a faulty test told them their child "was not the child [they] wanted"?

Though abortion is often presented as a solution to a fatal prenatal diagnosis, many courageous parents nevertheless eschew abortion, knowing that directly killing their child isn't a solution to illness or suffering. For instance, many parents who receive a diagnosis of anencephaly—a neural tube defect in which parts of a baby's brain and skull might be missing—reject abortion and spend whatever time they can with their newborn, though the condition often results in a child dying shortly after birth.

Even when parents receive a tragic diagnosis for their unborn child that ends up being correct, such as a diagnosis suggesting that their child might die shortly after birth, a 2015 study suggests that parents who rejected abortion in those cases had better psychological outcomes.[50] Research from 2018 in the *Journal of Clinical Ethics*, meanwhile, found that close to 98 percent of parents who received a diagnosis of a "life-limiting fetal condition" and chose not to abort their child reported being happy with their decision.[51]

While pregnant, Sonia Morales was told that her unborn child had anencephaly, and she was informed that most parents in her position choose abortion. But Morales continued her pregnancy and gave birth to her daughter Angela, who, despite her condition, lived until she was just a few months shy of her fourth birthday. Morales said she never considered abortion "because I already loved my child, and I knew I had to defend her right to life. My love for her didn't change after the diagnosis.... I was not the one who created the heartbeat, and I was not going to be the one ending her life."[52] After her daughter's death, Morales said she was grateful for her "extra time" with Angela, and she believes her daughter's life might give hope to parents who receive a similar diagnosis.

While some who support abortion in cases when a child is diagnosed with a disability might be motivated by sincere, if misguided, compassion, this worldview is undergirded by the evil logic of abortion, which insists that those in a position of power—in the case of abortion, the doctor and the pregnant mother—get to decide whether another human being's life is worth living. This is why abortion-rights groups are swift to oppose pro-life laws that would prohibit abortions chosen after a pregnant woman receives a Down syndrome diagnosis.

Though the United Kingdom limits elective abortions later in pregnancy, a woman may obtain an abortion at any point until birth if her child is diagnosed with "such physical or mental abnormalities as to be seriously handicapped," a category that includes nonfatal disabilities such as Down syndrome, clubfoot, or cleft palate. Though lawmakers, pro-life activists, and the disability-rights movement in the U.K. have fought to amend this law to protect unborn children diagnosed with these conditions, they have thus far been unsuccessful.

Here in the United States, the abortion industry has rabidly fought every pro-life effort to pass laws prohibiting discriminatory abortion. In 2016, Planned Parenthood of Indiana and Kentucky went all the way to the Supreme Court to block an Indiana law that, in part, forbade abortionists from knowingly performing abortions when the reason the mother sought an abortion was to lethally discriminate against her child based on sex, race, or disability. Opposing a similar ban on discriminatory abortions in Missouri,[53] Planned Parenthood's local affiliate portrayed the bill as a backdoor ban on abortion: "This bill is about one thing only: extremist politicians' determination to eliminate Missourians' access to safe and legal abortion. Abortion is a deeply personal and often complex decision that must be left to women, in consultation with their families, faith, and health-care providers. This bill inserts the state into the exam room in an effort to restrict access to abortion."[54] Planned Parenthood also asserted that the bill "would threaten women's lives and health by restricting abortion access for women who need them."[55]

When Ohio passed a bill banning the discriminatory abortion of unborn children diagnosed with Down syndrome, abortion-rights advocates immediately took action against it. Planned Parenthood activists lobbied against the bill at the state house.[56] The Center for Reproductive Rights called it "a dangerous attempt by anti-choice politicians to pit the disability rights community against the reproductive rights community."[57] The ACLU of Ohio said the law "does nothing to improve the lives of people with disabilities, nor does it increase their access to health care or other services, nor does it educate a woman and her family about having a child with a disability."[58] NARAL Pro-Choice Ohio executive director Kellie Copeland said, "This bill prevents a woman from having honest conversations about her options with her physician following a complicated medical diagnosis," while her deputy, Jamie Miracle, said it "callously disregards the unique circumstances that surround each woman's pregnancy."[59]

Neither Planned Parenthood nor any other abortion-rights group has provided evidence that women's health ever requires aborting an unborn child due to his or her race, sex, or genetic disorder. Planned Parenthood condemns sex-, race-, and disability-based discrimination in every other context, except when it occurs in the womb. Abortion proponents not only refuse to support laws protecting unborn children from discrimination based on race, sex, or disability, but they insist that being permitted to discriminate is a necessary component of "women's health care," and they take legal action to ensure that women can continue to choose abortion even for these reasons. The debate over fetal anti-discrimination abortion laws exposes the frighteningly consistent logic of the pro-abortion position: if abortion supporters were to admit that, in some cases, a woman might be choosing abortion for the wrong reasons—to admit, in other words, that some abortions are unacceptable—they would open themselves up to a debate about which reasons are good and which aren't. Of course, it is just as morally reprehensible to kill a healthy unborn child as it is to kill one who has a disability, just as it's as wrong to kill a child of the "right" sex as it is to kill one of the "wrong" sex. But their response to these discriminatory abortions illustrates how far abortion supporters will go to ensure that the law never protects unborn children, no matter the circumstances.

Abortion Supporters Are Not "Pro-Choice"

Many abortion-rights supporters insist that they don't want to be called "pro-abortion." Rather, they prefer the label "pro-choice." But in practice, the most vocal supporters of abortion rarely support options that enable expectant mothers to make any choice other than abortion. Since the Supreme Court created a right to abortion in *Roe v. Wade*, pro-lifers across the country have sustained pregnancy-resource centers, sometimes known as crisis-pregnancy centers, to help pregnant mothers in need welcome their babies into the world.

Confronted with the fact that many women choose abortion because they feel they have no other options, pregnancy-resource centers exist to present women with alternatives to abortion and to provide whatever assistance they need to continue their pregnancy, almost all of which is offered at no cost. For some mothers, this might be a pregnancy test or an ultrasound, or counseling to encourage her that motherhood is a worthwhile choice that she's capable of undertaking. For others, it might be learning the facts about adoption and receiving help in navigating the adoption process. Most pregnancy-resource centers offer women financial or material support that she isn't receiving from the child's father or from her own family, support that enables her to feel confident in choosing life.

Kathryn Jean Lopez describes the work of the Sisters of Life, a Catholic order of nuns whose particular mission is to minister to post-abortive women and help pregnant mothers in need:

> Founded 30 years ago, the Sisters are a Catholic community of women religious, with over 100 sisters in the New York metropolitan area, Toronto, Philadelphia, Denver, Phoenix, and Washington, D.C., who take the usual vows of poverty, chastity, and obedience. They also take a unique fourth vow: "to protect and enhance the sacredness of every human life." For almost two decades, Sister Magdalene has been at the helm of the Sisters' Visitation Mission in Lower Manhattan, where the Sisters frequently meet abortion-minded pregnant women and girls.
>
> Sister Magdalene is awed by the families willing to regularly open their homes to mothers and their children for temporary care and support. With a network of 20,000 co-workers across the United States and Canada, the Sisters regularly call upon about 3,000 of the most actively involved, whether it's to accompany a woman to a doctor's appointment or help her find a bed or offer long-term friendship and mentorship. "It's a few more peas in the soup, a little more spaghetti in the pot—let's just make this work," Maureen Cook's mother would always say.

If you stop by the Visitation Mission during the day, you will encounter women who have turned to the Sisters more than once. A few months ago, when I did just that, there was a mom with a toddler and an infant. She had seriously considered abortion in both pregnancies. But the love of the Sisters makes life possible. And when the moms visit in subsequent weeks, months, and years after birth, there is a deep and abiding affection, along with the material supplies that lift some of the financial burden of single motherhood. During the height of the COVID-19 shutdowns, through a generous ongoing donation from Goya Foods, the Sisters were able to make food deliveries to families.

The Sisters of Life convent in midtown Manhattan is a place where pregnant mothers, and mothers with their babies, can live until they are ready to leave on solid footing. The Sisters' work extends beyond preventing abortion and other threats to human life. They have been known to take teens who lived with them as infants on college visits. Sister Virginia Joy, S.V., who runs the Archdiocese of New York's Respect Life office, recently hosted a "feminine genius" brunch for women on the topic of mercy. The Sisters want all human beings to know they were made by love, for love. I call the Sisters of Life our pro-life credibility. But they are far from alone.[60]

There are about 2,500 pregnancy-resource centers across the country, with several major networks of pro-life groups supporting many of them. Nationally, pregnancy-resource centers outnumber abortion businesses by three to one, and in some states, by as much as eleven to one.[61] And research suggests that this model works. One 2021 study found that pregnant women who are considering abortion and visit a pregnancy-resource center are about 20 percent less likely to choose abortion than pregnant women who don't visit one.[62]

Despite the abortion-rights movement's insistence on the moniker "pro-choice," most abortion supporters don't seem thrilled by a woman's choice to visit a pregnancy-resource center and avoid abortion. In the same study that found women are less likely to choose abortion after visiting a pregnancy-resource center, the authors assert in their conclusion that the result must be at least in part because these centers are lying to women: "[Pregnancy-resource centers] may be providing resources to people who are considering continuing their pregnancy and/or they may be misleading people about the care and referrals they provide related to abortion."[63]

These researchers were hardly the first to insinuate, with no evidence, that pregnancy-resource centers offer fraudulent information to women and thereby convince them not to abort. A coalition of pro-abortion groups published a 2021 report called *Designed to Deceive: A Study of the Crisis Pregnancy Center Industry in Nine States*.[64] The report examined the websites of about six hundred pregnancy-resource centers in nine states and framed them as deceptive on the basis that they offer "virtually no medical care," despite using "language and imagery signifying they were providers of medical services." NARAL Pro-Choice America, meanwhile, has operated an extensive PR campaign painting pregnancy-resource centers as "fake women's health clinics." NARAL affiliates have conducted undercover "investigations" into pregnancy-resource centers called "Unmasking Fake Clinics," accusing pro-life centers of misleading women with "lies" such as this one: "More than 67% of the locations intentionally referred to the fetus as 'baby' and told our investigator she was already a mother because she was already pregnant."[65]

Abortion advocates often receive help from politicians in their crusade to discredit pregnancy-resource centers and limit their reach.

In California, Democrats passed the "Reproductive Freedom, Account-ability, Comprehensive Care, and Transparency Act," which was drafted with the assistance of Planned Parenthood and enforced by two successive state attorneys general, Kamala Harris and Xavier Becerra.[66] The law required pregnancy-resource centers to post large advertise-ments for the state's free or low-cost abortion program. These centers eventually won a challenge against the law at the Supreme Court, which returned the case to a lower court, ruling that California's statute likely violated the free-speech rights of the pro-life citizens operating the centers.[67] California wasn't alone in this project. Progressive cities across the country have tried to enact policies requiring pregnancy-resource centers to make disclosures that make them sound illegitimate and unqualified to serve pregnant women.[68]

While abortion supporters attempt to portray pregnancy-resource centers as somehow harming women or limiting their "right" to abor-tion, in fact they're merely offering something that abortion groups themselves don't provide. Compared with 354,871 abortions performed in 2020, Planned Parenthood itself reported that they offered only 8,626 instances of "prenatal care" and 2,667 adoption referrals.[69] In other words, for every instance of "prenatal care," Planned Parenthood clinics performed 41 abortions. For every adoption referral, they performed 133 abortions. Among services Planned Parenthood provided that specifically related to the woman's pregnancy decision—including abor-tion, prenatal or miscarriage care, and adoption referrals—abortion made up more than 96 percent.

In 2017, two former Planned Parenthood employees appeared in a Live Action video, revealing that the organziation imposes abortion quotas on its clinics and incentivizes workers to convince women to choose abortion.[70] Sue Thayer, former manager of the Planned Parent-hood clinic in Storm Lake, Iowa, told Live Action that executives would reward clinics with pizza parties or extra paid time off if they met their abortion targets. Clinics that didn't offer abortions were given quotas for abortion referrals made to other Planned Parenthood facilities. "I trained my staff the way that I was trained, which was to really encourage women to choose abortion and to have it at Planned Parenthood because it counts towards our goal," Thayer said.[71] Former Planned Parenthood nurse Marianne Anderson told Live Action, "I felt like I was more of a salesman sometimes, to sell abortions. We were constantly told we have quotas to meet to stay open."[72]

Thayer also said that clinic workers were trained to persuade pregnant mothers, especially hesitant ones, that abortion was their only option:

> If they'd say, "I'm not able to pay [my bill] today," then we would say something like, "Well, if you can't pay $10 today, how are you going to take care of a baby? Have you priced diapers? Do you know how much it costs to buy a car seat? Where would you go for help? There's no place in Storm Lake (or whatever town they were in), you know, where you can get help as a pregnant mom. So really, don't you think your smartest choice is termination?"[73]

Planned Parenthood bills itself as "pro-choice" and as a champion of women in need, but in reality the group prioritizes abortion. Pregnancy-resource centers, by contrast, are honest about their opposition to abortion, and they decline to refer women to abortion clinics. But they offer women real support, acknowledging their concerns about pregnancy and parenthood, and seek to meet whatever needs they can—diapers, cribs, car seats, formula, maternity clothes—to help mothers choose life. This service is especially important considering how lack of knowledge about alternatives, not to mention coercion from partners, can play a big role in women having an abortion.

One 2004 study of women who'd had an abortion found that about two-thirds of them had received no counseling ahead of time, and only 11 percent who did receive counseling said it was adequate. Just 17 percent said they were counseled on abortion alternatives, and about two-thirds reported feeling pressured to choose abortion. A majority said they weren't sure of their decision at the time they received an abortion.[74] Some women obtain an abortion under duress from their partner, whether literal force or other coercion such as financial pressure or threats to leave the relationship.[75] According to some surveys, a majority of women who seek abortion do so because of lack of support from a partner.[76] "I can't tell you how many [post-abortive black] women have fallen into my arms in tears because their significant other put a gun to their head or threatened to kill them or had someone escort them into an abortion clinic to keep them there to make them have an abortion," pro-life leader Catherine Davis, founder of the Restoration Project, told one of us (Alexandra) in a 2020 interview.[77]

These realities, often ignored or denied by abortion supporters, make it all the more important to reach women with abortion alternatives. For all their talk about the importance of the "right to choose," abortion advocacy groups evidently dislike that women might freely choose to continue a pregnancy and to find help in that choice from groups who tell them the truth about abortion.

Conclusion

Every abortion is discriminatory. Every time an unborn child loses his life in an abortion, it is because something about him has been deemed unworthy. He's not treated as the equal of the adult who kills him. Perhaps the argument is that he's too small or underdeveloped to count as a person. Perhaps a worker at an abortion clinic has dismissed him as a "clump of cells." Perhaps his parents have decided they're not ready for a baby or that finances are tight; he has to be eliminated because his life is an inconvenience.

But some abortions are evidence of a particularly nefarious type of discrimination, where the life of an unborn child is deemed not worth living because she may have a disability, or because her parents wish she were a he. Sometimes the discrimination is more subtle, affecting entire communities of black and Hispanic Americans, who have faced historic injustice and today have higher abortion rates than white Americans, a cycle of suffering that abortion can never hope to solve.

In the midst of that suffering, pro-lifers have spent decades working to help women of all races and all social classes, in all types of difficult situations, encouraging them and supporting them so they can avoid abortion and choose life for their unborn children. They do this important work often without praise, yet at every turn they face harsh opposition from abortion businesses and abortion-rights activists, whose hatred of pregnancy-resource centers can be explained only by the reality that they are pro-*abortion*, not pro-*choice*.

CHAPTER FOUR

Abortion Harms Medicine

As early as five weeks into pregnancy, a new mother is able to take home a picture of her unborn baby captured via prenatal ultrasound. This technology, allowing doctors to monitor the health of the child in the womb, was pioneered in Scotland in the mid-1950s, but it didn't become commonplace in the practice of obstetrics in the United States until the mid- to late 1970s.[1] This stunning technological development allows mothers and fathers to catch a glimpse of their unborn child almost as soon as they find out he or she exists.

Later in pregnancy, they're able to watch their child wave, suck his thumb, and cross his ankles. They're able to find out whether they're having a son or daughter well before birth. They can bring home sonogram photos at various stages of development to hang on the refrigerator and share with family. Many readers likely have seen a picture of themselves as an unborn child thanks to sonogram technology.

Because of this miracle of modern medicine, mothers and fathers are able to *see* their child—the exact same child who, if all goes well, will be placed in their arms after nine months in the womb.

Prenatal ultrasound isn't the only way in which scientific developments have improved our understanding of pregnancy and childbearing. We now know that what a pregnant mother eats and drinks, whether she exercises or smokes, can affect her unborn child. We know that if she takes certain vitamins or supplements while pregnant, it can help her baby remain healthy.[2] Technology has enabled doctors to help babies who are born prematurely survive at earlier and earlier stages of development, sometimes as early as twenty-one weeks' gestation, and go on to lead healthy lives. Even more remarkable, doctors have pioneered the ability to treat unborn children while they're still in the womb. In addition to less intensive interventions, physicians can operate on unborn children to ameliorate physical defects prior to birth and obtain better postnatal outcomes.

"Today, fetal therapy is recognized as one of the most promising fields in pediatric medicine, and prenatal surgery is becoming an option for a growing number of babies with birth defects," says the Children's Hospital of Philadelphia (CHOP), one of the industry leaders in the United States. The Center for Fetal Diagnosis and Treatment at CHOP recently celebrated the birth of the two thousandth child who benefitted from the hospital's fetal surgery practice.[3]

Scientific progress has enabled us to learn more than we could've imagined even a few decades ago about human life in the womb. Dedicated doctors, who understand that good medicine aims to eradicate disease and heal patients, can care for a human being well before birth. It's easy to see why the Hippocratic Oath, the doctor's gold standard of care for millennia, expressly forbids abortion: "I will neither give a deadly drug to anybody who asked for it, nor will I make a suggestion to this effect. Similarly I will not give to a woman an abortive remedy."[4]

And it's telling that most modern versions of the Hippocratic Oath, which some students take upon entering medical school, have been revised to omit the line about abortion.[5] There is perhaps no more fitting example of the way in which abortion has corrupted the medical profession.

Abortion contradicts all of the miraculous developments over the last century that have enabled health-care workers to care for unborn children more successfully than ever before. Rather than recognizing the child in the womb as a second patient, abortion targets the child for extermination. Rather than using the tools of medicine to heal, abortion uses drugs and surgical devices to end a child's life.

This corruption of the medical profession in defense of abortion has been underway since the very beginning of the campaign for legal abortion in the United States, and it has had serious consequences that affect all of us. In this chapter, we explain the important role that doctors played in the political effort pushing the Supreme Court to create a right to abortion in *Roe v. Wade* and how their argument was a crucial part of the Court's decision.

To illustrate how abortion has infiltrated and corrupted the medical field, we tell the story of the American College of Obstetricians and Gynecologists (ACOG), which transformed itself from a nonpartisan medical organization to a highly politicized abortion advocacy group that today lobbies for abortion at the federal level. We debunk the myth that Planned Parenthood, the nation's largest abortion provider, is a champion of women. Finally, we examine how the health-care industry's embrace of abortion has caused a number of society-wide harms, negatively affecting women's health care and instigating a broader devaluation of human life in the medical context.

The Medical Establishment's Push
for the Legalization of Abortion

Abortion proponents often use the language of women's empowerment when they speak about the right to abortion. What most people don't know—and what knowledgeable abortion supporters don't admit—is that the political push for the legalization of abortion was spearheaded in large part by a coterie of ideologically motivated doctors, not just women's rights activists.

As the abortion debate in the United States was heating up, a growing number of doctors wanted the freedom to perform elective abortions, but they were afraid of facing legal consequences. Prior to *Roe*, nearly every state had strict prohibitions against elective abortion, but none of those laws imposed criminal penalties on pregnant women *seeking* abortions; they punished the doctors who *performed* them.[6]

Those doctors—willfully ignoring the growing scientific evidence that confirmed the reality of human life in the womb—became a crucial force behind the campaign to legalize abortion. Leading up to the Court's decision in *Roe*, elite medical organizations, most notably the American Medical Association (AMA) and ACOG, rallied to the pro-abortion cause and used their influence as medical experts to lobby the Supreme Court, especially Justice Harry Blackmun—not because most doctors were pushing for it but because a small group of elite, activist doctors in leadership were. Neither of these organizations began as pro-abortion lobbying groups, but they became major players in the fight for the legalization of abortion, and they have remained prominent abortion advocates to this day.

It is impossible to overstate the influence that these medical professionals had on the Court ahead of *Roe*. One of the most influential *amicus curiae* briefs in the case was filed at the Court by ACOG and signed by nearly two hundred doctors arguing that abortion was necessary to enable good medical practice.[7] Several of the brief's signatories were doctors at the Mayo Clinic in Minnesota, and the brief most likely was aimed at influencing Blackmun, who had served as general counsel at Mayo in the 1950s prior to becoming a federal judge.

In their brief, these doctors argued that the Texas ban on abortion "interferes with a physician's practice of medicine by substituting the mandate of a vague legalism for the doctor's best professional judgment as to the medically indicated treatment for his pregnant patients." The brief went on to complain that "physicians treating pregnant women run the risk of criminal charges as the result of their professional decisions."[8]

Hiding their political advocacy behind the veneer of medical expertise, these doctors aimed to convince the Court that abortion bans inhibited them from exercising their medical judgment. Their argument worked. Both the ACOG brief and advice from the AMA, which had likewise begun endorsing relaxed abortion laws, appeared to significantly influence Blackmun's thinking. This is especially clear, as we'll see in the next chapter, from his opinion in *Roe*, which hardly mentions women's rights at all but focuses instead on deferring to the judgment of doctors: "For the period of pregnancy prior to this 'compelling' point [the end of the first trimester], the attending physician, in consultation with his patient, is free to determine, without regulation by the State, that, in his medical judgment, the patient's pregnancy should be terminated," Blackmun wrote.[9]

In his ruling, Blackmun also cited the AMA's 1970 declaration that "the Principles of Medical Ethics of the AMA do not prohibit a physician from performing an abortion that is performed in accordance with good medical practice and under circumstances that do not violate the laws of the community in which he practices."[10]

The influence of these doctors on Blackmun is especially clear if you contrast the ruling in *Roe* with the Court's 1992 ruling in *Planned Parenthood v. Casey*. In *Roe*, Blackmun grounded his rationale in large part on trusting physicians to decide whether abortion was necessary—so much so that feminists and scholars have criticized *Roe* for emphasizing the role of doctors to the exclusion of female autonomy.[11] Even Supreme Court justice Ruth Bader Ginsburg criticized *Roe* on those grounds: The decision, she said, was based on "the woman in consultation with her doctor. So the view you get is the tall doctor and the little woman who needs him."[12] *Roe* created a right to abortion, yes—but in Blackmun's telling, that right functioned more to protect doctors in their practice of medicine than to let women do as they pleased.

"The decision vindicates the right of the physician to administer medical treatment according to his professional judgment up to the points where important state interests provide compelling justifications for intervention," Blackmun wrote in *Roe*. "Up to those points, the abortion decision in all its aspects is inherently, and primarily, a medical decision, and basic responsibility for it must rest with the physician."[13]

This argument, like the claims from ACOG and the AMA, is nothing but smoke and mirrors. Even at the time of *Roe*, women were seeking abortions for reasons other than real medical need. With this rationale, the Court showed that it had bought the argument of these elite doctors, who subtly expanded the concept of "medical necessity," giving themselves cover to lobby for abortion laws that wouldn't punish them for performing abortions, no matter the circumstances.

Casey, by contrast, places women at the center of its logic and grounds the right to abortion in liberty and autonomy, so much so that the role of the doctor in abortion—the fact that abortion involves a doctor at all, even—all but vanishes. In *Casey*, the Court's reasoning essentially removes the abortion right from the context of a doctor's judgment and transforms it into an issue of female freedom and equality.

Prior to *Roe*, the desire among a subset of doctors to remove anti-abortion laws was so strong that it spurred physicians to peddle inaccurate maternal-mortality statistics in order to sway the Court. Along with other prominent abortion advocates, abortionist Bernard Nathanson—whose dramatic conversion story opened this book— lobbied against abortion restrictions prior to *Roe*, relying on the false claim that five thousand to ten thousand women were dying each year in "back-alley" abortions.[14] Legalizing abortion, this argument went, would allow women who were having illegal abortions anyway to have them safely. In other words, anti-abortion laws weren't preventing abortion; they were just preventing abortions from being safe. Allowing doctors to perform them legally would end up saving lives—those of the mothers.

After becoming pro-life, Nathanson admitted that his side had relied on these inaccurate maternal mortality statistics to make the situation seem far more dire than it was: "I confess that I knew the figures were totally false, and I suppose the others did too if they stopped to think of it. But in the 'morality' of our revolution, it was a useful figure, widely accepted, so why go out of our way to correct it with honest statistics? The overriding concern was to get the laws eliminated, and anything within reason that had to be done was permissible."[15]

As we noted in Chapter Two, a leading obstetrics textbook points out that if there were five thousand maternal deaths from abortion annually prior to 1973, that would amount to five times the total number of maternal deaths from all causes in any given year.[16] More reliable statistics suggest that, in the five years leading up to *Roe*, the number of abortion-related maternal deaths in the United States each year was less than 150.[17]

But that didn't stop doctors from bringing this false claim to the Supreme Court, pretending that a ruling in favor of abortion rights would end an epidemic of maternal deaths from illegal back-alley abortions. Their strategy worked. The Court's decision in *Roe* was the result of several factors, including the desire of several justices to legalize abortion no matter what legal gymnastics it required. But the ruling was due in large part to these doctors, whose abortion advocacy helped the Court justify its decision.

Corruption of Medical Practice: The Evolution of ACOG

In Chapter Two, we discussed the ways in which abortion can be harmful to women, including in terms of their physical and psychological well-being. We also noted how abortion providers and supporters often downplay this reality. Sometimes, those negative consequences for women are a direct result of negligence on the part of abortion providers. We don't know as much about these harms to women as we should in part because the abortion industry opposes laws requiring more oversight of abortionists and more careful reporting of abortion complications.

This state of affairs has obvious implications for the medical field. How did a procedure that ends the life of an unborn human being—and often harms the child's mother in the process—become regarded as standard medical practice? Why do major medical organizations insist that abortion is health care and yet reject typical health-care regulations and safety standards when it comes to abortion?

The answers to these questions are complex, but a significant part of how this happened can be explained in the story of ACOG. In *Roe*, the leaders of ACOG used their influence as medical professionals to push the Court to rule in favor of abortion, enabling the justices to argue that their decision was in line with the recommendation of doctors. Today, ACOG is one of the nation's foremost lobbying groups pushing for unlimited abortion on demand, under the guise of medical expertise.

But the organization wasn't founded as an abortion advocacy group. Instead, it was created as a nonpartisan professional organization to educate and assist obstetricians and gynecologists. The evolution of ACOG from a standard medical organization into one of the nation's most vociferous abortion-rights activists illustrates how abortion has infiltrated the medical field and enshrined abortion—an act of lethal violence—as supposed health care.

Founded in 1951, ACOG initially handled the brewing abortion controversy by advising doctors to perform abortions only "where the death of the mother might reasonably be expected to result from natural causes, growing out of or aggravated by the pregnancy, unless the child is destroyed."[18] In other words, in its early days, ACOG affirmed that it is unethical medical practice to perform elective abortions.

During ACOG's first decade of existence, its leadership maintained that the growing effort to legalize elective abortion was a matter for social debate, not a medical issue—and thus that it was not a debate in which ACOG should become involved. But by the late 1960s, pro-abortion members of ACOG's leadership began pushing the organization to use its influence as a medical group to lobby for legal abortion. Slowly, the group began to redefine "health" and "therapeutic" as they relate to abortion, subtly ushering elective abortions under the umbrella of medical necessity.

In 1968, ACOG's Committee to Study Liberalization of the Laws Governing Therapeutic Abortion issued a report announcing that doctors could perform "therapeutic" abortions "when continuation of the pregnancy may threaten the life of the woman or seriously impair her health." Crucially, the report added: "In determining whether or not there is such risk to health, account may be taken of the patient's total environment, actual or reasonably foreseeable."[19] This redefined "therapeutic" broadly enough to encompass any possible reason for desiring an elective abortion. It essentially amounted to ACOG's leadership sanctioning elective abortion by fiat, without consulting its members, at a time when performing elective abortions was illegal in most states. And ACOG's phrasing in this 1968 report bears a striking resemblance to the Court's ruling five years later in *Doe v. Bolton*.

The Court in *Doe* created a workaround for abortion restrictions by demanding maternal-health exceptions to any law regulating abortion. The Court defined health expansively, allowing doctors to exercise their medical judgment "in the light of all factors—physical, emotional, psychological, familial, and the woman's age—relevant to the wellbeing of the patient. All these factors may relate to health."[20] This rationale, coupled with the logic of *Roe*, has made it nearly impossible to enact any significant or effective regulations on abortion. The Court's move clearly had its roots in the idea ACOG had articulated: that doctors should be able to exercise judgment about abortion by accounting for a woman's health, defined broadly so as to cover nearly any reason they might decide she "needs" an abortion.

ACOG's shift toward supporting elective abortion didn't end with the 1968 report. In 1971, the group's executive committee formally approved the decision of ACOG president Clyde Randall to sign on to an *amicus curiae* brief filed at the Supreme Court in *Doe* by the pro-abortion James Madison Constitutional Law Institute.[21] Randall argued that ACOG should take a formal policy stance in favor of legal abortion, writing in a report, "The termination of pregnancy is one of the few areas in which laws now dictate what the physician may or may not do in the care of his patient."[22]

ACOG's own brief in *Roe* and *Doe* opposed the abortion laws at issue because they allowed abortions only to save the life of the mother, which ACOG claimed was "unconstitutionally vague."[23] The brief offered an expansive definition of the so-called life-of-the-mother consideration, arguing that "life may mean the vitality, the joy, the spirit of existence, as well as merely not dying," phrases meant to establish that an abortion could be necessary for a woman's life in some sense other than immediate physical danger. The brief insisted that decisions about whether abortion was medically necessary—even under this new, expansive definition—should be left to physicians and physicians alone.

With its involvement in *Roe* and *Doe* on behalf of the legalization of abortion, ACOG had begun its steady march toward what it is today: an abortion advocacy organization. Since placing its thumb on the scale in favor of legalized abortion in 1971, ACOG has weighed in on policy at every turn, always to insist that abortion restrictions are incompatible with good medicine. In more than a dozen Supreme Court cases, ACOG has filed *amicus* briefs advocating the least restrictive possible stance on abortion, and the Court has cited ACOG's contributions as representative of medical standards.[24] In two of the most recent cases, *Whole Woman's Health v. Hellerstedt* and *June Medical Services v. Russo*, ACOG argued against admitting-privileges requirements for abortion clinics, even though these requirements apply to all other forms of ambulatory surgical centers and even though ACOG's own guidance suggests that direct patient handoff reduces medical errors.[25] Its position on medical standards for abortion, in other words, stood in stark contrast to accepted medical standards and best practice for all medical circumstances other than abortion.

ACOG's unabashed support for unlimited abortion is apparent in most of its activity, but one example is particularly instructive. In 1996, when Congress was considering legislation to ban "intact dilation and extraction" abortions, otherwise known as partial-birth abortions, ACOG prepared a statement admitting that the group "could identify no circumstances under which this procedure…would be the only option to save the life or preserve the health of the woman."[26] But, after collaborating with the staff of President Bill Clinton—who was preparing to veto the partial-birth ban, and who later did so twice—ACOG included this blatantly political addendum: "An intact D+X, however, may be the best or most appropriate procedure in a particular circumstance to save the life or preserve the health of a woman, and a doctor should be allowed to make this determination."[27] This assertion was later quoted by the Supreme Court in *Stenberg v. Carhart* in defense of the Court's decision invalidating Nebraska's ban on partial-birth abortion.[28]

In 2007, ACOG issued an ethics statement suggesting that OB-GYNs should either perform abortions or refer women elsewhere to obtain one, a move that nearly led to doctors losing their board certification if they objected.[29] In 2010, the organization formed the American Congress of Obstetricians and Gynecologists, a lobbying organization that spends most of its time advocating unlimited abortion on demand, under the guise of medical expertise—and that all ACOG members are required to finance, even if they oppose abortion.[30]

ACOG was not the only medical organization to make this dramatic shift in the years leading up to and following *Roe*. The American Medical Association—the authoritative physician-lobbying group—had, like most of its members, opposed abortion from its founding in 1847 until 1967. In 1967, the AMA adopted a policy, at the urging of its Committee on Human Reproduction, that was "opposed to induced abortion" *except* when the pregnancy "threatens the life or health of the mother," in cases of rape or incest, or in cases of possible fetal abnormalities.[31]

This language, like that of ACOG in 1968, amounted to an endorsement of the idea that physicians alone could determine whether and when abortion was medically necessary. As we described earlier, Justice Blackmun in *Doe* cited the AMA's position favorably, noting too that in 1970 the AMA had doubled down on its support for abortion in a wider range of circumstances. Today, like ACOG, the AMA frequently weighs in against abortion restrictions of any kind. The group recently argued that Texas's heartbeat bill is objectionable because it interferes with the doctor–patient relationship and penalizes doctors for "providing care."[32] The group has even sued to invalidate North Dakota's informed-consent laws, which require abortionists to provide women with accurate medical information about risks and possible complications before performing an abortion.[33]

The evolution of ACOG and the AMA from nonpartisan medical groups into abortion cheerleaders is instructive. It demonstrates that physicians who were resistant to being regulated for their participation in abortion were a crucial part of pushing for abortion legalization. And it illustrates how, both before and after *Roe*, a critical mass of the elite medical community began to coalesce around more and more liberal abortion laws, pretending that such a position was medically necessary. They traded on their authority as medical doctors to advance what was essentially a political and moral conclusion. The expansion of abortion laws had success because, in American culture, the doctors and scientists are the high priests.

Abortion Is Not Health Care: Planned Parenthood

There is perhaps no better example of how this corruption of the medical profession has affected our debates over abortion and our conception of health care than the story of Planned Parenthood, our nation's largest abortion provider. Planned Parenthood has successfully cloaked itself in the pleasant veneer of hot pink and branded itself "essential women's health care." But the reality is that Planned Parenthood exists primarily to perform abortions, as well as to lobby for policies that make it easier to perform and profit from abortion. Planned Parenthood's business model exemplifies how, for abortion providers, turning a profit has displaced practicing medicine.

Planned Parenthood is, by far, the nation's largest abortion provider, performing somewhere between one-third and one-half of all abortions in the United States each year.[34] While the group also offers contraception, tests for sexually transmitted diseases, cancer screenings, and a handful of additional services, abortion is its most profitable procedure—and the one it defends most vigorously as a political matter.

Planned Parenthood Federation of America serves as the national umbrella organization for dozens of affiliates across the country, which operate more than five hundred clinics. But Planned Parenthood also has a lobbying arm, Planned Parenthood Action, which regularly opposes abortion restrictions, promotes even more expansive abortion policies than currently exist, and lobbies for increasing its own federal funding. Unsurprisingly, the group's PAC shells out tens of millions of dollars each election cycle in support of Democrats, who support unlimited abortion and increased government funding for Planned Parenthood.

Despite its prominent role in the abortion industry and in our politics, Planned Parenthood is a regular recipient of immense amounts of government funding. Each year, on average, the organization receives more than $618 million from federal and state governments, most of which comes in the form of reimbursements through Medicaid.[35] Most states also fund Planned Parenthood through their state Medicaid programs.

Though Planned Parenthood's supporters claim otherwise, government funding necessarily underwrites Planned Parenthood's provision of abortion, a topic we will address later in this section. In the 1980s, funding for abortion was a key political issue, eventually culminating in the 1991 Supreme Court case *Rust v. Sullivan*, in which a 5–4 majority ruled that the presidential administration could decide whether to allow abortion providers to receive funding under the Title X family-planning program.[36] But federal funding for abortion businesses, most notably Planned Parenthood, has in recent years become a political hot-button topic once again, with most Democratic politicians insisting on giving money to the group and most Republicans insisting that organizations that kill unborn human beings should not receive public support.[37]

Abortion funding became highly controversial after *Roe* was decided, leading to the bipartisan Hyde Amendment, which has long prohibited Medicaid tax dollars from funding elective abortions. But today, most Democrats no longer support Hyde and have joined Planned Parenthood in arguing that all abortions should be eligible for taxpayer funding.

Perhaps the best recent example of Planned Parenthood's dedication to abortion came during the presidency of Donald Trump. Under Trump, the Department of Health and Human Services (HHS) promulgated a new policy called the Protect Life Rule, dealing with the Title X family-planning program. The new rule established that, in order to be eligible for Title X funding, abortion providers had to financially and physically separate their provision of abortion from their other work—in other words, they had to separate into two distinct entities, with no financial crossover, and perform abortions in distinct facilities.

The policy was based on the rationale that because abortion is a grave moral evil, government policy shouldn't subsidize and thus financially incentivize it.[38] What's more, without such a separation, taxpayers were being forced to financially assist in the provision of elective abortion. Planned Parenthood immediately came out swinging, launching a huge campaign against the policy.

When the administration refused to back down, Planned Parenthood ultimately withdrew from the Title X program rather than separate its provision of abortion from the rest of its work. With this decision, the group forfeited about $60 million in federal funding.[39] Shortly after taking office, President Joe Biden directed his HHS to revoke the Protect Life Rule.[40]

This story illustrates that, despite Planned Parenthood's insistence that it is a women's health-care provider offering much more than abortion, when push came to shove, the group chose abortion. Had it financially and physically separated abortion procedures from the rest of what it does, the group could've continued performing abortions as a financially, physically distinct entity and continued receiving Title X funding for its other services. That Planned Parenthood chose not to do so confirms that it exists, first and foremost, to promote and perform abortions.

Despite that fact, Planned Parenthood maintains a glossy public image as an essential health-care provider. In service of this notion, Planned Parenthood executives and their supporters peddle a variety of myths, seeking to minimize the group's prominence in the abortion industry and in our politics. Below, we debunk each of these myths in turn.

"Abortion Is Just 3 Percent of What Planned Parenthood Offers"

Planned Parenthood's annual reports typically indicate that abortion is a mere 3 percent of the "medical services" the group provides each year. Planned Parenthood defenders often rely on this figure when they claim that Planned Parenthood is a health-care organization that offers much more than just abortion. But this statistic is a convenient fiction Planned Parenthood invented to obscure its role as the most prolific abortion provider in the country.

Planned Parenthood's own report provides the information with which to debunk the 3 percent claim. The group arrives at this statistic by dividing the number of abortion procedures performed each year by the number of "services" the group provided. A "service" is defined as a "discrete clinical interaction," such as the administration of an STI test.

Here's what this means in practice. If a woman visits a Planned Parenthood facility to obtain an abortion, and while she's there she also receives a pregnancy test (necessary before performing an abortion), an STI test (to see if the sex that resulted in pregnancy also resulted in an STI), and contraception (supposedly to preclude future abortions), Planned Parenthood would say that the abortion procedure was just 25 percent of the "services" she received—even though she came to the clinic primarily to obtain an abortion. In other words, the group downplays the prominence of abortion by inflating the importance of other "services" offered in the process of doing regular business. Using this deceptive formula, Planned Parenthood manipulates its data to make it appear as if abortion is a tiny fraction of its work, even though a higher percentage of patients are there to obtain an abortion. Planned Parenthood's annual number of "services," for example, is far higher than the number of patients who visit Planned Parenthood. Far more useful would be a figure showing what percentage of Planned Parenthood patients obtain an abortion; for the most recent fiscal year, it was about one in five women.

Meanwhile, even as Planned Parenthood has continued upping the abortions it performs each year, the group has begun providing what it calls "gender-affirming care," or hormone therapy for individuals suffering from gender dysphoria.[41] In its 2014 annual report, Planned Parenthood reported just twenty-six centers in ten states offering hormone therapy. As of 2019, that had jumped up to more than two hundred centers in thirty-one states, and according to the group's website, the number of clinics that provide hormone therapy has continued growing to include close to three hundred centers across thirty-eight states. It isn't clear from the group's reports exactly how many instances of "gender-affirming care" Planned Parenthood provides, as hormone therapy is grouped under "other services" with things like "adult preventive care" and "pediatric services." But in its 2018–2019 report, the "other services" category doubled from the previous report, up to about eighteen thousand.

It's not just that a significant portion of Planned Parenthood's work is abortion, but also that Planned Parenthood is the biggest abortion business in America. In 2019–2020, the most recent fiscal year for which Planned Parenthood produced an annual report, the group's facilities performed 354,871 abortions.[42] That accounts for more than half of all abortions in the United States as reported by the Centers for Disease Control (CDC), and more than a third of all abortions as estimated by the pro-choice research group the Guttmacher Institute. (The discrepancy is due to the fact that states aren't required to report abortion statistics to the CDC, and some large, abortion-friendly states choose not to do so. Guttmacher's estimates attempt to account for that reality.) Regardless of how many other "services" Planned Parenthood happens to provide, it remains the most prolific abortion provider in our country.

"Planned Parenthood Doesn't Use Taxpayer Money for Abortion"

During political debates over whether Planned Parenthood should continue to receive federal funding, the organization and its defenders routinely insist that taxpayer money never goes toward abortion. They claim that the organization somehow separates the money it receives so that its federal funding never reimburses providers for the cost of abortion procedures.[43] To make this argument, they point to the Hyde Amendment, which prevents federal Medicaid funds from directly covering the cost of elective abortions. While the Hyde Amendment is an admirable attempt to prevent public money from subsidizing unjust killing, the sad reality is that this amendment alone doesn't prevent federal money from funding abortion. That's because money is fungible. Even though Medicaid might not directly refund Planned Parenthood for the cost of performing abortions, any federal money Planned Parenthood receives assists the organization in keeping its doors open and thus in continuing to perform abortions.

A hypothetical example helps to illustrate the absurdity of Planned Parenthood's argument. If the federal government gave half a billion dollars to a tobacco company while also instructing it not to use the money to directly cover the production of tobacco products, no one would take such an arrangement seriously. The company might take the federal funding and use it to pay the lease, pay its staff, or cover the electric bills rather than directly funding the manufacture of tobacco products—but that half a billion dollars nonetheless assists the company in making its products. That money covering other costs enables the company to keep its doors open and put more of its other money into its work. The same is true for abortion and Planned Parenthood.

The fungibility of money is precisely why the Protect Life Rule required abortion providers to financially and physically separate abortion from their other work. Unless that stark separation was in place, any taxpayer money an abortion provider received would help them provide abortions, because it financially assists them as an organization. Any federal funding of an abortion provider essentially sanctions unjust killing and forces taxpayers to underwrite that provider's provision of abortion. The more than half a billion dollars in government funding that Planned Parenthood receives each year does fund abortion because it funds Planned Parenthood, and Planned Parenthood performs abortions.

Undercover Center for Medical Progress Videos
and Congressional Investigation

In the summer of 2015, the Center for Medical Progress (CMP)—
a group of pro-life citizen journalists and activists—began unveiling
a series of undercover videos that exposed Planned Parenthood's
involvement in the alleged illegal sale of fetal tissue. Posing as a potential fetal tissue buyer, CMP's founder, David Daleiden, captured
evidence suggesting that prominent abortionists, Planned Parenthood
executives, and biotechnology companies were selling and profiting
from the body parts of aborted babies, in violation of state and federal
laws.

The video footage was gruesome. Biotech employees talked about
harvesting fetal organs from aborted babies while working at Planned
Parenthood clinics. Planned Parenthood executives and abortionists
talked about modifying abortion procedures to obtain intact and thus
more-profitable organs from the babies they aborted—which, if true,
would be a violation of the law. Here's how one of us (Alexandra)
summarized the relevant details in a Spring 2021 article for the
Human Life Review:

> Planned Parenthood affiliates across the country were rou-
> tinely procuring body parts from aborted babies for biotech
> firms, which acted as middlemen for research groups
> looking to buy fetal tissue. With each transaction, the abor-
> tion provider took a payment from the tissue-procurement
> organization, which in turn made a profit for providing the
> body parts to universities and other medical researchers.
>
> While experimenting on aborted babies is legal in the
> U.S., profiting from the tissue and organ procurement process
> is not. That's why the bulk of Planned Parenthood's initial

response to the videos revolved around the claim that the fetal tissue in question had been donated, first by the women who chose abortion and then by the abortion organization.

But as the extensive comments captured on film illustrate, Planned Parenthood executives involved in the procurement process had no intention of offering their services for free. What's more, the videos and further investigation revealed that Planned Parenthood affiliates often didn't obtain informed consent from the women whose babies they shipped off to be used for research, flouting both legal requirements and the definition of "donation."

Meanwhile, Planned Parenthood workers rarely had been doing the organ or tissue procurement work themselves. Nevertheless, financial documents reveal that the group regularly accepted "reimbursement" fees from their biotech partners. For instance, in a partnership with StemExpress LLC—a biotech firm that subsequently sued Daleiden for exposing its role in this illegal marketplace— Planned Parenthood clinics involved in the fetal-tissue industry offloaded the work of organ harvesting to company technicians, then accepted a payment for each tissue sample, allegedly a reimbursement for labor, shipping, and handling costs.

Planned Parenthood affiliates were accepting payment for what, in the group's own words, was a "donation," as well as for samples that involved no work or transport for which the group would need to be reimbursed.[44]

At first, the videos received a huge amount of attention. Was Planned Parenthood, which holds itself out as a valued provider of women's health care, harboring some dark secrets? But, empowered by allies in the media, Planned Parenthood immediately rolled out a highly successful public-relations campaign to defend its public image. Despite all of this evidence—and even though the Senate Judiciary Committee ended up referring Planned Parenthood and several of its affiliates to the FBI and Department of Justice for further investigation and possible criminal prosecution—Planned Parenthood emerged largely unscathed.

This was due in large part to its propagation of the myth that the CMP videos had been "deceptively edited." Planned Parenthood spun this line and it was repeated in nearly every prominent media outlet, making it sound as though CMP somehow had managed to fabricate entire clips, using technology to make it appear as if Planned Parenthood executives had implicated themselves when in fact they hadn't. The *Huffington Post* labeled the CMP videos "debunked," *Newsweek* called them "a debunked anti-choice propaganda campaign," and ThinkProgress referred to them as "discredited sting videos."[45] *The Hill* and *U.S. News & World Report*, among other outlets, repeatedly cited Planned Parenthood's assertion that the videos were "heavily edited and misleading."[46]

On the contrary, the videos had never been discredited or debunked. In fact, quite the opposite. Shortly after releasing the videos, CMP published hours of full, unedited undercover footage, letting viewers access the entire context of each video. This refuted the lie that crucial context had been removed to make the statements on video appear incriminating. Two independent forensic reviews of CMP's footage confirmed that the audio hadn't been tampered with and that, compared with the full-length footage, nothing substantial or contextually necessary had been removed. One of those reviews was commissioned by Planned Parenthood itself and performed by Democratic research firm Fusion GPS.[47] Though Planned Parenthood pretended otherwise, even that analysis "did not reveal widespread evidence of substantive video manipulation."[48] Even the Fifth Circuit Court of Appeals has affirmed that the videos were not deceptively edited, permitting them to be used as evidence in a state's effort to defund Planned Parenthood.[49]

By the time congressional investigations confirmed that Planned Parenthood and others involved in fetal tissue trafficking appeared to have flouted numerous significant laws, most people had lost interest. Even though Planned Parenthood managed to make the issue all but disappear, it remains embroiled in a scorched-earth lawsuit seeking to punish Daleiden and his associates at CMP for exposing the group's misdeeds.

Legal Abortion Undermines Good Medicine

Elective abortion solves no medical problem and treats no disease. While it occasionally might be necessary to deliver a child early or perform a treatment on a pregnant mother that will result in the death of her baby, intentionally killing an unborn child is never medically necessary; today, every abortion is an elective one.[50] As the American Association of Pro-Life Obstetricians and Gynecologists (AAPLOG) has put it, "The fact that an elective abortion is performed by a physician with drugs or surgery does not turn an elective abortion into medical care any more than an attack with a scalpel turns an assault into medical care."[51]

It's impossible to overstate the cognitive dissonance produced within the medical field by the widespread acceptance of abortion as "health care." Consider just one example. In recent decades, enterprising doctors have pioneered a complex fetal-surgery procedure to treat unborn children diagnosed with spina bifida, in which the physician administers anesthesia to both mother and child and attempts to close the gap around the base of the child's spine, giving his tiny body a chance to develop normally before birth.[52] But if that very same unborn baby had parents who would prefer not to have a child with spina bifida at all, he might end up instead at an abortion clinic, where a doctor would use surgical tools to kill him and remove him from his mother's womb.

The only difference between those two cases is whether the child's parents, and especially his mother, want him to remain alive and want to care for him. In a society that has embraced the logic of abortion, that distinction is all it takes for doctors to shift from treating an unborn child as a patient to using those same medical tools to kill him.

This perversion of good medicine has had ramifications for all of us. One major harm has been to women's health care, and not only because of the direct negative effects to women of obtaining an abortion. The logic of abortion suggests that, at least in some cases, the unborn child doesn't belong inside his mother. The extension of this view is that pregnancy, at least some of the time, is a disease to be cured rather than the natural result of a female body functioning as it should.

This mindset, pervasive in the medical community in part because of its embrace of abortion, has led to an over-reliance on oral contraceptives, which likewise treat pregnancy as a disease to be prevented. Both second-wave and modern feminists hail easy access to birth control as a key component of female liberation, but, similar to abortion, contraceptive drugs treat the male body as normative and use chemical methods to alter the female body, thereby rendering sex sterile.

Hormonal contraceptives are not without side effects and health risks to women. According to researchers at Sweden's University Hospital, breast-cancer rates are two to three times higher among women who used the oral contraceptive pill for more than five years prior to their first pregnancy than among women who never used it.[53] Long-term oral contraceptive use, another study found, can be a cofactor that increases cervical-cancer risk by up to four times for women who carry cervical HPV DNA.[54]

In their 2012 peer-reviewed article, Georgetown University School of Medicine's Charles Norris and family medicine practitioner Rebecca Peck published a comprehensive review of the health risks of hormonal contraceptives. Their summary, based on decades of research, is worth quoting at length:

> Firstly, oral contraceptives (OCPs) have their own significant risks, namely, an increase in cardiovascular events (such as an increase in venous thromboembolism, pulmonary embolism, myocardial infarction, and stroke) especially in older women and smokers. Secondly, OCPs increase the risk of the world's most frequently occurring cancer, breast cancer. Thirdly, OCP use leads to an increase in human papillomavirus (HPV) infection and an increase in cervical cancer, which is the second most common cancer worldwide.

Therefore, they conclude, "OCPs fail the most important test of preventive medicine: they increase the risk of disease instead of decreasing it."[55] By way of comparison, the most recent clinical trial for an experimental form of male birth control was halted after a review panel determined that too many men were experiencing side effects.[56] After several decades of witnessing the effects of female contraceptives, some doctors now believe that these drugs are being overprescribed to women, to the detriment of their health and to the exclusion of actual health-care solutions.[57] In recent years, there has been an uptick in interest among women in natural fertility-awareness methods, which teach women about their reproductive function so they can seek treatment for health conditions rather than paper over problems with artificial hormones.[58]

Another major harm of abortion as "health care" is the devaluation of human life in a variety of medical contexts. At least in part because of how abortion dismisses the value of the unborn human being, elite organizations, advocacy groups, and politicians now advocate permitting destructive scientific research on human embryos. The same groups that threw their weight behind the legalization of abortion began lobbying for loosened regulations on embryo-destructive stem cell research, a topic hotly debated in the 2000s.[59] Once some number of medical experts have accepted the idea that killing an unborn child is an acceptable form of health care, it's easy to justify experimenting on embryos for the sake of scientific or medical progress.

A similar problem has occurred when it comes to assisted suicide and euthanasia, both of which devalue human life at the opposite end of the spectrum. Over the past few decades, "death with dignity" movements have begun pushing to legalize physician-assisted suicide, arguing that everyone should have the right to die when and how they wish—and that doctors must be allowed to assist in these suicides, or even forced to do so. As of 2021, ten states and the District of Columbia have legalized physician-assisted suicide.[60] These changes are enabled by a culture and a medical profession that have already embraced abortion, which denies the fundamental principle that every human life has intrinsic value. Furthermore, both abortion and physician-assisted suicide treat the medical profession as if it were a value-neutral task, requiring merely the application of expertise, a set of skills for using scalpels and syringes, pharmaceuticals and IV drips. In this framework, the question of whether that technical expertise is turned toward healing or killing is entirely up to the will of the physician—or even the will of the patient. Medicine is meant to be devoted to healing and wholeness, but this mindset treats doctors as if they are merely a technician for hire.[61]

As the medical profession has been transformed in this way, and as abortion has come to be treated as just another standard form of health care, the conscience rights of doctors have suffered. Once a critical mass of elite medical organizations began to deem abortion an acceptable medical practice, doctors who continued to affirm that abortion is unjust, lethal violence found themselves in a difficult position—and it has grown more difficult as time goes on. In 2007, ACOG issued guidance attempting to force all OB-GYNs to perform abortions or relocate their practice to be near a clinic that would do so.[62] As supporters of abortion began to describe abortion as a positive good worthy of celebrating, it was inevitable that they would attempt to force health-care providers to perform abortions and other procedures to which they are morally opposed and which they regard as detrimental to women's well-being.

This is slowly becoming a mainstream position among Democratic politicians. For example, the so-called Equality Act would amend the Civil Rights Act of 1964 to add "sex," "sexual orientation," and "gender identity" as classes protected by nondiscrimination statutes.[63] If enacted, the bill would have dire consequences for a whole host of policies, but one of the lesser-known problems is that it would mandate paying for and performing abortions.[64] The Equality Act redefines "sex" to include "pregnancy, childbirth, or a related medical condition," and federal agencies and courts already have determined that the phrase "related medical condition" can be interpreted to include abortion.[65]

The bill's text stipulates that those with "a related medical condition shall not receive less favorable treatment than other physical conditions," which would in effect make it illegal for physicians to decline to perform an abortion. As a result, the legislation likely would enable women who are denied an abortion, even as a result of a health-care worker's religious or conscience objections, to challenge the decision under the law—and most likely, they would succeed.

Similarly, as advocates of the Equality Act have admitted, those same provisions could be read to require taxpayer funding of elective abortions.[66] Because the federal government funds a wide range of health-care programs, and because the bill defines "establishments" broadly to include institutions other than actual health-care facilities, the government itself likely would be subject to the terms of the Equality Act. As a result, the law would almost certainly require both federal and state governments to cover the cost of abortion procedures.[67]

The desire to force Catholic health-care providers to cover abortion appears from time to time in left-wing commentary. In 2018, for example, the political website FiveThirtyEight ran a multipart series criticizing Catholic hospitals for refusing to provide abortions, contraception, and so-called sex-reassignment surgeries.[68] Later that same year, the *New York Times* ran a lengthy article on the same topic in which it "analyzed 652 websites of Catholic hospitals in the United States," and, finding that most decline to offer these procedures, lamented that patients might find some options "off limits."[69] These news reports reveal a raging debate over what constitutes good medicine, and some want to promote lethal violence as standard medical practice.

A similar mindset was evident when President Barack Obama's Department of Health and Human Services created a mandate as part of the Patient Protection and Affordable Care Act, requiring all employers—including a Catholic order of charitable nuns, the Little Sisters of the Poor—to provide coverage for contraceptives and abortion-inducing drugs in their employee health-care plans. The policy was undergirded by the view that contraception and abortion are necessary components of women's health care, and therefore that women must have easy access to them through their health-care plans. This ran roughshod over the religious freedom and conscience rights of employers who oppose birth control and abortifacients, forcing them to spend the past decade in court fighting for their right not to promote things to which they are morally opposed.

Conclusion

The Supreme Court created a constitutional right to abortion in *Roe v. Wade* in large part because of the lobbying of elite medical professionals, who insisted that legal abortion was necessary for them to do their work. Using the logic and statistics put forward by ACOG, the AMA, and other pro-abortion doctors, the Court in *Roe* granted its imprimatur to the idea that abortion is medically necessary and that it should be permitted on those grounds.

Once abortion was legal, the doctors who had pushed for it doubled down, becoming more radically pro-abortion over time and embracing the idea that abortion is an essential form of women's health care, at the expense of sound medical practice. This is clear both in the evolution of ACOG and the way Planned Parenthood operates its abortion business.

We are all worse off in a society where many believe that killing a human being is an acceptable and even necessary form of health care. True medicine aims to heal and never to harm. Abortion has perverted that norm, and none of us are exempt from its logic. Abortion's corruption of medicine has had significant negative ramifications, making it more difficult for women to obtain good health care, making it easier to defend unjust practices such as embryo-destructive research and euthanasia, and making it harder for health-care practitioners to avoid performing procedures they know are wrong.

CHAPTER FIVE

Abortion Harms the Rule of Law

In 2019, a dozen states passed some version of a heartbeat bill, a statute prohibiting abortion after an unborn child's heartbeat can be detected, usually around six weeks into pregnancy. The same year, several Democrat-controlled states enacted laws expanding access to abortion throughout all nine months of pregnancy. In New York, the Reproductive Health Act allowed abortion for any reason up to twenty-four weeks, defined the unborn as nonpersons under the law, and made it easier for women to obtain an abortion up until birth. In several other blue states, lawmakers passed statutes declaring abortion a fundamental right.

This legislative action indicated an uptick in interest in abortion as a policy matter, especially considering the impending possibility that the Supreme Court might overturn *Roe v. Wade*. But most revealing was what came next. Abortion providers and advocacy groups immediately sued the states with heartbeat bills, and one by one, each of those laws was blocked in court before it could save any lives. But while the pro-life laws were struck down, the laws expanding abortion after fetal viability and affirmatively declaring abortion a fundamental right remain in place to this day.

How did we end up in this lopsided situation, where Americans who support abortion are permitted to have their views enshrined in law, but pro-life citizens are blocked at every turn when their lawmakers try to protect unborn children?

This status quo is the poisonous fruit of the Supreme Court's ruling in *Roe v. Wade*, the 1973 decision that struck down Texas's longstanding protections for unborn children and created a constitutional right to abortion throughout the United States. The ruling removed nearly every question about abortion policy from the hands of the American people and placed the issue into the hands of unelected judges, even though the Constitution contains nothing that could remotely support a right to abortion.

Roe and the Court's subsequent abortion jurisprudence have created a legal minefield in which the supposed right to abortion is treated as sacrosanct and protected at every turn by rulings that have more in common with legislation than judicial opinions. What's more, these rulings don't follow traditional legal methods or settled standards. As Judge Amul Thapar of the Sixth Circuit Court of Appeals put it in a recent case: "There are rules for most cases, and then there are rules for abortion cases."[1]

Justice Sandra Day O'Connor, no staunch opponent of *Roe*, described it as the "abortion distortion"—the way in which our nation's highest court, when faced with abortion regulations, refuses to apply even the most elementary and uncontroversial legal rules and doctrines evenhandedly.[2] As she noted, the majority opinion in *Roe* "makes it painfully clear that no legal rule or doctrine is safe from ad hoc nullification by this Court when an occasion for its application arises in a case involving state regulation of abortion."[3] In other words, our legal system has been revolutionized to protect a right that the justices invented out of whole cloth.

In this chapter, we explain the backstory behind the Court's ruling in *Roe*. Many agree that *Roe* was bad constitutional law, but few understand the judicial willfulness that drove the ruling. We outline the legal, procedural, and factual flaws in the *Roe* decision and the way these mistakes have been perpetuated in the Court's subsequent abortion rulings, especially *Planned Parenthood v. Casey*. By the time we're done, it'll be clear that the only defensible path forward is for the Court to finally admit its mistake and overturn *Roe* and *Casey*.

Roe v. Wade Harmed the Rule of Law

To take stock of where we are so far: The supposed constitutional right to abortion has harmed unborn children, as we saw in Chapter One, and women, as we saw in Chapter Two. It has put the most vulnerable—racial minorities, baby girls, and children with disabilities—at greatest risk, as we saw in Chapter Three, and it has dramatically corrupted the practice of medicine, as we saw in Chapter Four. It has also damaged our system of constitutional self-government and the rule of law. The U.S. Constitution simply does not protect a right to choose abortion. The justices who first created such a right in *Roe* perverted the Constitution and imposed their own moral-political opinions about the desirability of abortion on the nation. And supporters of abortion have spent the past fifty years using lies and distortions to prop up this ideological ruling.

Justice Clarence Thomas perhaps put it best, calling *Roe* a purely political maneuver without "a shred of support from the Constitution's text."[4] But even scholars and lawyers who support legalized abortion as a policy matter agree that *Roe* was a bad decision.[5] Writing in the *Yale Law Journal* in 1973, renowned law professor John Hart Ely, later dean of Stanford Law School, derided the decision as "bad because it is bad constitutional law, or rather because it is not constitutional law and gives almost no sense of an obligation to try to be."[6] Laurence Tribe observed in the *Harvard Law Review* that "one of the most curious things about *Roe* is that, behind its own verbal smokescreen, the substantive judgment on which it rests is nowhere to be found."[7]

Meanwhile, Edward Lazarus, a former law clerk to Harry Blackmun (the Supreme Court justice who authored *Roe*) who went on to serve as an Obama administration official, explained, "As a matter of constitutional interpretation and judicial method, *Roe* borders on the indefensible." It's worth noting that Lazarus describes himself as "utterly committed to the right to choose." The late Justice Ruth Bader Ginsburg called *Roe* "heavy-handed judicial intervention," and the prominent progressive law professor and Obama administration official Cass Sunstein believes *Roe* "way overreached."[8] The decision in *Roe* and subsequent decisions upholding it were judicial activism in service of a ruling that was egregiously wrong. *Roe* and *Casey* created a "constitutional right" to abortion out of thin air. The majorities in those cases did not actually find textual, historical, or traditional evidence for any such right. Instead, the justices created a right to abortion out of whole cloth to satisfy their own political desires.

None of the Court's rationales for a constitutional right to abortion were agreed to, either in practice or principle, by the framers and ratifiers of the Fourteenth Amendment, where the justices claimed to find them—nor in any other provision of the Constitution. Indeed, prominent pro-life scholars such as Robert P. George of Princeton, John Finnis of Oxford, and the late Charles Rice of Notre Dame have argued that the proper interpretation of the Fourteenth Amendment entails that laws denying legal protections to the unborn and laws that protect abortion are themselves unconstitutional, as they deny unborn persons the equal protection of the laws.[9] Texas made this very argument in support of its abortion law back in 1972, and we'll have more to say about the Fourteenth Amendment in our conclusion.[10]

The Court's conclusions in *Roe* contradict every element of sound constitutional law and theory, overstepping the role of the Court and undermining the rule of law. When *Roe* was decided, "living constitutionalism" was on the rise. At the beginning of the twentieth century, as political progressivism was becoming common in the elected branches of government, only one thing stood in the progressive movement's way: the Constitution. Supreme Court justices once were willing to strike down pieces of New Deal legislation, but over time—through intimidation and, more important, through the appointments of justices who shared a different vision of constitutional law—the Court relented. After that point, the Court was more willing to uphold constitutionally dubious New Deal and Great Society legislation, but it became increasingly eager to strike down laws that conflicted with the justices' social vision of progress, particularly on moral, religious, and sexual matters. In short, a significant number of the justices believed that the sexual revolution needed an accompanying judicial revolution.

Living constitutionalism thrived during this era. This legal theory encourages judges to update the law to contemporary mores, with only peripheral regard for the text or original meaning of the Constitution. What many now derisively call judicial activism was back then seen as a virtue, a way of updating an out-of-date document, ushering it into modernity.

Woodrow Wilson, a proponent of living constitutionalism, argued that the government of the founders was like a machine following predetermined laws of nature. He believed the government should operate more like a living organism—"accountable to Darwin, not to Newton," as he put it—that would need to be manipulated to meet modern challenges. Wilson's flawed reading of the founders aside, it is clear how this theory applies to the legal field. "All that progressives ask or desire is permission," Wilson said, "in an era when 'development,' 'evolution,' is the scientific word—to interpret the Constitution according to the Darwinian principle."[11] In other words, progressives wanted judges to reinterpret the Constitution, to update it, to let it evolve, to claim that it meant what they wanted it to mean, rather than discern and apply what it actually meant.

When it came to *Roe*, rather than seek a constitutional answer to the question of abortion, living constitutionalist justices began from their desired conclusion—legal abortion in some form—and reasoned backward to pretend that the Constitution licensed their decision. Striking down a Texas ban on abortion, the seven-justice majority in *Roe* invented a constitutional right to abortion, which they wanted to find before the Court even agreed to hear the case.

■   ■   ■

In *Roe*, the justices held that the Due Process Clause of the Fourteenth Amendment includes protection for a woman's right to abortion, and they invented a framework dividing pregnancy into trimesters in an attempt to balance the interests at stake. According to the decision, a woman's right to abortion is absolute in the first trimester and cannot be regulated by states. In the second trimester, the abortion right can be regulated only in ways that are aimed at protecting maternal health. After fetal viability, which roughly corresponded with the third trimester, the justices said the state could enact regulations designed to protect the life of the unborn child, as long as they made exceptions for the mother's life and health.

It is important to note that *Roe* had a companion case decided on the same day, *Doe v. Bolton*, considering the constitutionality of Georgia's abortion law. The decision in *Doe* effectively erased even the viability line, thus entailing that even in the third trimester states couldn't effectively protect the child in the womb. In *Doe*, the Court defined the scope of *Roe*'s mandatory "health exception" (which must apply to restrictions on abortion at *all* gestational stages) to include not merely physical well-being but also "factors physical, emotional, psychological, and familial."[12] Moreover, the abortionist was given the sole authority to determine whether any such aspect of a woman's well-being warrants an abortion. Accordingly, the Court essentially nullified the ability of states to restrict abortion even after a child could survive outside the womb.

Roe grounded the supposed right to abortion in the constitutional right of privacy—a right that is not found within the text of the Constitution but rather was discovered by the Supreme Court in "emanations" from the "penumbras" of the Bill of Rights.[13] The "right to privacy...is broad enough to encompass a woman's decision whether or not to terminate her pregnancy," wrote Justice Harry Blackmun, the author of the majority opinion in *Roe*.[14] This assertion at the heart of *Roe*, paired with the trimester framework—which has far more in common with a policy scheme than a legal test—is perhaps the best evidence that the justices had begun from their desired conclusion and invented a baseless constitutional theory to justify it. Certainly there is no way to start with the Constitution and somehow discern a trimester system from it.

As *Roe*'s author, Justice Blackmun is widely considered the architect of the decision. But two other justices—William Douglas and William Brennan, the latter of whom was the foremost advocate of living constitutionalism on the Court at the time—did much more behind the scenes to pave the way for the Court's eventual ruling.

Several years before *Roe,* Douglas had written the majority opinion in *Griswold v. Connecticut,* which found a right to marital privacy in the "penumbras, formed by emanations" from the Bill of Rights, and prohibited states from regulating married couples' use of contraception—a holding that later became foundational in *Roe.*[15] When the court agreed to hear *Roe,* Brennan was already writing the majority opinion in *Eisenstadt v. Baird,* in which he extended *Griswold*'s privacy right to cover a variety of sexual matters for both the married and unmarried alike.

Brennan could "extend" *Griswold* in this way only by utterly repudiating the logic behind it. Somehow, the right to marital privacy created in *Griswold* became a right to sexual privacy in *Eisenstadt*—and the Court treated "privacy" as freedom from legal restrictions, regulations, or bans on the commercial sale of various items. How marital privacy guarantees public commercial protections is anyone's guess. How marital privacy might be extended to the unmarried defies logic.

Here's how Brennan put it in *Eisenstadt*: "If the right of privacy means anything, it is the right of the individual, married or single, to be free from unwarranted governmental intrusion into matters so fundamentally affecting a person as the decision whether to bear or beget a child."[16] *Roe* was already pending when Brennan wrote those words, and Brennan himself said that this language would be useful in substantiating the Court's eventual decision finding a right to abortion.[17] Indeed, Blackmun would go on to quote that passage in *Roe.*

Grounding the right to abortion in the right to privacy was a hobbyhorse of Brennan's, and he advocated it forcefully during the debate over the *Roe* decision. In a memo to Douglas on December 30, 1971—shortly after the first oral arguments in *Roe*—Brennan said that their aim should be to strike down all restrictions on abortion "except for the requirement that the abortion be performed by a licensed physician."[18]

In his memo, Brennan admitted that justifying legal abortion would be an uphill battle, and he charted a course for addressing some of the procedural, precedential, and constitutional issues at stake while dismissing others and finessing the rest.[19] The decision of "whether to abort a pregnancy," Brennan added, "obviously fits directly within each of the categories of fundamental freedoms I've identified and, therefore, should be held to involve a basic individual right."

More likely than not, these are the "penumbras of the Bill of Rights" to which Blackmun referred in the *Roe* decision, when he argued that the right to privacy had a distinguished constitutional pedigree. In support of including abortion under the umbrella of privacy, Blackmun cited, to a one, the very same cases Brennan had mentioned in his memo.[20]

The notion that a right to privacy encompasses a right to lethal violence is baseless, and the argument that the justices offered for it was not an argument at all. Rather, Blackmun simply asserted the connection and cited cases that did not support this proposition. He cited, for example, *Pierce v. Society of Sisters*, which protected the right of parents to direct the education of their children—a right that does not in any logical way license abortion.[21] It is hard to see how a case upholding the authority of parents over their children's education could be used to support a purported right of mothers to kill their children.

Another significant error in *Roe* was its assertion that abortion could fairly be regulated via the use of a trimester framework hinging on fetal viability—or when a child could survive outside the womb—which was around the end of the second trimester when the case was decided. This standard is entirely arbitrary, and the justices knew it.[22] Indeed, while working on the opinion, Blackmun wrote to his fellow justices, "I have concluded that the end of the first trimester is critical." He went on to say, "This is arbitrary, but perhaps any other selected point, such as quickening or viability, is equally arbitrary."

The Constitution, of course, entails nothing at all about trimesters of pregnancy, quickening, or viability. From a moral standpoint, there is no difference in value between a newly conceived child, a twenty-four-week-old fetus, and a newborn baby. To draw lines as Blackmun did was not only morally incoherent but also a policy judgment rather than a legal decision—with no basis in the Constitution. No legal principle can explain why the state's interest in protecting the life of the unborn child only becomes substantial enough after the child can survive outside the womb. The state has the very same interest in protecting that child's life whether he is inside or outside the womb, whether he is "viable" or "dependent." In December 2021, during oral arguments in *Dobbs v. Jackson Women's Health Organization*, advocates for *Roe* and *Casey* were unable to explain why viability is a principled standard, echoing the *Roe* and *Casey* Courts by merely asserting that viability is critical.

Though the majority in *Roe* feigned ignorance about when unborn life begins—calling it "a difficult question" and asserting that the Court was "not in a position to speculate as to the answer"— Blackmun asserted that "there has always been strong support for the view that life does not begin until live birth." While claiming not to answer the question, the Court effectively took a stance against unborn life, avoiding directly answering the question but basing its decision on flawed science, potted history, and half-baked philosophy that denied personhood to the unborn.

Perhaps partly responsible for this deficiency is the fact that the Court did not have before it an evidentiary record on abortion when the justices debated and decided *Roe*. This is just one of several glaring errors in how the case was handled.

The Court originally agreed to hear *Roe* as a procedural case, not a case to settle the abortion question.[23] When the justices first took *Roe* and *Doe* in April 1971, they agreed only to address the proper scope of federal-court intervention into state criminal proceedings. The Texas case touched on abortion only insofar as abortionists wanted to protect themselves from state regulation by demanding court intervention on their behalf. *Roe* came to deal with the merits of abortion much later, after the Court had first resolved this jurisdictional question in a different case.[24] As a result, *Roe* arrived at the Supreme Court without a factual or evidentiary record on abortion—lower courts hadn't been asked to consider the merits of an abortion right.

The process was even more shoddy than the case development would suggest. Blackmun himself admitted this, calling the process by which they reached a decision "a serious mistake" and acknowledging that the Court "did a poor job."[25]

Three months before the first set of oral arguments in *Roe*, Justices Hugo Black and John Marshall Harlan retired. Hastily, the remaining justices denied Texas's motion to postpone oral arguments until after two new justices could be confirmed. The seven-justice bench heard arguments on December 13, 1971, focusing on the role of federal courts in state criminal law proceedings. Three days later, on December 16, the Court conferenced to vote and assign opinions.

The final vote tally among the seven justices in conference after those initial arguments was unclear, but we do know that out of the conference emerged Blackmun's first draft opinion. That draft was much narrower than the decision in *Roe* ended up being.[26] While it struck down the Texas abortion law as unconstitutionally vague, it did not rule on the merits of an abortion right.

But this draft never became the ruling of the Court. Before the Court could issue its decision, President Nixon had appointed, and the Senate confirmed, two replacement justices, Lewis Powell and William Rehnquist. Chief Justice Warren Burger, as well as Blackmun, Powell, White, and Rehnquist, began pushing to rehear oral arguments before the full Court.[27] This troubled Douglas, who still hoped to create a constitutional right to abortion and who feared that the new Court might not reach his desired outcome. He refused to rehear arguments until he obtained certain promises from Blackmun.

A 1991 interview with Blackmun revealed how it happened. "Douglas literally exploded," Blackmun explained. "He may have thought the two new appointees...might vote the other way, and Burger, who was shaky in his vote, might switch his vote and influence me in so doing. Bill made a lot of noise and it was rather ugly."[28] Historian James Simon summarized what happened next: "Douglas refused to withdraw his dissent [from rehearing] until Blackmun personally assured him that his position of declaring the abortion statutes unconstitutional was firm, and that he had no intention of reversing that position after re-argument. Blackmun gave Douglas that assurance."[29]

This pressure campaign achieved its desired result, and after a second round of oral arguments, the Court's liberal bloc was able to convince Blackmun to produce a majority opinion creating a constitutional right to abortion. Only Justices Byron White and William Rehnquist dissented. White's criticism of the majority's ruling was straightforward: "I find nothing in the language or history of the Constitution to support the Court's judgment. The Court simply fashions and announces a new constitutional right for pregnant mothers and, with scarcely any reason or authority for its action, invests that right with sufficient substance to override most existing state abortion statutes."[30]

In his dissent, Rehnquist argued convincingly that the *Roe* majority had applied the concept of "privacy" incorrectly:

> I have difficulty in concluding, as the Court does, that the right of "privacy" is involved in this case. Texas, by the statute here challenged, bars the performance of a medical abortion by a licensed physician on a plaintiff such as Roe. A transaction resulting in an operation such as this is not "private" in the ordinary usage of that word. Nor is the "privacy" that the Court finds here even a distant relative of the freedom from searches and seizures protected by the Fourth Amendment to the Constitution, which the Court has referred to as embodying a right to privacy.[31]

He insisted, too, that the Constitution did not sanction what the Court had done:

> The decision here to break pregnancy into three distinct terms and to outline the permissible restrictions the State may impose in each one, for example, partakes more of judicial legislation than it does of a determination of the intent of the drafters of the Fourteenth Amendment. The fact that a majority of the States reflecting, after all, the majority sentiment in those States, have had restrictions on abortions for at least a century is a strong indication, it seems to me, that the asserted right to an abortion is not "so rooted in the traditions and conscience of our people as to be ranked as fundamental." ... To reach its result, the Court necessarily has had to find within the scope of the

Fourteenth Amendment a right that was apparently completely unknown to the drafters of the Amendment.[32]

These two dissents shed light on why *Roe*, despite carrying a majority of the Court, still haunts our legal system.[33] It is not constitutional law, properly speaking, but rather the imposition of a few justices' opinions about what our nation's abortion law should be.

Planned Parenthood v. Casey and the Aftermath of *Roe*

Due in large part to its lack of constitutional or historical grounding, *Roe* has proven far from settled. There is perhaps no better confirmation of *Roe*'s failure than the 1992 Supreme Court case *Planned Parenthood v. Casey*, in which a plurality claimed to uphold what it described as the "central holding" of *Roe*—a constitutional right to abortion before viability—but largely abandoned the reasoning of *Roe*. Gone were *Roe*'s shoddy historical claims about the common law and the motivations for various abortion laws. There was little attempt to defend *Roe* as rightly decided and much appeal to *stare decisis*. Instead of emphasizing privacy, the *Casey* plurality attempted to ground the abortion right on the new philosophical footing of "liberty" with a new judicial test: the "undue burden" standard.[34]

The decades between *Roe* and *Casey* illustrate that the Court had succeeded in creating more questions than answers. States attempted to pass a variety of abortion laws in subsequent years, trying to force the Court to illuminate the contours and boundaries of what it had done. What kinds of abortion regulations would the Court allow before fetal viability? Exactly how far could a state law go in regulating abortion without contradicting *Roe*'s vague legal logic? These questions had to be tested by sending state legislation back to court.

This uncertainty came to a head in 1992, when the Court agreed to hear *Planned Parenthood v. Casey*, which involved several Pennsylvania abortion regulations signed into law by the state's pro-life Democratic governor, Robert Casey Sr. The provisions included an informed-consent law, a spousal-notification law, a twenty-four-hour waiting period, and a law requiring minors to obtain parental consent for abortion.

Casey was the first time that the Court revisited its central holding in *Roe*, and by 1992 the Court had a very different composition. Only three justices remained of the nine who had been present for *Roe*: Blackmun, the author of *Roe*, and the two dissenters, Rehnquist and White. The six new justices, meanwhile, all had been appointed by Republican presidents. The pro-life movement was optimistic that the Court would dispatch with *Roe* entirely.

That's far from what happened. Instead, the Court produced one of the most confused rulings in its history. In *Casey*, a plurality of three judges managed to uphold *Roe* and the right to abortion while in essence replacing *Roe*'s reasoning. Here's how Harvard Law professor Mary Ann Glendon and Notre Dame Law professor O. Carter Snead summarize it:

> Despite the justices' statements to the contrary, *Casey* over-ruled *Roe* in nearly every key respect. It shifted the normative justification for abortion rights from "privacy" to "liberty." It downgraded the right to abortion from "fundamental" to a seemingly less robust "liberty interest," in effect repudiating *Roe*'s nearly insurmountable "strict scrutiny" standard of review for evaluating abortion restrictions. Lastly, it abandoned Justice Blackmun's trimester framework, providing in its place the rule that, prior to fetal viability, states may not impose an "undue burden"

on a woman's right to an abortion. After viability, the
justices declared states free to prohibit abortion, so long as
the law includes exceptions for the life and health of the
mother—again, where "health" was understood to encompass so much as to render any limit on abortion null. The
upshot was to leave the legal standing of abortion effectively unchanged, even as the justices tried to re-ground
that standing in a new justification.[35]

Even as the plurality in *Casey* upheld most of the Pennsylvania
abortion regulations at issue, it insisted that the Court could not
overturn *Roe* because to reverse its own precedent would damage the
credibility of the Court, and because, as we discussed in Chapter Two,
women had come to rely on abortion.

The doctrine of *stare decisis* has held that for the sake of stability
and predictability, the Court should hesitate to reverse its previous
rulings, but the doctrine has never been understood to forbid the
Court from ever reversing itself. Indeed, as Justice Brett Kavanagh
pointed out in oral arguments in *Dobbs*, some of the Court's most
cherished decisions entailed overruling wrongly decided cases, such
as *Brown v. Board of Education*, which overruled *Plessy v. Ferguson*.
Nearly all of the Court's rulings that the Left champions on LGBT
issues—*Lawrence v. Texas*, *U.S. v. Windsor*, and *Obergefell v.
Hodges*—entailed overruling prior precedents. *Stare decisis* for thee
but not for me seems to be the message from progressives.

In the abortion cases following *Roe*, most especially *Casey*, justices have twisted the concept of *stare decisis* to justify preserving the
Court's abortion jurisprudence, despite substantial criticism and *Roe*'s
obvious unworkability. In *Casey*, the Court argued that because of
stare decisis, the constitutional right to abortion invented in *Roe* had
to remain in place, even though key parts of the decision had been

wrong. This was their excuse for preserving the right to abortion, even as they drastically altered their rationale from *Roe* to *Casey*.

Casey rejected *Roe*'s grounding of the abortion right in a generalized right of privacy and found it instead in the Due Process Clause's guarantee of liberty. The justices insulated the abortion right from legislative interference by inventing a new "undue burden" standard, which held that states could place no "undue burdens" on abortion access prior to fetal viability. After viability, states could prohibit abortion as long as the laws had exemptions for the health of the mother, where health of the mother was interpreted so broadly as to negate any prohibition.

Here's how the *Casey* plurality defined "undue burden":

> A finding of an undue burden is a shorthand for the conclusion that a state regulation has the purpose or effect of placing a substantial obstacle in the path of a woman seeking an abortion of a nonviable fetus. A statute with this purpose is invalid because the means chosen by the State to further the interest in potential life must be calculated to inform the woman's free choice, not hinder it. And a statute which, while furthering the interest in potential life or some other valid state interest, has the effect of placing a substantial obstacle in the path of a woman's choice cannot be considered a permissible means of serving its legitimate ends.[36]

In other words, under *Casey*, states cannot regulate abortion before fetal viability in any way that amounts to a "substantial obstacle"—and any outright prohibition would certainly entail a "substantial obstacle." But many lesser regulations would violate *Casey* should they place a "substantial obstacle" on abortion access, itself a standard that judges would have to determine. This empowered judges more than ever to determine which abortion regulations were acceptable. Note, too, how *Casey* speaks of the state's interest in "potential life," as if the unborn child were only a potential child, not an actual one. As we noted in Chapter One, the child in the womb is a human life with potential, not a potential life.

Casey's bewildering outcome did little to improve the situation *Roe* had created, but the decision illustrates that a majority of the Court was determined to preserve the right to abortion, no matter how unworkable its jurisprudence had proven to be. Constitutional-law scholar Michael Stokes Paulsen has called *Casey* "the worst constitutional decision of the Supreme Court in our nation's history," noting that

> the Court that committed *Casey* committed it with full knowledge of what it was doing. Some of the Justices, it can be said with reasonable certainty, did it while simultaneously believing that *Roe* was wrongly decided and with a full understanding as well that *Roe*'s result produced exactly the described substantive evil of the killing of millions of embryonic human lives. But they did it anyway, out of concern for the Court's own image and power, lest the Court be embarrassed, and individuals on it perhaps disparaged, for departing from a precedent that a substantial portion of elite opinion cherished and continues to cherish. They did it, that is, out of vanity and self-interest. And they did it on the basis of a doctrine of *stare decisis* that is deceptively appealing, but in the end became, in the *Casey* Court's hands, an arbitrary and dishonest tool of enhanced judicial power, designed to entrench the Court's specific judgment, its future judgments, and (if successful) to

de-legitimize resistance to the Court's judgments, even when—especially when—it has departed grotesquely from its constitutional duties and powers.[37]

Even after two decades, a majority still couldn't agree on how to ground the abortion right in the constitutional tradition or on the correct judicial tests to impose on lower courts. The two most recent Supreme Court cases dealing with abortion, prior to *Dobbs*, illustrate this confusion.

In 2016, shortly after the death of Justice Antonin Scalia, the Court in *Whole Woman's Health v. Hellerstedt* struck down Texas abortion regulations aimed at protecting the safety of women seeking abortions by establishing safety standards for abortion clinics and requiring abortionists to maintain admitting privileges at a nearby hospital. Writing for the majority, Justice Stephen Breyer created yet another test with no basis in the Constitution. To determine when a law creates a "substantial obstacle" to abortion, Breyer's new, more freewheeling test would require judges to balance a law's burdens and benefits to determine its lawfulness. He created, in short, another policy-style judgment in the guise of a judicial test.

Four years later, in the Court's 2020 decision in *June Medical Services v. Russo*, a reshaped Court ruled on a strikingly similar abortion regulation out of Louisiana.[38] Once again, the Court struck down the law as unconstitutional, but this time the judges were split quite differently. The plurality opinion, written by Breyer, implemented the test from *Hellerstedt* and found that Louisiana's law imposed a substantial obstacle to abortion access without a health-related benefit.

But the decisive vote was cast by Chief Justice John Roberts, who had *dissented* in *Hellerstedt* just four years earlier. Citing the judicial principle of *stare decisis*, Roberts pointed to precedent to strike down the Louisiana law that was in essence the same as the Texas law from four years earlier. But while Roberts cast the deciding vote to strike down the Louisiana law, he didn't embrace Breyer's new test recasting *Casey*, and in fact reiterated the original *Casey* test, writing, "Nothing about *Casey* suggested that a weighing of costs and benefits of an abortion regulation was a job for the courts."[39] In the main, Roberts rejected *Hellerstedt*, and he dissented from the application of Breyer's balancing test. As Notre Dame law professor O. Carter Snead wrote shortly after the decision, the ruling in *June Medical* "was a grave disappointment and a missed opportunity," but in the view of many, "Roberts's concurrence—the controlling opinion for purposes of precedent—leaves pro-life litigants on a better jurisprudential footing than before."[40]

Even so, it is little surprise that such a confused outcome has produced more confusion. In the mere two years since *June Medical*, there already have been several significant circuit-court splits on how to interpret the Court's ruling.[41] This judicial chaos is the predictable fruit of five decades of the Court injecting itself into a policy debate, seeking to prop up the failure of *Roe* and place it on firmer footing in each successive iteration. So far, it has yet to find a way to ground the supposed right to abortion in the Constitution such that the issue will be resolved once and for all—because there is no legitimate way to do so.

Conclusion

In *Roe v. Wade*, the Supreme Court distorted the Constitution in service of legalized abortion, a policy goal that several justices favored before the case ever reached their chambers. In so doing, the Court removed what is perhaps the most controversial issue in American public life from the hands of the people, attempting to put an end to the brewing controversy. Most objectionable is that the Court took abortion from the democratic process in order to decide the issue the wrong way; if the Constitution can be read to apply to the question of abortion at all, it is in the sense that abortion is an unconstitutional denial of due process and equal protection of the laws to the unborn.[42]

By issuing a decision that distorted the Constitution, the Court overstepped its constitutionally prescribed role and transformed itself into something of a super-legislature. Seven unelected justices got the Constitution wrong and committed a grave injustice against the unborn that has been perpetuated for half a century.

Rather than ending the abortion debate, *Roe* threw a burning match onto the kindling. Nearly five decades later, the issue has become more polarizing than ever, and the Court's subsequent abortion decisions have revealed exactly how unsettled *Roe* remains as a matter of law. That status quo has infected every aspect of our legal system, making it nearly impossible for states to restrict abortion and entangling the judiciary in endless battles over whether particular abortion regulations are permissible under the fabricated, confusing frameworks articulated and rearticulated by the Court.

None of this is the fruit of a well-reasoned Court decision. Instead, it is the poisonous result of a ruling that cloaked a policy judgment in the thin veneer of law, thereby perverting our system of constitutional self-government.

CHAPTER SIX

Abortion Harms Politics and the Democratic Process

While campaigning for president in 1992, Bill Clinton devised a cagey way of describing his support for abortion: he said he believed the procedure should be "safe, legal, and rare."[1] This was, to be sure, a deceptive slogan even on its own terms. But the phrase stuck. For decades, even as Democratic politicians became more accepting of abortion in the years following *Roe*, they used this phrase to indicate support for abortion while still appearing to recognize that there is something less than desirable about it.

Today, even this fairly permissive phrase has fallen out of favor with the Democratic Party. During a Democratic presidential primary debate in 2019, Tulsi Gabbard faced swift backlash from left-wing activists for uttering the "safe, legal, and rare" formulation to describe her stance on abortion. Pro-choice groups immediately rejected Gabbard's position as out of step with the abortion-rights movement, insisting that it was wrong to suggest that abortion should be rare because it suggests that abortion is a bad thing.[2]

It is this sentiment, not the once-popular slogan, that is fully in line with today's Democratic Party. This swift march to full, vocal abortion radicalism has been unfolding rapidly over the past decade. Even when the slogan had been "safe, legal, and rare," the Democrats' official platform had hinted at the need for abortion funding, saying the party supported "the right of every woman to choose [abortion]...regardless of ability to pay."[3]

But in recent years, the party's leadership has become far more willing to display explicit support for federally funded abortion on demand. In 2008, Democrats excised the word "rare" from the abortion section of the party platform, and they added language even friendlier to abortion in 2012.[4] By 2016, the party had amended its platform to formally call for the repeal of the Hyde Amendment, which since the 1970s has forbidden federal Medicaid funds from covering elective abortion.[5] In 2021, Democrats began passing the first spending bills in decades that didn't have Hyde attached, an effort to open the floodgates for federal taxpayer funding for abortion businesses and, implicitly, to induce demand for abortion procedures.[6]

The Democratic Party wasn't always this way, likely because our country was once largely pro-life. When Roe was handed down, thirty states had laws prohibiting nearly all abortions.[7] In many of those states, legislatures had already debated abortion policy and decided in favor of protections for the unborn. Roe obliterated those democratically crafted laws, as well as laws that some states had passed loosening—but not entirely eliminating—restrictions on abortion. Even ostensible compromise on abortion was unconstitutional as the result of Roe.

Under the predominant understanding of Roe and Casey, states must allow elective abortions throughout all nine months of pregnancy, for virtually any reason. Because of the expansive maternal-health exception the Court demanded in Doe, even abortion regulations permitted by courts must include a carve-out that allows abortion for reasons such as psychological, financial, or even familial health—in effect sanctioning unlimited abortion on demand, especially considering that the health determination in question is to be made at the sole discretion of the abortionist.

If this sounds extreme, that's because it is, especially compared to the rest of the world. To be sure, any legalized abortion is extreme, because it permits lethal violence against innocent human beings. But American law is particularly outside the norm. The United States is one of only seven countries—along with North Korea, China, Vietnam, Canada, Singapore, and the Netherlands—that permit elective abortion after twenty weeks of pregnancy.[8] U.S. abortion policy is far more permissive even than the policies in most European countries. Thirty-nine of the forty-two European countries that allow elective abortion permit it only in the first twelve weeks of pregnancy.[9]

Opinion polling over the past few decades indicates that America's permissive abortion policy is unpopular with the American people, most of whom would prefer to see each state set its own laws regarding abortion and most of whom would like to see abortion regulated more strictly than it is now. While this outcome certainly would be an improvement on what we have today, merely aligning our policies with today's public opinion on abortion still would not produce a just outcome. Incrementalism in abortion law must be in service of the goal of full abolition. That is, if political circumstances allow us to pass a law that will protect more unborn children than the current law does, even if they do not allow us to pass a law that will protect all unborn children, we should pass the most protective law we can—while still working to persuade our fellow citizens that we must protect all unborn human beings at every stage of development. Even so, it is notable that *Roe* enshrined a status quo on abortion policy that most Americans disagreed with at the time and that most Americans still believe is far too permissive.

Nevertheless, in the decades since *Roe*, the Democratic Party has perpetuated that status quo, embracing *Roe* and *Casey* and making abortion on demand a key piece of the party's official platform. Nearly all Democratic politicians—including those who once were pro-life—today favor unlimited elective abortion, fully funded by the U.S. taxpayer. Democrats have rejected the truth about what it means to be human and established a position that contradicts the views not only of the average American but also of their own voters.

While previous chapters focused on the ways in which abortion harms unborn children, women, vulnerable populations, good medicine, and the rule of law, in this chapter we explain how the Court's decision to remove the abortion debate from the hands of voters has harmed the political process and contradicted the will of the people. We tell the story of how the Democratic Party came to embrace *Roe* and unlimited abortion as a signature policy position. Finally, we examine how this commitment to abortion has corrupted the judicial confirmation process, as Democrats have refused to fairly consider nominees who they fear won't uphold *Roe* and *Casey*.

Abortion and Public Opinion

Public opinion does not determine truth, and current public opinion on abortion in the United States is not that of a society that respects the dignity of every human life. No amount of abortion is acceptable, and a culture that values human life would favor protecting every unborn child from abortion. But we're not there yet.

Even so, it's notable that abortion law in the United States today remains far more permissive than most Americans would prefer. In defense of abortion, activist organizations such as Planned Parenthood and NARAL commonly peddle the statistic that seven in ten Americans support *Roe v. Wade.* It's true that Americans often say they favor leaving *Roe* in place. But polling suggests, first, that most Americans don't know what *Roe* actually held and, second, that most Americans disapprove of the abortion policy imposed by *Roe* and *Casey.* That is, while many Americans don't actually know what *Roe* did, a majority doesn't support the legal landscape that the case created.

For one thing, a sizable percentage of voters don't even know that *Roe* had to do with abortion. One Pew Research poll, for instance, found that only 62 percent of Americans knew *Roe* dealt with abortion, and among respondents under thirty years old, that percentage fell to just 44 percent.[10] If so few Americans know that *Roe* was about abortion, imagine how few fully understand what the ruling meant for abortion law.[11] Surely even fewer are aware that *Roe*, *Doe*, and *Casey* make it nearly impossible to limit abortion in any serious way—and polling suggests that most Americans would prefer to protect the unborn far more than these decisions allow.

In September 2021, a Fox News poll found that 65 percent of Americans said they want *Roe v. Wade* to remain in place, compared to 28 percent who said they want the decision overturned.[12] But the very same survey found that respondents were perfectly split on whether abortion should be legal, tied at 49 percent. Roughly half of the country reported that they wanted abortion to be illegal either all of the time or in certain circumstances, but only a quarter realized that such an outcome would be impossible without overturning *Roe.* A substantial number of Americans, in other words, both want to protect unborn children and mothers from the harms of abortion and to preserve the jurisprudence that makes it impossible to do so. Such an outcome is possible only if many Americans have no idea that, in order to make good laws on abortion, *Roe* must go.

Far more helpful than asking voters for their view on *Roe* is asking what they think of specific abortion policies. Based on that type of polling, it's clear that most voters deeply disagree with the status quo created by *Roe* and perpetuated by *Casey*. Even though a majority tends to favor allowing abortion in at least some circumstances, just 13 percent of Americans support elective abortion in the last three months of pregnancy, the policy mandated by our abortion jurisprudence.[13]

Each year, the Knights of Columbus commissions Marist College to ask Americans what they think of a variety of abortion policies. For several years in a row, the survey has found that Americans across the political spectrum favor protecting unborn children far more than the status quo allows. In 2021, Marist found that more than three-quarters of Americans favor far stricter abortion laws than we have now. A quarter would prohibit abortion after the first three months of pregnancy, nearly 40 percent would allow abortion only in cases of rape or incest or when a mother's life is at risk, and 12 percent would prohibit abortion entirely. A plurality also said it would prefer to see abortion law decided at the state level.[14] Under the *Roe* regime, none of these positions can be enacted into law.

Perhaps most interesting, it's not just Republicans who oppose our current abortion policy as established and enforced by the judiciary. Marist polling has found that even a majority of Americans who call themselves "pro-choice" want to limit abortion to the first three months of pregnancy or the so-called hard cases of rape and incest, or when a mother's life is at risk.[15] A YouGov poll commissioned by Americans United for Life in 2019 found that 66 percent of pro-choice Americans oppose abortion in the third trimester, 68 percent oppose abortion the day before a child is born, and 77 percent oppose removing medical care from a viable child.[16]

Opinion surveys consistently find that the Democratic Party is out of step even with its own voters when it comes to abortion. About a third of Democrats describe themselves as pro-life, and according to Gallup only 18 percent of Democrats say they support abortion for any reason in the last three months of pregnancy, as the Democratic Party does.[17] There was a time when most of the Democratic Party opposed abortion and the party was the natural home of pro-life voters. Those days are long gone.

Abortion Has Corrupted the Democratic Party

While one might fairly accuse some Republican politicians of merely paying lip service to the cause of life, it is thanks in large part to the Democratic Party's embrace of an unlimited right to abortion that *Roe v. Wade* has been in place for nearly fifty years.

Of course, neither the longevity of *Roe* nor the Democratic Party's support of it was predestined. When *Roe* was decided in 1973, political analysts reasonably could have prognosticated that the GOP would become the pro-abortion party and Democrats the pro-life one. Historically, the Democratic Party prided itself on being the party of the little guy, and protecting the unborn child from the violence of abortion would've fit well into that paradigm. For many years it did—until *Roe*.

Around the time that *Roe* was decided, the Democratic Party remained largely opposed to abortion. In 1972, pro-life Democrat Edmund Muskie was an early frontrunner for the presidential nomination, suggesting substantial pro-life sentiment in the party. Even though the more socially liberal George McGovern eventually became the nominee rather than Muskie, he selected pro-lifers as his running mates: first Thomas Eagleton and then, as Eagleton's replacement, Sargent Shriver, a pro-life Catholic. That same year, when left-wing feminists attempted to add a pro-abortion item to the Democratic platform, it was rejected by a majority of delegates.[18]

In 1976, pro-life Catholic Democrat Ellen McCormack, who had no prior experience as a politician, ran for the Democratic presidential nomination with a platform focusing solely on the need to abolish abortion. She won 238,000 votes in 18 Democratic primary contests, including 9 percent of the vote in Vermont, 8 percent in South Dakota, and more than 5 percent in both Indiana and Kentucky. McCormack's long-shot campaign earned 22 delegates at the 1976 Democratic convention.[19] Even after *Roe*, in other words, a significant faction of the party remained opposed to abortion.

One of the best examples of this was Bob Casey Sr., who served as Democratic governor of Pennsylvania from 1987 to 1995. A Catholic, Casey remained staunchly pro-life for his entire political career—in stark contrast to his son, Bob Casey Jr., who currently serves as Democratic senator from Pennsylvania and calls himself "personally pro-life" but votes in line with Planned Parenthood and NARAL nearly all the time.[20]

Casey Sr. actually opposed abortion as a matter of law and policy—a necessary part of being a pro-life politician. In fact, Casey Sr. was the same Casey who defended the abortion regulations at stake in the landmark 1992 case *Planned Parenthood v. Casey*. "By embracing abortion," Casey said in 1992, "the Democratic Party is abandoning the principle that made it great: its basic commitment to protecting the weakest and most vulnerable members of the human family."[21]

For his defense of the unborn, Casey was sidelined by his own party, which was well on its way to fully embracing abortion. Though he was a highly successful two-term governor from one of the nation's largest states, Casey was denied the chance to speak at the Democratic National Convention in 1992, which nominated Bill Clinton, a supporter of unlimited abortion. Journalist Bill McGurn recalls the message the DNC wanted to send: "Clinton officials refused a place at the podium for the Democratic governor of America's fifth-largest state while also providing speaking slots for six pro-choice *Republican* women. To make sure the point was delivered, one of these was a pro-choice woman who had campaigned for Casey's Republican opponent."[22]

Casey's exclusion was a death knell for pro-life Democratic politicians across the country, who all but dwindled out of existence over the next few decades. Once, the notion of a Catholic Democrat was a mainstay in American politics and a foundational part of the Democratic Party. Prominent Democratic leaders, including many Catholics, expressed opposition to abortion before *Roe* was decided, often citing the teaching of the Catholic Church. Here's how Massachusetts senator Ted Kennedy put it to a constituent in a 1971 letter:

> While the deep concern of a woman bearing an unwanted child merits consideration and sympathy, it is my personal feeling that the legalization of abortion on demand is not in accordance with the value which our civilization places on human life.
>
> Wanted or unwanted, I believe that human life, even at its earliest stages, has certain rights which must be recognized—the right to be born, the right to love, the right to grow old. When history looks back at this era it should recognize this generation as one which cared about human beings enough to halt the practice of war, to provide a decent living for every family, and to fulfill its responsibility to its children from the very moment of conception.[23]

As late as 1979, Kennedy was still singing from the same hymnal: "I am opposed to abortion on demand whether it is to be paid for by private funds or public funds—whether the woman is rich or poor," he wrote at the time.[24] In 1982, Delaware senator Joe Biden, another Catholic Democrat who once opposed abortion, voted in committee for the Hatch Amendment, which would have overruled *Roe* and given both Congress and states the right to protect the unborn.[25] In 1989, yet another Catholic Democrat, Illinois senator Dick Durbin, said he continued "to believe the Supreme Court's decision in *Roe v. Wade* should be reversed."[26]

But shortly thereafter, these politicians began to change their tune. A growing number of Americans cheered for *Roe* and wanted to see abortion further protected under law—and a growing number of Democratic politicians, including these Catholics, began to say they wouldn't want a future Court to reverse the ruling, because it was becoming increasingly politically expedient to support *Roe*'s invention of a supposed right to abortion.

Motivated by the desire for political plaudits, these prominent Democrats offered weak rationales for changing their minds and embracing abortion. Some of them suggested that, having reflected on the importance of women's autonomy, they had determined that politicians shouldn't interfere with that decision-making process. Others said they had decided they couldn't impose their faith through policy.

A crucial turning point in the Democratic Party's trajectory on abortion came in 1984, when New York governor Mario Cuomo delivered a high-profile speech at the University of Notre Dame. In it, Cuomo pioneered the now-common claim that a Catholic politician could oppose abortion in his personal life while not opposing it politically—a facile argument that proved essential in Democratic politicians' efforts to rationalize their newfound support for *Roe*.[27]

"The question whether to engage the political system in a struggle to have it adopt certain articles of our belief as part of public morality, is not a matter of doctrine: it is a matter of prudential political judgment," Cuomo said. His prudential judgment, as it turned out, was that seeking to prohibit abortion as a Catholic politician would be

"rationaliz[ing] our own laxity by urging the political system to legislate on others a morality we no longer practice ourselves."[28]

This language began to percolate through the Democratic ranks,
as politicians who had once been pro-life sought to explain why they
had reversed themselves. Here's how Dick Durbin subsequently justified his change of heart: "I still oppose abortion and would try my
best to convince any woman in my family to carry the baby to term.
But I believe that ultimately the decision must be made by the woman,
her doctor, her family and her conscience."[29] Durbin's explanation
might sound reasonable to some, but it led him to radical places. In
2003, for example, he was one of several Catholic Democrats in the
Senate to vote against a federal ban on gruesome partial-birth abortion procedures.[30]

Perhaps the best example of Democratic politicians' corruption
when it comes to abortion is Joe Biden, who since the 1980s has
echoed Cuomo's line, calling himself personally pro-life but saying
he supports abortion as a political matter. In addition to voting
for the Hatch Amendment that would have reversed *Roe*, Biden
spent his decades in the Senate supporting the Hyde Amendment,
which prohibits federal Medicaid funds from directly paying for
elective abortion. "Those of us who are opposed to abortion should
not be compelled to pay for them," Biden said of his position on
Hyde in 1997.[31]

But during his campaign for the Democratic presidential nomination in 2019, Biden reversed this position he had held for decades.
Under pressure from left-wing feminists and his fellow Democratic
primary contenders, Biden embraced his party's new position opposing
Hyde and came out in support of elective abortion throughout pregnancy, for any reason, funded by the U.S. taxpayer.[32]

These same Catholic Democrats have been known to cite their
faith in defense of their other policy positions, such as support for

stringent environmental-protection laws, unwillingness to enforce immigration laws, or their support for universal health care and expansive federal welfare programs. As we noted in our first chapter, there's nothing wrong with a politician's faith and moral values informing his policy preferences. In fact, it's a good thing. We want our laws to be shaped by sound moral convictions, and most people's moral convictions are shaped by theological or other metaphysical commitments. Any attempt to prevent moral and metaphysical convictions from shaping law and policy is destined to fail. The only question, then, is whether true morality and sound metaphysics will inform our laws—or whether false morality and unsound metaphysics will.

Arguments from Catholic Democrats advocating the separation of their moral views from their legal and political views on abortion have always rung hollow, not least because true separation of one's morality from one's political preferences is impossible. That Democrats admit their faith informs their stance on issues other than abortion suggests either that their supposed personal support for the Church's moral teaching on abortion is insincere—or that they're willing to reject their Church's moral teaching when it precludes them from aligning with their party's preferences. Either way, the end result is that they support injustice.

■   ■   ■

Biden's reversal on the Hyde Amendment during his successful presidential campaign marked the decisive end of the long-time bipartisan agreement—a shift that had been set in motion during the 2016 election cycle, when the Democratic National Committee formally endorsed federally funded elective abortion in the party platform. Such a change had been a long time coming. As recently as the 1990s and early 2000s, Democratic politicians were arguing that abortion should be "safe, legal, and rare." But in 2019, when Democrat Tulsi Gabbard repeated that phrase while running for president, she was rebuked by pro-abortion groups, which rightly noted that "safe, legal, and rare" no longer represents the mindset of the abortion-rights movement.

The rhetorical shift was accompanied by a shift in policy. First, national Democrats removed the word "rare" from their party platform, then they called for federal funding of all abortions, and finally, they began passing congressional spending bills to officially license that funding.[33]

These policy changes mark a significant shift from the rhetoric of Democratic politicians even a decade ago. Barack Obama, in a 2009 speech at the University of Notre Dame, at least paid lip service to the importance of finding common ground with pro-life Americans and working to reduce the demand for abortions.[34] In 2008, Hillary Clinton used the phrase "safe, legal, and rare," tacking on the line "and by 'rare,' I mean *rare*."[35] But by the time she became the Democratic Party's presidential nominee in 2016, Clinton had ceased using the phrase, rejected Hyde, and, in the third debate, doubled down on her support for partial-birth abortion.

As Biden's shift indicates, today's Democratic officials near uniformly oppose Hyde and all forms of conscience protections on abortion, to say nothing of actual abortion restrictions. In 2021, Democrats in the House passed the Women's Health Protection Act, which would block any state law limiting abortion, even after fetal viability. In February 2022, the Senate voted on the same legislation, and only one Democrat opposed the bill.[36] Some Democratic politicians have voiced support for packing the Supreme Court to prevent the overturning of *Roe*. During her own run for president, current vice president Kamala Harris proposed that the Department of Justice spearhead a preclearance regime for any state laws regulating abortion, meaning that pro-life states would have to receive approval from the executive branch before attempting to enforce new pro-life laws.[37] Such calls will intensify when *Roe* is finally overturned.

Another good example of the Democratic Party's embrace of *Roe* and unlimited abortion is the story of Dan Lipinski, a former Democratic congressman who represented Illinois's third district. Lipinski was first elected in 2004, representing a blue-collar, highly Democratic constituency, which his father had represented for the previous twenty years. Both father and son were faithful Catholic Democrats, strongly opposed to abortion.[38]

In 2020, Lipinski was unseated in the Democratic primary by progressive feminist Marie Newman, who challenged Lipinski on the grounds that opposing abortion is no longer acceptable in today's Democratic Party. Heavily funded by abortion advocacy groups, Newman defeated Lipinski—and though she won by less than three thousand votes, her win suggested that support for unlimited abortion had become a non-negotiable issue for Democratic politicians at the national level. The narrow margin suggested that Lipinski remained popular in his district, but his opposition to abortion enabled Newman to secure the crucial support of national progressive groups, which ultimately spelled doom for the pro-life incumbent.[39]

This was in stark contrast to Casey Sr. in the 1990s, who remained comfortably in office even as the broader party shifted to support elective abortion. Most Democrats were happy to let Casey retain his seat, even though they wouldn't let him speak at the DNC. Today, national Democratic groups support abortion so strongly that they couldn't countenance allowing a single pro-life Democrat to remain in the House.

After losing the primary, Lipinski penned an op-ed insisting that he had no regrets about standing his ground. "Abortion advocacy groups poured millions into my opponent's campaign. If I had simply changed my position on abortion, there probably wouldn't have been a contest. Abortion proponents wanted to hear me express regret about sticking with my pro-life beliefs," Lipinski wrote.[40]

At the press conference Lipinski hosted after his loss, a reporter asked him, "There are some pro-life Democrats, like Tim Kaine, who have found a way to come to terms with the fact that they do not believe in abortion but they also support a woman's right to choose, so they have been able to kind of maneuver—there isn't just black and white, there is some flexibility. Did Tim Kaine ever talk to you about that?" In his op-ed, Lipinski wrote, "I replied that if you believe life exists in the womb, you have to support policies that protect that life."[41] His courage stands in stark contrast to the many Democrats, whether "personally pro-life" or otherwise, who have placed their desire to remain in office ahead of defending the right to life of the unborn child.

National Democrats made this growing obsession with abortion on demand explicit during the 2019 presidential primary. Several times, pro-life Democratic voters asked the candidates whether they were welcome in the party despite their opposition to abortion. The answer they received was, in short, "No."

"Do you want the support of . . . pro-life Democratic voters?" Kristen Day, president of Democrats for Life of America, asked Pete Buttigieg during a town hall. "And if so, would you support more-moderate platform language in the Democratic Party to ensure that the party of diversity, of inclusion really does include everybody?"[42] In response, Buttigieg offered only equivocations: "The best I can offer is that if we can't agree on where to draw the line, the next best thing we can do is agree on who should draw the line. And in my view, it's the woman who's faced with that decision in her own life."[43] In other words, "Take a hike."

Confronted with a similar question, socialist senator and Democratic primary frontrunner Bernie Sanders was less equivocal: "I think being pro-choice is an absolutely essential part of being a Democrat. By this time in history…when we talk about what a Democrat is, I think being pro-choice is an essential part of that."[44] This signaled a shift even for Sanders, who as recently as 2017 had endorsed a Democratic candidate who was deemed "anti-choice" for supporting a ban on abortion after twenty weeks and a law that required giving women the option to view an ultrasound before an abortion.[45]

The 2020 Democrats' repudiation of pro-lifers within their own party was so complete that the leaders of Democrats for Life penned an op-ed ahead of the Democratic National Convention titled "The Democrats Biden Doesn't Want." In it, they argued that today's Democrats no longer even support helping pregnant women because such policies, "previously central to Democratic values, violate the core tenet that 'abortion is normal.' "[46]

In a homily ahead of the 2022 Walk for Life West Coast, San Francisco archbishop Salvatore Cordileone noted the religious dimension of modern support for abortion:

> The new secular religion of our own time takes on this practice in an almost sacramental way: indeed, abortion has become, for them, their blessed sacrament, what they hold most sacred, the doctrine and practice upon which their whole belief system is built. That is why we see such visceral and violent reaction to any even minimal regulation of abortion in the law, regulations that even those who believe it should be kept legal would see as reasonable, such as informed consent and parental consent. It should come as no surprise that the first to challenge the Texas Heartbeat Bill was the Satanic Temple, and precisely on the grounds of deprivation of religious liberty: they need abortion to carry out their religious rituals.[47]

Ahead of the 2022 March for Life in Washington, D.C., abortion activist group Catholics for Choice—dedicated to the inaccurate proposition that Catholic theology can be understood to endorse abortion—projected a pro-abortion message on the side of the Basilica of the Immaculate Conception.[48] For these abortion activists, the zeal with which they embrace and promote abortion has become something akin to religious fervor. It isn't just the Catholic Church that has been afflicted by deep confusion and perversion when it comes to abortion. Growing acceptance of abortion has also decimated mainline Protestantism, to the point where some abortionists explicitly cite their Christian faith as the reason for their work.[49] In January 2022, Georgia Democratic senator Raphael Warnock shared this pro-abortion sentiment—cloaked in his prior role as a Christian pastor: "As a pro-choice pastor, I've always believed that a patient's room is way too small for a woman, her doctor, and the United States government."[50]

Bob Casey Sr. presciently warned his fellow Democrats against this leftward march on abortion in his autobiography, which he penned just a few years after being excluded from the national platform at the DNC to nominate Bill Clinton:

> Many people discount the power of the so-called "cultural issues," and especially of the abortion issue. I see it just the other way around. These issues are central to the national resurgence of the Republicans, central to the national implosion of the Democrats, central to the question of whether there will be a third party. The national Democrats may, and probably will, get a temporary bump in the polls, even, perhaps, one more national election victory from their reactive strategy as the defenders of the elderly and poor who rely on Medicare and Medicaid. But the

Democrats' national decline, or better, their national dis-
integration, will continue relentlessly and inexorably until
they come to grips with these values issues, primarily
abortion.[51]

In the span of fifty years, the Democratic Party shifted from being
a home for pro-life Americans to a party unwilling to accept that
some of its own voters oppose abortion. Why did this happen? In
large part, it was the result of powerful pro-abortion activists and
special interest groups who recognized that left-wing politicians were
increasingly supportive of abortion and who used their growing influence to ensure that the Democratic Party would fully embrace the
pro-abortion agenda.

Our politics and our society would be better served if neither of
our major political parties formally supported abortion, a gross injustice and a blatant violation of fundamental human rights. Any political society in which a sizable contingent supports lethal violence
against some of its innocent members, especially the most vulnerable,
is simply degraded. The Democratic embrace of abortion as a positive
good is unjust in and of itself.

Furthermore, the excuses made for this embrace of abortion have
denigrated the role of morality and religion in our politics. We should
want our man-made laws to comport with the natural and eternal
law. As Martin Luther King Jr. put it in his "Letter from Birmingham
Jail," "A just law is a man-made code that squares with the moral
law, or the law of God. An unjust law is a code that is out of harmony
with the moral law."[52] The rhetoric used by abortion-supporting
Democrats, particularly the Catholic ones, has severed our legal
system from its natural and divine sources. It has left us operating
with a political culture in which might makes right and the popular
vote, detached from moral truth, determines legal justice.

Finally, the Democratic Party's embrace of abortion has made our political process hostage to abortion. It would be far better for pro-life citizens to have a meaningful political choice between two political parties, neither of which was committed to gross injustice. In an ideal situation, no party would embrace immoral policy positions, thus enabling citizens to choose between morally acceptable options. The difference, then, would be one of prudential judgment, and the debates would be over prudential policy choices rather than basic morality. As it stands, the immoral position of Democrats on abortion has led many voters to feel restricted to the Republican Party, despite other policy disagreements, because Democratic policies on abortion are morally unacceptable. In many circumstances, this has allowed Republican politicians to take pro-life voters for granted, knowing that they have no real alternative. A world in which both major parties were pro-life—or at least tolerant of pro-lifers—would force the parties to compete for votes on other important issues.

The Corruption of the Judicial-Nomination Process

The legal status quo created by *Roe* has done significant damage to several other aspects of the American political order. In large part because of the Democrats' embrace of abortion, we have witnessed tremendous corruption of the process by which new justices are nominated and confirmed. Because the Court declared abortion a constitutional right without any grounding in the Constitution, the American people have their eyes fixed on the Court, waiting for further edicts on abortion policy. It has caused the third branch of our federal government to take on an outsized and inappropriate role in American political life.

As a result, judicial nominations and the Senate confirmation process have grown increasingly rancorous, especially as pro-abortion politicians and activists resist—even to the point of outright corruption—the confirmation of any judge who they fear might oppose *Roe*. Early on, Republicans weren't particularly good at selecting justices—recall from the last chapter that *Casey* was decided by a Court with eight justices nominated by Republican presidents. Part of the change since then is that the Republican Party grew more sophisticated in how it vetted and nominated justices. In the words of one progressive writer at *Vox*, "One of the main reasons conservatives got to the point where *Roe*'s defeat seems plausible is that they learned to be more like Democrats."[53] He continues:

> Republicans won most of the presidential elections in the first two decades after the *Roe* decision came down, and Republican presidents got to fill every Supreme Court vacancy that opened up in that span. But they did not reliably appoint anti-abortion justices. Several Republican appointees—John Paul Stevens, Sandra Day O'Connor, Anthony Kennedy, and David Souter—ended up voting to uphold *Roe*, which is why it wasn't overturned decades ago.
>
> In contrast, though there have been fewer Democratic appointees since *Roe*, every one of them turned out to be reliably pro–abortion rights.
>
> The political triumph of conservative activists, then, was in taking over their own party—pressuring George W. Bush and Donald Trump to rethink how Supreme Court appointments were made, and to only appoint nominees they'd vetted and deemed reliably anti-abortion.[54]

Such vetting, it seems, was based not on the judge's policy stance with respect to abortion but on his judicial philosophy and interpretive methodology when it came to the Constitution. It is this judicial theory—one that rejects the living constitutionalism and judicial activism of the mid-twentieth century—that Democrats decided they couldn't countenance, because they knew it would place *Roe* on the chopping block.

Partisanship has always played a role in the Senate, but its members used to take the chamber's constitutional role seriously and agreed on the importance of the constitutional order, even when doing so made it more difficult to achieve their own policy goals. And while the mid-century Court grew partisan and policy-outcome oriented with the rise of progressive politics, it hadn't always been that way. There was a time when both Republicans and Democrats defended the Court's impartiality.

In 1937, shortly after Franklin Roosevelt unveiled his plan to increase the number of justices on the Supreme Court in order to secure the New Deal against judicial interference, the Democrat-led Senate Judiciary Committee issued a stern rebuke to its own party's leader: "The bill is an invasion of judicial power such as has never before been attempted in this country.... It is a measure which should be so emphatically rejected that its parallel will never again be presented to the free representatives of the free people of America."[55]

Thankfully, that Court-packing never occurred. Yet it is impossible to imagine such a spirited defense of our institutions from today's Senate Judiciary Committee, especially when *Roe* is on the line. Instead, the Democrats on the committee today care most about one thing: blocking candidates who are not affirmatively pro-*Roe*. As Notre Dame law professor Gerard V. Bradley has noted, "Even when the terms of debate were proxies, such as 'originalism' vs. 'judicial activism,' everyone knew it was mainly about abortion. Just review the video of the Senate committee's grilling of any Supreme Court nominee over the last 20 years."[56]

Once, it was customary for judicial nominees to be confirmed in near-unanimous bipartisan votes. In 1986, Justice Antonin Scalia was confirmed unanimously, in a 98–0 vote, and even as late as 1993, Republicans upheld this custom, as Justice Ruth Bader Ginsburg was confirmed by a vote of 96–3.[57] But as Democrats began to embrace abortion on demand, their judicial confirmation behavior changed. Since *Roe*, several Republican-nominated Supreme Court nominees, including Robert Bork, Clarence Thomas, and Brett Kavanaugh, have incurred the wrath of Democratic senators, in what liberal legal commentator Tom Goldstein has called "scorched-earth ideological wars."[58] And it's not as though the confirmation hearings for John Roberts or Samuel Alito were cakewalks, either.

Justice Amy Coney Barrett's confirmation hearing in 2020 was slightly less contentious, partly because Democrats didn't have the votes to block her and partly because they had already tried and failed to discredit Barrett on the basis of her Catholic faith when she was nominated to the Seventh Circuit Court of Appeals.[59] California Democratic senator Dianne Feinstein's comment that the "dogma lives loudly" in Barrett became a conservative rallying cry, and supporters dubbed her the "Glorious ACB," a response to progressives who hailed Justice Ruth Bader Ginsburg as the "Notorious RBG." Coupled with backlash to the debacle in which Democrats smeared Supreme Court nominee Brett Kavanaugh, Democrats were unable to tarnish Barrett, a well-qualified judge with an impressive personal story—and opposing a pro-life woman posed unique challenges. It is notable that, despite her stellar qualifications and excellent performance in her hearing, not a single Democratic senator voted to confirm her.

The Kavanaugh confirmation in 2018, meanwhile, revealed to a new generation of young Americans the extent to which sitting politicians will defy the norms of the confirmation process and vilify those who they think imperil the supposed constitutional right to abortion.

In this episode, Feinstein—or perhaps a member of her staff—chose to sit on Christine Blasey Ford's shocking allegation that Kavanaugh had sexually assaulted her some thirty-five years earlier, keeping it under wraps until it was politically advantageous to publicize.

No one was well-served by such a gambit. Sexual assault is a horrendous offense, and if true, Ford's allegation rightly would have called into question Kavanaugh's confirmation.[60] Treating the accusations as a political football minimized the seriousness of sexual assault and created a political circus. Perhaps Feinstein or a staff member didn't act on the allegations initially because the veracity of Ford's claims was unclear. Indeed, inconsistencies in Ford's own testimony; contradictions from supposed witnesses, including a life-long friend; and an inconclusive federal investigation suggested that the allegation simply wasn't true. Furthermore, there is no evidence that the two had ever met each other.[61] Regardless, Senate Democrats used her story to try to destroy Kavanaugh's public reputation and indulged in even more grotesque and unfounded allegations against him, in large part motivated by abortion activists, including Planned Parenthood, NARAL, and the ACLU, which took the allegations as fact and refused to acknowledge evidence to the contrary.[62]

But the truth is, Democrats and these activist groups opposed Kavanaugh almost as vociferously long before Ford's allegations emerged. When his nomination was announced, Planned Parenthood urged the Senate to reject him: "There's no way to sugarcoat it: with this nomination, the constitutional right to access safe, legal abortion in this country is on the line."[63] During the first round of confirmation hearings, before Ford's story became public, committee Democrats showed little interest in seriously considering the nomination. Protesters in the Senate chamber, many dressed like oppressed women from the dystopian novel *The Handmaid's Tale*, tried to shout down the proceedings, and had to be removed by Capitol police. There were more than two hundred arrests during the first week of the hearings for disorderly conduct attempting to oppose Kavanaugh's confirmation on the basis of his presumed opposition to *Roe*.[64]

Kavanaugh was simply the latest in a long line of victims of such treatment. Decades before Kavanaugh, Judge Robert Bork experienced similar opposition when nominated to the Supreme Court by President Ronald Reagan in 1987. Bork, a well-respected federal judge and former Yale Law School professor, was widely known for his belief that the Constitution does not protect the kind of privacy right that the Court invented in *Griswold* and *Eisenstadt*.

At NARAL's 1987 annual convention, the group's executive director, Kate Michelman, called the Bork nomination, without a sense of irony, "the fight of our lives."[65] Ralph Neas, executive director of the Leadership Conference on Civil Rights, insisted that abortion supporters were prepared to take down Bork: "This is about what people have worked their whole lives for."[66] These activists set the tone for the lawmakers.

Not one hour after Reagan announced his nominee, Democratic senator Ted Kennedy warned in an infamous, fearmongering speech, "Robert Bork's America is a land in which women would be forced into back-alley abortions."[67] Joe Biden, who at the time was a senator from Delaware and chairman of the Senate Judiciary Committee, promised Bork a fair hearing, but at the same time promised pro-abortion groups that he would block the nomination.

Chairing the confirmation hearing, Biden treated Bork not as a serious nominee but as the representative of a harsh conservative social agenda, attacking him for his views on privacy and his broader legal thinking.[68] Bork's widow Mary Ellen later recalled that Biden had "orchestrated a vicious lying assault" and described his conduct this way: "Then-Sen. Biden presided over a rigged hearing full of an unprecedented level of lying and distortion of a man known for his integrity and judicial wisdom. Democrats flagrantly lied about Bob's record of opinions."[69]

This ideologically motivated, fact-free tenor cast a pall over the hearings. Criticisms of Bork dealt with more than abortion, but fear about losing *Roe* drove the tireless resistance and led to the defeat of Bork's nomination. And they got what they wanted: Reagan's eventual choice, Anthony Kennedy, went on to write the plurality decision in *Casey*. In tanking Bork's nomination, activists achieved precisely what they intended, and the way the nominee had been treated led to the creation of the verb "borking" to describe unfair treatment aimed at blocking a judicial nominee.

When President George H. W. Bush nominated Clarence Thomas to the Supreme Court, he came before a Senate Judiciary Committee, still led by Biden, that was prepared to move from unjust ideological opposition to character assassination. As he had done with Bork, Biden promised Thomas a fair hearing, but behind the scenes he was preparing to torpedo the nomination on the pretext of Thomas's belief in natural law, which many believed was another way of describing opposition to *Roe*.

But rather than focusing opposition to Thomas on those grounds, Democrats ended up fixating on allegations from Anita Hill, his former colleague, who claimed he had made sexually suggestive comments to her. Her allegations were unsubstantiated at the time and remain so to this day, yet the committee dragged Thomas through a hearing to discuss them in minute detail, a process Thomas decried as "a high-tech lynching for uppity blacks who deign to think for themselves."[70] Thomas was confirmed by a Democrat-controlled Senate, but not before some Democrats and activists succeeded in damaging his reputation and further tarnishing the confirmation process.[71] As columnist David Harsanyi has written, "If Biden should apologize to anyone, it's Clarence Thomas, or maybe the American people, for allowing judicial confirmation hearings to be turned into partisan-fueled character assassinations, weaponized to destroy the legitimacy of the Supreme Court—all in the service of nothing more noble than the killing of the unborn."[72]

When you consider what Democrats and their allies have done to Thomas, Kavanaugh, and others, you have to ask: What center-right jurist would want to go through such a process? Indeed, Democrats have made it such that the process is the punishment. These confirmation battles for Republican-nominated jurists have become fever-pitched because Democrats have aimed to make it more difficult for presidents to nominate any candidates who aren't "moderate" enough—in other words, candidates who don't support abortion. By making the hearings so politically costly and unpleasant, Democrats have attempted to intimidate Republican presidents into avoiding candidates who are faithful to the Constitution, which, of course, protects no right to abortion.

Confirmation proceedings have become an embarrassment for the Senate, and the politicization of the process has had a negative effect on our broader political landscape. Standing outside the Supreme Court after oral arguments in *June Medical*, Senate Democratic leader Chuck Schumer threatened the recently confirmed justices: "I want to tell you, Gorsuch. I want to tell you, Kavanaugh. You have released the whirlwind and you will pay the price. You won't know what hit you if you go forward with these awful decisions."[73]

Unlike during FDR's presidency, if Biden pushes a reform to expand the Supreme Court—especially in the wake of a decision overturning *Roe* and *Casey*—he is likely to find plenty of support within his party. Many have already indicated they'll be the first to play ball. To the modern Democratic politician, the game for legal abortion is much more important than our constitutional order. As Archbishop Cordileone noted, abortion has become "their blessed sacrament, what they hold most sacred."

Conclusion

Even though the Supreme Court in *Roe v. Wade* intended to settle the issue and end the public debate over the controversial question of abortion, it has remained unsettled for nearly five decades. In part, that's because most Americans don't support abortion on demand—a significant number remain strongly pro-life, and a majority would prefer to limit abortion far more than is permissible under *Roe* and *Casey*.

But rather than realizing this political reality and working to right the wrong of *Roe*, most Democratic politicians slowly began to embrace it, becoming hardened in their support of abortion thanks to the advocacy of staunch abortion-rights supporters who found a home in the left wing of our politics. Younger generations of politicians got the message, as the sad devolution from the heroism of Bob Casey Sr. to the cowardice of Bob Casey Jr. reveals. Those who didn't get with the program were driven out of the party—just ask Dan Lipinski.

This has caused tremendous harm not only to the Democratic Party but also to its voters, many of whom remain pro-life or want more protections for the unborn than their politicians will consider. It has also harmed our politics, offering voters only one major party that recognizes the harm of abortion and espouses support for the right to life of the unborn child. In perhaps the most fitting of consequences, it has undermined the Court's own credibility, turning judicial confirmation hearings into media circuses. The only way to begin fixing this set of harms is to overturn *Roe*.

CHAPTER SEVEN

Abortion Harms Media and Popular Culture

O n January 22, 2019, the anniversary of the Supreme Court decision in *Roe v. Wade*, New York governor Andrew Cuomo signed
the pro-abortion Reproductive Health Act. The law recognized a
"fundamental right to abortion," moved abortion from the state's
criminal code to the public-health code, permitted abortion for any
reason up to twenty-four weeks' gestation, and created broad health
exceptions effectively allowing elective abortion throughout the rest
of pregnancy.[1]

But signing the bill wasn't the only thing Cuomo did that day.
He also directed state landmarks to light up in pink "to celebrate
this achievement and shine a bright light forward for the rest of the
nation to follow."[2] In Manhattan, that meant lighting up the spire
of One World Trade Center, or Freedom Tower, built beside the spot
where the Twin Towers once stood. Directly beneath Freedom
Tower, two memorials to the victims of the September 11 terrorist
attack bear the names of eleven pregnant women who were killed.

Beside each of those names, etched in stone, are the words "and her unborn child."[3]

The 9/11 memorial in Manhattan bears witness to the value of every person we lost that day, including the unborn; it bears witness to the reality of human life in the womb. But when Cuomo demanded that the city emblazon Freedom Tower in pink to celebrate his bill, he was directing New York City to hail a law that denies the humanity of unborn children and allows them to be killed, for nearly any reason, until the moment of birth.

This celebration of abortion on demand was possible only in a culture that has normalized abortion, a society in which most media organizations, the entertainment industry, social-media companies, and major corporations promote the lie that abortion is unobjectionable—and even that abortion is a social good. This corruption of our media and popular culture contributes to a vicious cycle in which the glorification of abortion fuels further belief among citizens that abortion is normal.

As a result, many Americans will never hear the truth about abortion. If they get their news from major outlets such as the *New York Times* or the *Washington Post*, they are unlikely ever to encounter most of the facts we've presented in this book. If they get their information on social media, they might miss out on pro-life content as the result of censorship or biased moderation, to say nothing of the self-selected echo-chamber nature of much of social media.

Ordinary Americans, in other words, may never encounter the truth—and they're liable to be led astray by reporting and commentary that obscures or excludes important details about the effects of abortion in our country. If you go to public schools, watch mainstream news, and aren't particularly religious, there's a good chance you've never been presented with a compelling pro-life argument. And it's nearly impossible to escape the pro-abortion bias filtering through much of our culture, especially in our online world, perpetuating the idea that abortion is safe, unobjectionable, and even beneficial.

This has consequences for what people believe about abortion, both as a personal and a political matter. Citizens in a self-governing republic need to be presented with basic truths to inform their views and their votes. Supporters of abortion fear that a knowledgeable citizenry would react negatively to the reality of abortion, so they choose to distort and hide that reality, aided by cultural institutions that have embraced abortion. This skewed playing field makes it far more difficult to find common ground and make incremental improvements. In a post-*Roe* America, the pro-life movement will need to persuade Americans to support law and policy protecting unborn human beings. This project will require the ability both to speak the truth and to reach those who don't know it. As we have witnessed over the last several decades, the news media, social media, Hollywood, and our corporate culture are key to that effort—and their opposition can easily undermine the cause.

In this chapter, we survey how legacy media outlets have uniformly come to support abortion, regularly covering abortion with bias and excluding or distorting essential facts. We explain how major technology and social-media companies have targeted pro-life groups, limiting the ability of pro-lifers to share information online. We examine how many parts of our popular culture have embraced abortion on demand, as celebrity advocacy and the entertainment industry attempt to sway public opinion in favor of abortion. Finally, we describe how big corporations have put their thumb on the scale for legal abortion, wielding their cultural power to normalize abortion and prevent the enactment of pro-life laws.

Media Outlets Have Embraced Abortion
and Perpetuate Falsehoods

Most of us are aware that our nation's most well-known media companies are owned and operated by progressives—and that a progressive worldview filters through much of the reporting and commentary available today. This is especially true when it comes to abortion, as legacy media outlets and their supposedly neutral reporters compromise basic journalistic standards when covering the issue. In recent years, this problem has become more like a gaslighting campaign, a full-scale effort to hide the extremism of abortion supporters while exaggerating the supposed dangers of the pro-life point of view.

Though many of us have learned not to trust these sources, media distortions of the truth make self-government more difficult, as citizens are presented with inaccurate information about abortion law and policy and the effects of abortion on our culture. What citizens read and what they see on TV affects how they shape their opinions and make decisions, including decisions about whether they support abortion, how they might vote, and even whether they think about abortion at all. Our media sustain a widespread abortion distortion, perpetuating a culture in which abortion is increasingly regarded as normal and acceptable.

This distortion of the truth is especially stark when it comes to political coverage. Journalists offer kid-glove treatment to politicians and groups that support abortion while subjecting pro-lifers to unfair scrutiny and criticism. Politicians or candidates who favor abortion, for example, are never asked basic questions about what takes place during an abortion or why they believe that lethal violence should be legal. Reporters often avoid discussing abortion altogether, and when they do raise it, they ask questions such as this one, posed during a Democratic presidential primary debate in 2019: "Let's turn to women's reproductive rights. If states prevail on restricting abortion what's your plan to stop them?"[4]

Partial-Birth Abortion Ban

This isn't new. To explore just one case study, consider how the media have covered partial-birth abortion bans. At a 1992 meeting of the National Abortion Federation, an abortionist named Martin Haskell gave a presentation on dilation and extraction (D&X) abortions, which he said he used "routinely" for abortions between twenty and twenty-four weeks. Haskell said the procedure begins by pulling the unborn child partially out of the woman's uterus by the feet.[5] What happens next was best explained by one of Haskell's former nurses in a 1995 letter to her Ohio congressman about what she witnessed in one such procedure:

> The baby's body was moving. His little fingers were clasping together. He was kicking his feet. All the while his little head was still stuck inside [the uterus]. Dr. Haskell took a pair of scissors and inserted them into the back of the baby's head. Then he opened the scissors up. Then he stuck the high-powered suction tube into the hole and sucked the baby's brains out.[6]

Senator Daniel Patrick Moynihan, a liberal Democrat from New York who despite being "personally pro-life" supported abortion as a political matter, described this procedure as "not just too close to infanticide; it is infanticide, and one would be too many."[7]

In 1995, Congress began debating a bill to ban D&X abortion procedures, colloquially referred to as "partial-birth abortions," a reference to how the unborn child is partially delivered prior to being killed. Even though the pro-abortion American College of Obstetricians and Gynecologists would admit in hearings on the same proposal several years later that it "could identify no circumstances under which this procedure...would be the only option to save the life or preserve the health of the woman," abortion advocates, including ACOG itself, opposed the ban, insisting that women need this gruesome procedure.[8]

During the debate, advocacy groups and their media allies attempted to downplay the horror of what happens in partial-birth abortions. Barbara Radford, former executive director of the National Abortion Federation, conjectured, "Much of the negative reaction...is the same reaction that might be invoked if one were to listen to a surgeon describing step-by-step almost any other surgical procedure involving blood, human tissue, etc."[9] Planned Parenthood emphasized that D&X abortions are rare and, alongside NARAL, claimed that anesthesia given to the mother would kill the child prior to delivery.[10] According to contemporaneous testimony, the *New York Times*, the *Los Angeles Times*, the *Baltimore Sun*, and *USA Today* all ran pieces framing the issue as one of the government displacing sound, even "lifesaving" medical judgments.[11]

The 1995 ban passed the Senate by a vote of 98–1 but was vetoed by President Bill Clinton.[12] When similar bans were reintroduced in subsequent years, abortion supporters found their media allies ready to assist. Writers at Slate insisted that partial-birth abortion is not objectionable because "every abortion is gross, but the technique is not the issue" and claimed that "partial-birth abortion" is a misnomer because the procedure "is not a birth."[13] Covering the ban proposed in 2002, the Associated Press asserted that the bill aimed to protect a "fetus outside a woman's body."[14] There's a word for a "fetus" outside a woman's body: newborn.

These perversions persisted even after the ban finally became law. Slate writer Dahlia Lithwick argued that the "biggest problem with the words 'partial-birth abortion' is that they have neither a precise legal definition nor an exact medical one."[15] This line originated with abortion-rights groups, which derided the phrase "partial-birth abortion" for being insufficiently medical, an obvious effort to avoid terminology that describes the D&X procedure clearly.[16] These arguments over rhetoric are common from abortion supporters, who spend a lot of time berating pro-lifers for using phrases such as "partial-birth" or "late-term" when describing abortion, because disputing terminology is easier than discussing what actually happens in these procedures.

This distortion on partial-birth abortion is alive and well today. During his 2021 confirmation hearing to head the Department of Health and Human Services, Biden appointee Xavier Becerra was confronted about his vote against the partial-birth ban when he was in the U.S. House of Representatives. Asked whether he agreed that partial-birth abortion is illegal as a result of that ban, Becerra said there "is no medical term like 'partial-birth abortion' " and there is "no law that deals specifically with the term 'partial-birth abortion.' "[17] Pennsylvania representative John Joyce was quick to point out that the relevant section of the U.S. Code is titled "partial-birth abortions prohibited." The media gave Becerra a pass.

To be sure, partial-birth abortions are no more morally wrong than abortions performed in a more sterile manner or abortions earlier in pregnancy. But the public debate over the D&X procedure was a particular threat to abortion supporters because it vividly exposed what takes place in all abortions: an innocent human being is killed. Likewise, it exposed how radical the pro-abortion movement is, unwilling to forgo even this gruesome type of late abortion, used for no medical reason and only when the child could easily survive outside the womb.

Media Outlets Defend Abortion-Rights Proponents and Attack Heartbeat Bills

In 2019, several pro-life states passed some form of a heartbeat bill, prohibiting most abortions after the heartbeat of an unborn child could be detected. At the same time, several progressive states considered bills providing state-level protections for abortion. In New York, it was the Reproductive Health Act (RHA). In Vermont, Illinois, and Rhode Island, it was legislation declaring abortion a "fundamental right." In Virginia, it was a bill loosening restrictions to allow abortion up to the moment of birth, or even during labor, a bill that thankfully did not pass. The disparity between how national media outlets covered these two types of states was egregious, as writers were swift to defend the abortion-rights supporters and portray pro-lifers in a negative light.

Media all but cheered the Reproductive Health Act. CNN emphasized that the bill "puts in measures to protect access to abortion."[18] (The phrase "access to abortion" is a political euphemism, used by abortion-rights activists and advocacy organizations—and now most media outlets—to subtly communicate the assumption that abortion is acceptable and that access to it should be guaranteed.) A *New York Times* report about Cuomo's vow to expand abortion rights was laudatory: "With Hillary Clinton to his right, female elected officials seated before him and cheering women filling the audience, Gov. Andrew M. Cuomo on Monday promised to protect women's reproductive rights by expanding the state's abortion laws within the first 30 days of the new legislative session."[19] And when Cuomo signed it into law, *New York* magazine's Sarah Jones praised him for updating what she characterized as New York's "archaic" abortion laws, a reform that "couldn't come at a better time," as the Trump administration was "waging a multipronged attack on reproductive rights."[20]

Media cheered similar legislation in other states, even when infanticide was on the table. In Virginia, Democratic state representative Kathy Tran proposed a bill lifting most restrictions on abortion after fetal viability.[21] During debate over the bill, Tran admitted that her bill would allow a woman to obtain an abortion even during labor.[22] Asked about his support for Tran's legislation the day after her comments, Democratic Virginia governor Ralph Northam, a physician, suggested that it would be acceptable to deny medical care to a newborn who had survived an abortion, at least in some circumstances: "The infant would be kept comfortable, the infant would be resuscitated if that's what the mother and family desired, and then a discussion would ensue between the physicians and the mother."[23] In other words, an infant born alive after a failed abortion procedure does not have the right to basic legal protection—his rights depend on the desires of his parents and the judgment of the doctor.

News organizations rushed to defend Tran and Northam. A piece from The Cut denounced what it called "the false outrage over Kathy Tran's 'infanticide' bill."[24] A *New York Times* op-ed titled "Fake News about Abortion in Virginia" insisted that there was nothing objectionable about either Tran's bill or Northam's comments.[25] *Newsweek* and the *Washington Post* ran reports focusing not on Tran and Northam but rather on the conservative response to them, saying Republicans "seized upon" Northam's remarks and that the Virginia bill "drew GOP outrage."[26] Reuters fact-checked Northam's critics, saying they had misrepresented his comments by removing "key contextual references."[27] As it happens, the full context only makes the brutality of his thinking even clearer.

These defenses of abortion radicalism stand in stark contrast to media criticism of pro-life heartbeat bills, which primarily downplay the reality of the fetal heartbeat. After Georgia passed its heartbeat bill in 2019, *Wired* magazine's Adam Rogers published an article claiming that "'Heartbeat' Bills Get the Science of Fetal Heartbeats All Wrong," placing the word "heartbeat" in scare quotes as if to suggest that no such thing exists. Rogers used clinical phrases such as "cardiac rhythm," "fetal cardiac activity," and "a cluster of pulsing cells" to describe the heartbeat of the unborn child. He quoted abortionists, billed as medical experts, who said the phrase heartbeat is misleading and described it instead as "a group of cells with electrical activity" and "fetal pole cardiac activity."[28] The goal of this phrasing is obvious: replace the word "heartbeat" with clinical terminology that sounds sterile and impersonal rather than humanizing.

"Fetal pole cardiac activity" became so popular among abortion supporters that actress Alyssa Milano—whose ardent pro-abortion activism we'll address in greater detail later—demanded that the press refer to all heartbeat bills exclusively as "fetal pole cardiac activity" bills.[29] Among others, *Time* reporter Madeleine Carlisle obliged, explaining that Georgia's law would prohibit "most abortions after a doctor detected fetal cardiac activity."[30] *The Guardian* updated its style guide to replace the phrase "heartbeat bill" with "six-week abortion ban." Justifying its decision, *The Guardian* cited ACOG, which "does not use the term 'heartbeat' to describe these legislative bans on abortion because it is misleading language, out of step with the anatomical and clinical realities of that stage of pregnancy."[31]

In its coverage, the *Washington Post* quoted unnamed doctors who asserted that "what appears to be a heartbeat...is simply a vibration of developing tissues that could not exist without the mother. This vibration is a medical term called 'embryonic cardiac activity.'"[32] Likewise, *New York* magazine ran a piece titled "Embryos Don't Have Hearts," referring to the heartbeat as "pulsing cells" and supposedly debunking the "unscientific" notion of a fetal heartbeat.[33] The *New York Times* went with "the pulsing of what becomes the fetus's heart" and "embryonic pulsing."[34] In 2021, on the heels of

Texas's heartbeat bill, four *Times* reporters explained that they would not use the phrase "heartbeat" in their coverage because "there is no heart at this stage of development, only electrical activity in developing cells. The heart is not fully formed until later in pregnancy."[35]

While it is true that the unborn child's heart does not become fully formed until about ten weeks into pregnancy, his or her heartbeat nevertheless can be detected as early as five or six weeks' gestation.[36] A heart can beat even before a heart is fully formed—a reality that pro-abortion activists seem intent on ignoring. In fact, the presence of a fetal heartbeat early in pregnancy is one of the chief indicators of whether a pregnancy is progressing well and whether the child will be born healthy. According to one study, once an ultrasound has confirmed an unborn child's heartbeat at eight weeks' gestation, the risk of miscarriage is only 3 percent.[37] Another study found that, among women with a history of recurrent miscarriage, only 3 percent experienced a subsequent miscarriage after a fetal heartbeat had been detected.[38] A heartbeat is a reassuring sign of life and health in every context other than abortion.

The Texas heartbeat bill prompted a fresh round of media outlets attempting to debunk the existence of a fetal heartbeat. NPR cited "physicians who specialize in reproductive health," the first of whom is an ACOG abortion provider, to claim that the phrase fetal heartbeat is "misleading." Another group of so-called experts explained to NPR that at six weeks' gestation, we can't detect a heartbeat but rather a "grouping of cells that are initiating some electrical activity."[39]

These reporters might be surprised to find out that Planned Parenthood, in contrast to the mainstream refusal to use "heartbeat," says on its website that a "very basic beating heart" develops in the unborn child at six weeks.[40] When Ryan and Anna heard their son's heartbeat during their first ultrasound appointment, the technician repeatedly used the word "heartbeat" and never once said "electrical activity" or "fetal pole cardiac activity." No pregnant mother has ever had an ultrasound technician, midwife, or OB-GYN use any word other than "heartbeat" in this context—and if she did, she would rightly find a new health-care provider immediately.

Of course, what makes the unborn child a human person whose life is worthy of protection is not the presence of a fully formed heart or heartbeat. The human being in the womb is valuable even before he or she has a heartbeat, just as each of us is valuable regardless of whether our heart is functioning well or poorly. But news organizations evidently realized what makes heartbeat bills so powerful: they remind us that the child in the womb is a living human being, a whole organism with its own heartbeat, distinct from his mother. This truth threatens the pro-abortion argument, which is why these media outlets have been so helpful in minimizing it.

Born-Alive Abortion Survivors Protection Act

In 2019, shortly after Northam's comments, Nebraska senator Ben Sasse introduced the Born-Alive Abortion Survivors Protection Act. The bill, meant as a response to Northam and his defenders, did not restrict abortion, contrary to what opponents claim. Instead, it required doctors to provide the same standard of medical care for newborns who survive an abortion that they would for any other newborn of the same gestational age.[41]

Sasse was building off the logic of an earlier bill. In 2002, President George W. Bush signed into law the Born-Alive Infants Protection Act (BAIPA), which included "born-alive infants" under the legal categories of "person," "human being," "child," and "individual."[42] The law was intended to protect newborns delivered alive after a failed abortion procedure, but it had no enforcement mechanism. Indeed, it required nothing at all; it merely stated that newborns count as legal persons. But the law unfortunately did nothing to stop doctors from letting babies who survived an abortion die from lack of medical care, which is far more common than directly killing babies who survive an abortion. Law is a teacher, and the bill's architects acknowledged that, because civil penalties were dropped from the original proposal, it was primarily meant to educate the public. The bill would, its main expositor Professor Hadley Arkes argued, "break to the public news that most people would find jolting. Most people did not know that under *Roe v. Wade* and [*Doe*], the right to abortion would extend through the entire length of the pregnancy...even when a child survived the abortion."[43]

Sasse's bill aimed to put the logic of BAIPA into action by explicitly requiring doctors to care for newborn infants who survived an abortion. It also would have instituted reporting requirements to keep track of when this lethal neglect occurs. For three years in a row, Senate Republicans brought the born-alive bill up for a vote, and all three years, Democrats blocked the legislation. They claimed that the born-alive law was unnecessary, arguing that infanticide never happens and is already illegal, anyway—both demonstrably false claims.[44] But they faced little blowback for their votes, due in large part to the assistance of reporters who regurgitated Democratic talking points and gave them cover.

Major news networks, including CNN, ABC News, NBC News, and MSNBC, ignored the born-alive bill almost entirely.[45] Mainstream outlets that covered the bill spun it as a Republican scheme to demonize the Left. "Trump, Pence Lead GOP Seizure of Late-Term Abortion as a Potent 2020 Issue," one *New York Times* headline declared.[46] The *Washington Post* went with the same theme: "Trump and Republicans are trying to paint Democrats as radical on abortion," and "Republicans seize on liberal positions to paint Democrats as radical."[47] CBS "abortion access" reporter Kate Smith did the same, claiming that the bill was part of "a push by the conservative right to reframe the reproductive rights debate toward third-trimester abortions" to make Democrats appear extreme.[48]

Most major outlets described the bill as "anti-abortion," even though it doesn't regulate or restrict abortion at all—rather, it's about what is owed to a newborn child who has survived an abortion.[49] *Politico* reporter Alice Miranda Ollstein described it as an attempt by Republicans to "jam" and "squeeze" Democrats.[50] She also placed "attempted abortion" and "abortion survivors" in scare quotes, as if to suggest that unborn children never survive abortion procedures.[51]

Covering the reintroduction of the bill in 2020, CNN's Caroline Kelly explained that it "would require abortion providers to work to 'preserve the life and health' of a fetus that was born following an attempted abortion."[52] Absent pro-abortion bias, any normal person would use the word "newborn" rather than the bizarre phrase "a fetus that was born." After significant criticism, CNN removed the phrase, stating in an editor's note that the story had been "updated to more precisely reflect the language used in Sasse's bill."[53]

As troubling as these examples are, they only scratch the surface of how deep the rot goes when it comes to media coverage of abortion. Mainstream publications are hostile to pro-lifers, as when they fail to cover the annual March for Life, despite the fact that it's one of the largest annual D.C. protests, or cover it only to criticize its speakers or participants. But they bend over backwards, often by distorting or ignoring key facts, to defend the pro-abortion movement.

Social-Media Giants Shut Down Pro-Life Information

The most powerful technology companies in the United States, companies such as Google, Facebook, and YouTube, have revealed their support for abortion by using their power to target pro-life groups and suppress their informational campaigns. This trend hasn't been limited to large companies but has also cropped up at smaller ones such as Pinterest and GoDaddy. These companies have manipulated search results, prohibited pro-life videos, banned advertisements from pro-life groups, and even suspended or removed the official accounts of pro-life groups from their platforms. Oftentimes, these companies review and walk back their decisions after facing scrutiny, but these incidents reveal that powerful tech companies and social-media groups are overseen by people biased against the pro-life cause.

Susan B. Anthony List (SBA List), a prominent pro-life group working on the front lines of politics, has chronicled many instances of social-media censorship, as well as other examples of bias.[54] Several specific examples suggest that these companies have intentionally used their moderation and curation powers to make it more difficult for pro-life groups to share accurate information about abortion. Ahead of the 2018 midterm elections, when several key Senate seats were up for grabs, Facebook deleted SBA List advertisements contrasting Democratic support for taxpayer-funded abortion with the pro-life positions of Republicans.[55] Some of the ads shared the stories of two babies who had survived premature births, which Facebook deemed improperly "sensational."[56] Facebook later apologized and reinstated the advertisements after public backlash.[57] One year earlier, Twitter had axed SBA List advertisements that included the phrase "killing babies." SBA List's president Marjorie Dannenfelser recalled: "No advertiser is permitted to use the phrase 'killing babies.' That's what Twitter told us when they censored one of our videos."[58]

Throughout 2017, Twitter was particularly hostile to pro-lifers, removing an ad from the Senate campaign of Republican Marsha Blackburn that highlighted her work to stop Planned Parenthood from selling fetal body parts. Twitter also stopped SBA List from running ad campaigns after the group urged Republican congressman Mark Meadows to defund Planned Parenthood, though the site permitted Planned Parenthood's Twitter campaign to advocate the defeat of the same bill—and Twitter also prevented Live Action from running ads altogether unless they removed pro-life ads that Twitter deemed objectionable content, such as information about fetal development and Planned Parenthood's abortion business.[59]

In December 2018, Slate writer April Glaser criticized YouTube for allowing pro-life videos to appear in the search results for the word "abortion." Glaser demanded that YouTube explain "why anti-abortion videos saturated the search results for 'abortion,' and if the platform thought accurate, health-focused information had a place there."[60] Her inquiry proved fruitful. "Before the company got back to me," Glaser reported, "the search results had changed to include a number of news outlets among the top results." The results continued to be updated, she noted, to include more pro-abortion videos at the top of the page.[61] Some of the videos to which Glaser objected were those explaining what happens in an abortion procedure, a reality that abortion activists are eager to hide and that YouTube assisted them in suppressing.[62]

In September 2021, Google banned all of Live Action's advertising and its promotion of a new video showing an unborn child's development in the womb, citing supposed "unreliable claims," "health in personalized advertising," and "misleading content."[63] The ban applies to such Live Action advertisements as one informing users about abortion-pill reversal, a safe and effective medical procedure that can halt a chemical abortion if the pregnant woman decides she wants to keep her baby before taking the second dose of the chemical-abortion drug.[64] Google described Live Action's content as misleading even though abortion-pill reversal has been quite successful, saving more than three thousand unborn children.[65]

In 2018, Live Action accused YouTube of modifying search results to effectively bury the pro-life group's videos.[66] A year later, the social-media site Pinterest banned Live Action's entire account, claiming that its "pro-life educational and political content" qualified as "pornographic." Facebook's fact-checkers, meanwhile, labeled as "false" and "inaccurate" two Live Action videos stating that abortion is never medically necessary.[67] As it turned out, the fact-check team consisted of two abortion-rights advocates, both of whom have formal ties to abortion-rights groups: NARAL board member Dr. Daniel Grossman and Dr. Robyn Schickler, a fellow with the abortion advocacy group Physicians for Reproductive Health.[68] Both Grossman and Schickler are abortionists. "We should remember that while these medical reasons for abortion are very serious, all reasons for deciding to seek abortion care are valid; no one reason is better than another," Schickler said in her statement explaining the fact-check. Facebook eventually reviewed the decision, removed Schickler's comment from the statement, and reinstated the videos in question.[69]

Though these social-media decisions are often walked back after the fact, these incidents reveal the bias of tech companies, which disadvantages the pro-life movement and makes it harder for users to share accurate information about abortion—making it less likely that the truth will reach people who need to hear it.

Abortion Distortion in Popular Culture

Television and movies have long been a home for social-reform messaging. In the past, abortion was almost always depicted in a negative light, and it often remains that way today. But increasingly, spearheaded by abortion-rights activists, depictions of abortion are becoming bold and casual, and celebrating abortion is sometimes even the heart of the plot.

Abortion supporters know that what Americans watch changes the culture and that culture shapes people's beliefs, so they are hard at work pushing the people who create America's films and shows to change how people think about abortion. In 2019, the *Washington Post* ran a feature on Caren Spruch, "Planned Parenthood's woman in Hollywood—or, in official terms, its director of arts and entertainment engagement."[70] Spruch "encourages screenwriters to tell stories about abortion and works as a script doctor for those who do (as well as those who write about any other area of Planned Parenthood's expertise, such as birth control or sexually transmitted infections)." The *Post* reports that roles like Spruch's are becoming "increasingly welcome in Hollywood," and Spruch says her work is increasingly successful:

> In the past year or two, word of Spruch's services has started to filter through the film industry. "Nobody used to call me," she says. "I would be watching TV and going to the movies and figuring out who I thought might be open to including these story lines. Now I have a couple of repeat clients. Now people call me." She estimates that Planned Parenthood has advised on more than 150 movies and shows since that first effort with "Obvious Child." Writers who have relied on her advice tell me they feel a secret kinship with one another. "We could see hints of her in all the TV shows coming out, from 'Shrill' to 'Jane the Virgin,'" says Gillian Robespierre, writer-director of "Obvious Child." "It's really wonderful. She's like Planned Parenthood's secret weapon."[71]

Activists such as Spruch work to ensure that TV depictions of abortion are both celebratory and realistic, that they instruct viewers about the supposed downsides of limited abortion access, and that they include both at-home chemical and in-clinic surgical abortions.[72]

The effects of this work are becoming apparent from the viewing options available. In a famous 2015 episode of the TV show *Scandal*, Olivia Pope (played by Kerry Washington, herself a Planned Parenthood supporter) underwent an abortion set to the soundtrack of "Silent Night," while her friend Mellie filibustered a Senate bill that would defund Planned Parenthood. The episode was later praised by Planned Parenthood, and show creator Shonda Rhimes was honored with Planned Parenthood's 2017 "Champions of Change" award.[73] BuzzFeed ran an article saying that 2016 was the "year abortion was destigmatized on TV," observing that *BoJack Horseman, Jane the Virgin, You're the Worst*, and *Crazy Ex-Girlfriend* all included "consequence-free, even comedic abortion storylines."[74]

But this still wasn't good enough for abortion supporters. Stephanie Herold and Gretchen Sisson—both researchers at Advancing New Standards in Reproductive Health (ANSIRH), a program within the UCSF Bixby Center for Global Reproductive Health—argued in a 2020 op-ed that despite progress, producers still aren't getting abortion right. "We've found that Hollywood tends to dramatically exaggerate the medical risks associated with abortion," they write, "while downplaying real barriers to access."[75] Writing for the *New Statesman*, Katharine Swindells agreed:

> We have come a long way since the portrayals of pain and suffering of 50 years ago, but current depictions still tend to be neither realistic nor nuanced. Instead of using outdated moral turmoil as a dramatic device, abortion stories could explore the many barriers that still face those trying to access it both in the US, the UK and across the world.[76]

Swindells's piece came *after* 2020, a banner year for abortion plots. The distastefully titled HBO movie *Unpregnant*, released in

September 2020, depicts a pregnant, Ivy League–bound teenager who discovers she can't have an abortion in her home state of Missouri without parental consent. Her solution? Driving with her friend to New Mexico, pawning the engagement ring with which her boyfriend proposed to her *after* finding out about the pregnancy, obtaining the abortion, then calling her mother to ask for a plane ticket home. Actress Barbie Ferreira, who plays the main character's friend, said of the film, "I just hope that people come out of *Unpregnant* feeling good."[77]

Celebrating abortion is also filtering into comedy. In 2017, NARAL sponsored a sketch called "Comedians in Cars Getting an Abortion," attempting to make light of how hard it is to get an abortion.[78] More recently, in 2021, actress Cecily Strong portrayed "Goober the Clown (who had an abortion when she was 23)" in a bizarre three-minute sketch on *Saturday Night Live* supposedly meant to show solidarity with women who have had abortions.[79]

Hollywood Cheers for Planned Parenthood and Abortion

Hollywood's support for abortion is also evident in widespread celebrity support for Planned Parenthood. Whenever Republicans renew their campaign to remove federal funding from Planned Parenthood, celebrities take to social media to support the organization—a fact that suggests the abortion business could survive just fine on their donations alone.[80] At the 2017 Oscars, in response to the election of Donald Trump, prominent actresses sported Planned Parenthood pins.[81]

Perhaps no one exemplifies celebrity support for Planned Parenthood better than Alyssa Milano, who conducts herself as if she's Planned Parenthood's unpaid spokeswoman, in addition to her activism against pro-life laws.[82] Some of this support for abortion among actresses seems to be undergirded by their personal reliance on abortion as a means of participating in the Hollywood economy. Milano herself, for instance, has spoken about having had two abortions in the span of a few months, a story she shares to explain her support for abortion.[83]

At the Golden Globes in 2020, actress Michelle Williams said she "couldn't have succeeded without the right to choose." Williams described the award as "the acknowledgement of the choices I've made" and said she was "grateful to have lived in a moment in our society where choice exists, because as women and as girls, things can happen to our bodies that are not our choice."[84] Watched by about eighteen million viewers and hailed by feminist writers after the fact, Williams appealed to young women, and though she didn't mention the word "abortion" at all in her speech, it was telling that she used her moment in the spotlight to insist that women can't achieve success without the right to kill their unborn children.[85]

Shortly after Texas passed its heartbeat bill, Paxton Smith, valedictorian at a high school in Dallas, Texas, dedicated her remarks to celebrating abortion, saying, "There is a war on my body and a war on my rights, a war on the rights of your mothers, a war on the rights of your sisters, a war on the rights of your daughters."[86] Smith was praised by prominent progressive women such as actress Jennifer Aniston and Hillary Clinton.[87] We don't know whether Smith watched Michelle Williams receive her Golden Globe, but she certainly sounded like someone who grew up in a culture that celebrates abortion as the epitome of female freedom:

> I have dreams and hopes and ambitions. Every girl graduating today does, and we have spent our entire lives working towards our future, and without our input and without our consent our control over that future has been

stripped away from us. I am terrified that if my contraceptives fail, I am terrified that if I am raped, then my hopes and aspirations and dreams and efforts for my future will no longer matter.[88]

Abortion supporters know that the internet and social media have immense power to shape hearts and minds, especially those of young people. Perhaps that's why Shout Your Abortion co-founder Amelia Bonow produced a video telling young children about her abortion and encouraging them to celebrate it.[89] "They just suck the pregnancy out," Bonow explains in the video. "It was like a crappy dentist appointment or something." "Do we want people to just have all those babies?" Bonow asks one of the kids. When he shakes his head no, evidently being led in this direction by her questioning, Bonow asks, "So what do we do with them?" The child, clearly baffled, suggests, "Put them up for adoption?" Bonow is not pleased: "I feel like if I am forced to create life, I have lost the right to my own life. I should be the one to decide if my body creates a life."

Celebrity advocacy alone can't convince people to support abortion, but culture is the water in which we swim, shaping opinions and changing hearts, often without anyone noticing. As much as we might like to think that everyone sits down, reads up on the facts, and makes a rational decision about an issue as important as abortion, that isn't how public opinion is formed. Many people go with the flow and follow popular culture. For those of us who are convinced that abortion is wrong, pop-culture advocacy might be a mere annoyance that causes us to roll our eyes, flip the channel, or avoid particular films. But for those who don't have strong convictions about abortion one way or the other, this type of advocacy is powerful, and the hold abortion has on our culture has left its mark on our entertainment industry.

Corporations Put Their Thumb on the Scale for Abortion

In recent years, big business has put its thumb on the scale for unlimited elective abortion. Major companies now wield their cultural power against pro-life states, most recently in response to heartbeat bills. In March 2022, banking giant Citigroup announced that it would cover travel costs for employees who travel out of their home state to obtain an abortion. The company said the policy is a "response to changes in reproductive healthcare laws in certain states in the US," and, though it did not explicitly mention abortion, said that the reimbursements would "facilitate access to adequate resources."[90] This move was the latest example of a major corporation not only publicly supporting abortion but using financial and cultural power to undermine state pro-life laws. In 2019, after Georgia passed its heartbeat bill, Netflix, AT&T's WarnerMedia, Disney, NBC, CBS, AMC, Sony, and Viacom all threatened to pull their business out of the state if the law went into effect.[91]

Nearly two hundred major companies took to the pages of the *New York Times* calling abortion restrictions "bad for business." The full-page advertisement—signed by chief executives from Twitter, Yelp, Slack, Postmates, and more—argued that these restrictions threaten "the health, independence, and economic stability of our employees and customers" and "are against our values."[92] Senator Tom Cotton criticized the ad on the Senate floor, calling it "disgusting" for using the phrase "bad for business." "All these politically correct CEOs want company men and women, not family men and women," Cotton said. "They'll support your individuality and self-expression just so long as you stay unattached and on the clock."[93]

In fall 2021, major companies reacted with similar outrage to the Texas heartbeat bill. Several corporations, including software company Salesforce, offered to pay to relocate employees who wanted to leave Texas. Rideshare companies Lyft and Uber said they would cover legal fees for drivers who faced legal action under Texas law for driving a woman to get an abortion.[94] Lyft also pledged $1 million to Planned Parenthood, and the company's general counsel Kristin Sverchek defended the move, saying, "It's important that corporate America holds government accountable and speaks out on important issues."[95]

"Corporate America holds government accountable." Progressives used to demand that government hold corporate America accountable. Indeed, when it comes to issues other than abortion, progressives typically spend a lot of time complaining about the effects of "big business" and "dark money" on politics. But with the rise of woke capitalism, with abortion as its most sacred rite, we hear nary a peep.

Perhaps most interesting: no major companies threatened to boycott the state entirely. They pledged money to abortion businesses and promised to help their employees deal with the effects of the law, but they didn't so much as gesture at pulling out of the state—likely because doing so would undercut the bottom line. Texas's biggest businesses, including American Airlines, AT&T, ExxonMobil, Dell Technologies, and Oracle, remained totally silent on the subject. This suggests that, at least some of the time, there is an element of virtue signaling in companies' public commentary on abortion when they believe it will help business, and when they fear it will hurt, they stay silent.

Lamenting the Texas law, Christopher Miller, head of global activism strategy at ice-cream giant Ben & Jerry's, offered a hint at why companies have stepped up their pro-abortion activism: "If you're operating in a state like Texas, it puts you at a competitive disadvantage. It makes it difficult to deliver on pay equity and recruiting and retaining talented leaders when there is a blatant attack against women."[96] Though Miller is being cagey, he seems to be arguing either that female employees prefer not to work in states with pro-life laws or, more sinister, that when women have less access to abortion, more women become mothers, which is bad for business. Several dozen companies affirmed Miller's point when they published a statement responding to the law, proclaiming their support for "reproductive healthcare" and suggesting that the Heartbeat Act "bans equality." The signatories included Yelp, Lyft, Madewell, Bumble, Ben & Jerry's, Asana, and Vice Media. The statement argues that "policies that restrict reproductive health care go against our values and are bad for business," and it alleges that state restrictions on abortion "cost state economies $105 billion dollars per year."[97]

You might think this ideological commitment to abortion would be part of a larger commitment to female equality. You'd be wrong. In recent years, the *New York Times* has published two major exposés chronicling instances of discrimination against pregnant women at major U.S. companies. The first *Times* piece "reviewed thousands of pages of court and public records and interviewed dozens of women, their lawyers and government officials." According to the authors' summary, "A clear pattern emerged. Many of the country's largest and most prestigious companies still systematically sideline pregnant women. They pass them over for promotions and raises. They fire them when they complain."[98]

Several of the examples in the piece are particularly troubling. Otisha Woolbright, a Walmart employee, asked for permission not to lift heavy trays after she got pregnant, based on her doctor's advice. Her supervisor insisted that she continue, on threat of being fired, which led to her getting injured on the job. Three days after asking about the company's maternity-leave policy, Woolbright was fired. Rachel Mountis, a top saleswoman at the pharmaceutical company Merck, was fired three weeks before giving birth. Mountis has joined a lawsuit accusing Merck of paying women less than men and denying them professional opportunities, brought by Kelli Smith, a Merck saleswoman who alleges her career was derailed when she got pregnant. In 2010, drug company Novartis settled a class-action lawsuit brought by thousands of current and former sales representatives who claimed the company discriminated against women, including expectant mothers, in pay and promotions. Erin Murphy, a senior employee at Glencore, the world's largest commodity-trading company, alleges that, after she told her boss about her first pregnancy, he said it would "definitely plateau" her career. Murphy also alleges that when she was eight months pregnant with her second child, she asked her boss about her career trajectory, to which he allegedly replied, "You're old and having babies so there's nowhere for you to go." She claims that, after returning from maternity leave, she was instructed to pump breastmilk in a supply closet.

A second *New York Times* exposé focused solely on Planned Parenthood, which was found to have a systemic workplace culture disfavoring pregnant women. This included both illegal discrimination, such as taking account of pregnancy in hiring decisions, or subtle discrimination, such as not permitting women to take doctor-recommended breaks.[99] The report found that "most Planned Parenthood offices do not provide paid maternity leave, though many let new mothers take partially paid disability leave."[100] "A former hiring manager at a Planned Parenthood in California said that when internal promotions came up, supervisors openly debated whether candidates were likely to get pregnant in the near future and preferred those who were not," the *Times* article says. "They declined to hire one pregnant woman and to promote one new mother, the employee said."[101]

Though none of these examples deals directly with abortion, they suggest that the corporate culture at several major companies tends to become unfriendly to women who choose to become mothers rather than remain entirely unencumbered by family life and thus maximally available for work. Big business's support for legal abortion is ideologically driven, but we shouldn't discount self-interest.

As we discussed in previous chapters, abortion treats pregnancy as a disease and establishes the male body as the norm, a reality that disadvantages women as a result of their asymmetrical role in reproduction. In the corporate world, this can create a culture in which women are incentivized to behave like men to succeed, making marriage and childbearing decisions in service of their career instead of the other way around. Rather than accommodating women's capacity for childbearing and, often, natural desire for childrearing, our laws permit abortion on demand and our culture encourages women to succeed in the workplace by behaving like immature men: delaying marriage and childbearing and minimizing the effects of motherhood on their performance in the workplace.[102] For corporations that care little about their employees as human beings, viewing them instead as essential components of the company's success, childbearing and parenthood are inconveniences. The easy availability of abortion makes it possible for women to engage in the workplace as if they were men, workers who are always available and not burdened by the demands of children or the desire to be a mother.

Conclusion

The truth about abortion—the reality that every abortion takes the life of an innocent human being—is the strongest argument against it. There are plenty of sophisticated and sophistical academic debates about whether this form of killing might somehow be permissible or whether the government ought to restrict it. But the basic reality of what abortion is, when it's unfiltered and presented directly to the American people, is a compelling one—and that's why abortion supporters will do everything in their power to obscure it.

In a post-*Roe* United States, pro-lifers will need to convince our neighbors that unborn children deserve protection under the law. And convincing our fellow citizens that the child in the womb deserves legal protection will require cultural power, the ability to speak the truth in the public square without being silenced. It will require fighting the tide of corruption evident in so many of our cultural institutions, which have put their weight behind abortion, lying about what abortion is and spreading fear about what a world without abortion might look like.

Conclusion

Shortly after getting married, Alice began taking birth control, and she didn't realize she had conceived until she had been pregnant for several months. When she told her husband, he wasn't pleased. "Don't worry about it; I've been through this before and it's no big deal," he told her. His idea of a solution was to take her to get an abortion. Here's how Alice later described her experience:

> Going into the clinic—that hollow, hollow feeling in the pit of your stomach. I didn't want to look anyone in the eye. All the girls sitting around like statues, trying to talk. The sound of that stupid machine. I'm sure I had a suction abortion, but I was pretty far along, three or four months. I don't remember getting anything for pain. I was crying out....
>
> The doctor was rushing, and it seemed like he was just tearing me apart. Afterwards I felt so weak. I think the

weakness comes not just from the physical but from the emotional ordeal. In the recovery room the other girls looked white as sheets, and I thought, "I must look just as pale." I just felt ugly, having to sit there and wait for a half-hour before we could go.... We never talked about it. I guess it was denial; I just pushed it back in my mind.[1]

"Tearing me apart." That, in a phrase, is the devastation that abortion causes. It tears apart the bodies of unborn children, and it tears apart the bodies of their mothers. It places an act of violence at the center of the fundamental, vulnerable relationship between a mother and her child. It causes rifts between men and women, mothers and fathers. The promise of abortion—that it would set women free and make them equal, that it would improve our society—is nothing but a lie, a falsehood that has torn us all apart.

Abortion has enabled lethal discrimination in the womb, targeting unborn children of an "unwanted" sex and those diagnosed with a disability. Rather than supporting women in need, the supposedly "pro-choice" movement has revealed itself to be merely pro-abortion, opposing every effort to help pregnant mothers choose life for their babies. Abortion has corrupted our medical system, treating pregnancy as a disease to be cured and using tools meant for healing as lethal weapons. Abortion on demand, imposed by the highest court in our nation, has undermined the rule of law and constitutional self-government, turning our politics into a circus. Those who want to preserve *Roe v. Wade* and unlimited abortion at all costs have used judicial nominations as a political football and created a toxic mess out of the confirmation process. Because of how abortion has polarized our politics and corrupted Democratic politicians, citizens have become alienated from one of our major political parties and dependent on the other, even when they disagree with Republicans on other issues. Abortion has corrupted our culture—the popular culture that increasingly glorifies abortion, the legacy media outlets that cover abortion with obvious bias, the virtue-signaling corporations that promote abortion as good for business, and the social-media companies that use their moderating power to limit the spread of pro-life information.

The only proper response to the past five decades of destruction is to dismantle every part of the system that perpetuates abortion. As it has done since *Roe v. Wade*, the pro-life movement must work to make abortion not only illegal but also unthinkable. There are no simple solutions to bring about that goal, but there is plenty that each of us can do. Consider the immense power that even one maternity home or pregnancy-resource center has to transform the life of a mother in need, helping her reject the lie that abortion will solve her problems. One such mother, Mikaela, tells the story of discovering that she was pregnant just after starting college:

> I had a bright future ahead of me but, at 18 years old, I discovered I was pregnant. When I told my parents, they were shocked—and not in a good way.
>
> My dad suffered greatly from depression and insomnia in the months afterward, and my mom started having chronic migraines. My father was angry with me at first and wanted me to have an abortion. He would no longer allow me to live at home. My mother didn't agree with him and wanted to help me, but didn't have the resources on her own.
>
> I had nowhere to turn. My boyfriend wouldn't let me move in with him unless I agreed to an abortion. So I went to an abortion clinic but felt conflicted about it. My mother understood my doubts and found one of the maternity home programs across the country that support women facing pregnancy in difficult circumstances.

I was nine weeks pregnant when I reached Mary's Shelter in Virginia that September, and was able to live there until and after the birth of my baby.

The home I lived in operates out of a community of houses and actually allows women to stay for up to three years while they further their education or seek a career. I learned so much there that prepared me for my daughter's arrival and life in general, including basic cleaning, courtesy toward others and budgeting wisely. I pursued counseling for myself as well. Everyone at Mary's Shelter was incredibly supportive and one staff member in particular became almost a second mother to me.

Today, I'm grateful to say I have reconciled with my father who adores his granddaughter. And the baby's father is supportive and he loves his daughter. I love being a mom and I am attending college, with the goal of becoming a history teacher after graduation.[2]

Women like Mikaela deserve so much better than abortion, and babies like hers deserve to live. Creating a society in which every unborn child will be welcomed into the world is going to require major shifts in our law and our culture. In each domain, our efforts should prohibit the evil of abortion and affirm the goods of life and family. Making abortion illegal and unthinkable will require the work of politicians and policymakers, pregnancy-resource centers, churches, other groups that assist families in need, and each of us within our communities.

Of course, a few short pages are hardly enough space to solve the immense challenge ahead of the pro-life movement; here we sketch out only a few ideas that could fill an entire book. Much of what we offer should be a matter of charitable discussion among pro-lifers. We must agree on our final goal: abolition of abortion both through law and culture, a world where abortion is both illegal and inconceivable. But there are a multitude of ways to achieve it, and prudence will be necessary. Achieving consensus will be easier on the measures necessary to prohibit abortion—no pro-lifer can support lethal violence in the womb—but there is a legitimate diversity of views about which measures best address the so-called demand side of abortion. We should not establish litmus tests for what constitutes a "real" pro-life solution for any given cultural or legal proposal in this regard. Pro-lifers can hold a range of views on, for example, paid family leave or child tax credits. We should debate these policies on the merits, not use them to cast others out of the pro-life movement. All the while, we should keep in mind that the challenge of ending abortion requires a "both-and" approach on a number of levels, not an "either-or." We need plans for shifting our laws and our culture, efforts to care for babies and mothers, work from state and federal governments—and all of these efforts should aim at ending the supply of abortion and the demand for it.

After *Roe* and *Casey* are gone, states will scramble to respond. Pro-lifers should concentrate on advancing laws as protective of unborn children as possible, keeping in mind that we can't let the perfect be the enemy of the good. In many states, this will require patience and incrementalism, enacting more and more protections for the unborn over time while continuing to convince our fellow citizens that nothing short of full protection will satisfy the demands of justice.

When *Roe* and *Casey* are gone, abortion will remain legal in many states, either because they have "codified" a supposed right to abortion or because their state supreme court has invented such a right. Pro-lifers will need to undo these laws and rulings, as well as prevent them from being passed and invented in the future. In deep-blue states, pro-lifers may not be able to pass abortion restrictions at first, but we can focus on marginal improvements such as

conscience protections, ensuring that doctors don't have to participate in abortion, that the government doesn't fund abortions, and
that employers, insurers, and taxpayers don't have to cover them. In
California, for example, pro-abortion lawmakers are working to
require funding—including public spending—to reimburse the travel
expenses of women seeking abortions in the state. Pro-lifers will need
to aggressively oppose expansions such as this one. While advocating
laws that protect all unborn children, pro-lifers in these states can
continue what they already do so well: assisting women in need and
looking for opportunities to pass "compromise" bills, less protective
than we might prefer but better than what we have now.

There are also dozens of states with pro-life laws already on the
books, ready to take effect should the Court finally admit its mistake
in *Roe*. Public officials must enforce these laws, and pro-life citizens
must hold them accountable if they don't. In states with little legislation
one way or another on abortion, the pro-life movement should enact
pro-life policies that can take effect as soon as possible. It will be particularly important for pro-life legislators to focus on the new frontier
of abortion-rights activists: expanding reliance on chemical abortion,
prescribed via telemedicine, sent via mail, and self-administered by
women alone in their homes. In pro-life states especially, laws will be
needed to prevent cross-state transportation of abortion pills, protecting both unborn children and their mothers.

Though much pro-life progress will take place at the state level,
the federal government has an important role to play. Both Congress
and the president—and, by extension, executive agencies—have constitutional authority to protect unborn children from the violence of
abortion. That's the premise of the federal partial-birth abortion ban
and federal bills attempting to prohibit abortion after twenty weeks
of pregnancy. In a post-*Roe* America, there will be new possibilities
for abortion regulations via congressional statute and executive
action, because the Fourteenth Amendment empowers the federal

government to ensure that no person is deprived of life without the due process of law or denied the equal protection of the law. Litigators should press this line of argument in court, too.

We must remember that politics is the art of the possible; what Congress, the Court, and the president can accomplish depends on the votes and on who controls the White House. With prudence in mind, all of the following should be on the agenda, at a minimum: eliminating government subsidization of abortion businesses; strengthening conscience protections for health-care workers and taxpayers; and protecting unborn children and infants through existing legislation such as the Born-Alive Abortion Survivors Protection Act and the Pain-Capable Unborn Child Protection Act, which prohibits abortion after twenty weeks of pregnancy.[3] Pro-life legislators should also introduce a federal version of the heartbeat bills that many states have tried to enact. Even if it would serve only as a teaching and messaging bill for the time being, lawmakers should put forward legislation to abolish abortion entirely.

Until hearts and minds have shifted a great deal, there will be times when pro-lifers won't exercise total control over the federal government. Under a pro-abortion administration, a pro-life Congress should exercise rigorous oversight of executive agencies, which would likely protect abortion and taxpayer funding for abortion in any way they can. If pro-lifers are in the minority in Congress, they should work to block any legislation that includes abortion funding or that attempts to preserve the *Roe* status quo even after the Court's abortion jurisprudence is gone. In September 2021, shortly after the Texas heartbeat bill took effect and shortly before the Court heard oral arguments in *Dobbs*, the House of Representatives passed a bill to codify *Roe*. The bill died in the Senate, but it is sure to return—and pro-lifers must defeat it.

Pro-life presidential administrations, meanwhile, should work within the scope of their constitutional role to treat unborn children as persons. The executive branch should enforce existing conscience protections for pro-life doctors, employers, insurers, and other groups who might otherwise be coerced into providing or funding abortions. Abortion businesses should not receive funding through programs administered by executive agencies. Presidents should lobby Congress to defund abortion and protect conscience rights and should oppose efforts to codify legal abortion or fund abortion. Pro-life candidates at both the state and federal levels must be asked whether they'll follow through on these goals—dependent on which office they're seeking—if elected.

Another pro-life policy goal might be a constitutional amendment to ensure that unborn children are explicitly protected as persons under the Fourteenth Amendment, precluding pro-abortion politicians from legalizing abortion at the federal level. At first, working to pass such an amendment would largely be a messaging effort, but if enacted it would serve as a more permanent solution than federal laws and policies protecting unborn children, which could shift depending on which party controls the executive and legislative branches. Some legal scholars argue that the Fourteenth Amendment, on an originalist reading, already includes unborn children as legal persons under its protections.[4] As pro-life litigators work to persuade a majority of the Supreme Court of that view, pro-life legislators should work to enact an amendment explicitly stating that unborn children are persons under the Fourteenth Amendment and are entitled to its protections.

But even after our laws begin to change for the better, we will never fully curtail abortion until our society is able to recognize how much abortion harms all of us. We must shape a culture that helps the people around us reject the lie that abortion is any kind of solution to human brokenness and pain. It is impossible to overstate the importance of marriage and stable families in that project. Many women seek abortion because they lack support from the father of their child—indeed, because far too many men behave as though pregnancy is a woman's problem and abortion a woman's decision.[5] The breakdown of marriage and family since the sexual revolution, fueled by a false ideology that portrays freedom as mere license, has created conditions that make abortion appear like a solution to very real cultural ailments.[6]

Making abortion unthinkable will be possible only when our society finally comes to terms with the disaster of the sexual revolution. So long as we fail to reckon with the damage done by widespread acceptance of sex outside of marriage—whether in the form of hookup culture or adultery—there will continue to be demand for abortion. Abortion is the ultimate backstop for "free sex" because it enables adults to engage in sex solely for pleasure and without commitment, erasing the consequences—their child—by means of lethal violence. A recovery of a sound sexual culture is the ultimate foundation for a culture of life.

While there are no big-picture ways to immediately resolve these systemic problems, pro-lifers can shape a pro-life culture through the same avenues that abortion supporters are working to dominate. We can produce TV shows and music that celebrate life and that reject the logic of the sexual revolution. We suspect that, if they were well-crafted to avoid that hokey after-school-special feel, productions such as these would find a receptive audience—and an enterprising production studio and network would make a sizeable profit. More Americans than Hollywood executives realize hunger for entertainment that respects life and the family. Likewise, we should use our Facebook and Twitter accounts to promote the truth about abortion, write letters to the editor and op-eds, and use whatever means are at our disposal to persuade our neighbors—perhaps passing along a copy of this book. In all of these efforts, we have to focus not only on preventing abortion but on helping our fellow Americans to understand how evil abortion is.

More important, we have to show how good life is—particularly family life. This will require a commitment not only to opposing abortion but to rebuilding the family and rejecting the sexual revolution. For every abortion clinic in our country, there should be dozens of pregnancy-resource centers helping women reject abortion. Much of this project will be a continuation and expansion of what the pro-life movement has done for decades to support mothers in need. When laws protect the hundreds of thousands of unborn children killed by abortion each year, pregnancy-resource centers will have to expand dramatically to meet demand. What Mary's Shelter has done for women in Virginia should be multiplied everywhere.

We can't neglect the responsibility that each of us has on an individual level to build a culture of life, finding small ways to create the kind of pro-life society within which we want to live. Much of what we can do will depend on our state in life; none of us can do everything, but each of us can do something. We need men and women to commit to each other in marriage and then commit to their children—allowing their own family to be a witness to life. We will need pro-life doctors and journalists, lawmakers and ultrasound technicians, lawyers and engineers, parents and preachers and priests. Some of us might personally support a mother in need or welcome our own child in difficult circumstances. Some are called to give witness to life by counseling or praying on the sidewalk outside an abortion clinic. Others might volunteer at a pregnancy-resource center or offer donations to support its work. And finally, each of us must arm ourselves with courage, resolving to help our neighbors open their eyes to the truth of what abortion is and how it harms all of us.

Acknowledgments

We owe our gratitude to countless people who helped this project come into being, especially our agent Keith Urbahn and our publisher Tom Spence, without whom this book would not exist. Thank you to the Ethics and Public Policy Center, *National Review*, and Alliance Defending Freedom for their support of our research and writing. We are especially thankful to the many friends who reviewed some or all of our manuscript and who deserve credit for our finer points but no blame for any errors: Erika Bachiochi, Timothy Bradley, Charles Camosy, Mallory Carroll, Dan Casey, Josh Craddock, Joseph DeSanctis, Chuck Donovan, Kevin Donovan, Maureen Ferguson, Christina Francis, Rick Garnett, Robert P. George, Sherif Girgis, Denise Harle, Donna Harrison, Erin Hawley, Kathryn Jean Lopez, John McCormack, Calum Miller, Ramesh Ponnuru, Tara Sander Lee, Frank Scaturro, Carrie Severino, Tom Shakely, Carter Snead, Christopher Tollefson, Ian Tuttle, and Quentin Van Meter. To Nicholas Tomaino for lending his keen editor's eye to our final draft. To Nicholas Marr for all his help, including but not limited to marshalling our endnotes. And to Anna Anderson for holding down the fort (and the farm) while Ryan was toiling at the computer in the basement.

Notes

Introduction

1. Patty Knap, "The Remarkable Conversion of an Abortionist," *National Catholic Register*, April 14, 2016, https://www.ncregister.com/blog/the-remarkable-conversion-of-an-abortionist.

2. Carolee McGrath, "Converted Hearts," *Columbia* online edition, December 29, 2011, https://www.kofc.org/en/columbia/detail/2012_01_converted_hearts.html.

3. Ibid.

4. Robert P. George, "Bernard Nathanson: A Life Transformed by Truth," Public Discourse, February 27, 2011, https://www.thepublicdiscourse.com/2011/02/2806/.

5. Ibid.

6. Brief of Mother Teresa of Calcutta as Amicus Curiae Supporting Petitioners, *Loce v. New Jersey*, 630 A.2d 792 (N.J. Super. Ct. App. Div.), cert. denied, No. 93-1148 (February 28, 1994).

7. See O. Carter Snead, *What It Means to Be Human: The Case for the Body in Public Bioethics* (Cambridge, Massachusetts: Harvard University Press, 2020).

8. Brief for 240 Women Scholars and Professionals et. al as Amicus Curiae Supporting Petitioners at 23a–33a, *Dobbs v. Jackson Women's Health Organization*, No. 19-1392 (U.S. December 1, 2021) (Hereafter Brief for 240 Woman Scholars and Professionals).

9. See Erika Bachiochi, *The Rights of Women: Reclaiming a Lost Vision* (Notre Dame, Indiana: University of Notre Dame Press, 2021).

10. Frederica Mathewes-Greene, "When Abortion Suddenly Stopped Making Sense," *National Review*, January 22, 2016, https://www.nationalreview.com/2016/01/abortion-roe-v-wade-unborn-children-women-feminism-march-life/.

11. Eric Kniffin (@ekniffin), "For those unable to join us in person...," Twitter, January 7, 2022, 11:27 a.m., https://twitter.com/ekniffin/status/1479489889322348549?cxt=HHwWisC53eaNmogpAAAA.

Chapter One: Abortion Harms the Unborn Child

1. It wasn't just Ryan and Anna's ultrasound technician. Health-care professionals routinely use the word "baby" rather than "fetus" when referring to an unborn child, especially in the context of health risks to the baby. See Helena Anolak, Charlene Thornton, and Deborah Davis, "What's Wrong with Using the F Word? A Systematic Integrative Review of How the Fetus is Talked about in Situations of Fetal Demise or High Risk of Fetal Loss," *Midwifery* 79, no. 102537 (September 23, 2019), https://pubmed.ncbi.nlm.nih.gov/31580999/.

2. Biologists know that life begins at fertilization, too. Ninety-five percent of biologists affirm that a new organism is created at fertilization, including large majority of self-described "pro-choice" and even "very pro-choice" biologists. The same paper found that 65 percent of the public thinks that biologists are the experts on when life begins. See Steven Andrew Jacobs, "The Scientific Consensus on When a Human's Life Begins," *Issues in Law & Medicine* 36, no. 2 (2021): 226–29, https://papers.ssrn.com/sol3/papers.cfm?abstract_id=3973608.

3. See Robert P. George and Christopher Tollefsen, *Embryo: A Defense of Human Life* (New York: Doubleday, 2008); see also Maureen Condic, "When Does Human Life Begin? The Scientific Evidence and Terminology Revisited," *University of St. Thomas Journal of Law and Public Policy* 8, no. 1 (2013): 47–61; and see Maureen Condic, "The Origin of Human Life at Fertilization: Quotes Compiled from Medical Textbooks and Peer-Reviewed Scientific Literature," November 2017, https://bdfund.org/wp-content/uploads/2016/05/Condic-Sources-Embryology.pdf.

4. Keith Moore and TVN Persaud, *The Developing Human: Clinically Oriented Embryology*, 7th. ed. (Philadelphia, Pennsylvania: Saunders, 2003), 16.

5. With fraternal twins, two eggs are fertilized. In the case of identical, monozygotic twins, one fertilized egg later branches off into two human beings. See Donna Krasnewich, "Identical Twins," National Human Genome Research Institute, https://www.genome.gov/genetics-glossary/identical-twins; see also Maureen Condic, *Untangling Twinning* (Notre Dame, Indiana: University of Notre Dame Press, 2020).

6. Even in the case of monozygotic (identical) twins their DNA isn't 100 percent the same due to genetic mutations.

7. Alexandra DeSanctis, "CNN Contributor: 'When a Woman Is Pregnant, That Is Not a Human Being inside of Her,'" *National Review*, May 7, 2019, https://www.nationalreview.com/corner/cnn-contributor-when-a-woman-is-pregnant-that-is-not-a-human-being-inside-of-her/.

8. Christopher Kaczor, *The Ethics of Abortion: Women's Rights, Human Life, and the Question of Justice* (London: Routledge, 2010), 15.

9. Peter Singer, *Rethinking Life & Death: The Collapse of Our Traditional Ethics* (Cambridge: Cambridge University Press, 1994), 218.

10. Mary Anne Warren, "On the Moral and Legal Status of Abortion," *The Monist* 57, no. 4 (1973): 5.

11. Ibid., 6.

12. On these personhood arguments in general, and their application to abortion in particular, see Patrick Lee and Robert P. George, *Body-Self Dualism in Contemporary Ethics and Politics* (Cambridge: Cambridge University Press, 2007), 118–50.

13. Gilbert Ryle, *The Concept of Mind* (Chicago: University of Chicago Press, 1949), 17.

14. Edward Feser, *The Philosophy of Mind* (London: Oneworld Publications, 2005); Patrick Lee and Robert P. George, *Body-Self Dualism in Contemporary Ethics and Politics* (New York: Cambridge University Press, 2008); Robert P. George and Christopher Tollefson, *Embryo: A Defense of Human Life* (New York: Doubleday, 2008); David Braine, *The Human Person* (Eugene, Oregon: Wipf and Stock Publishers, 1994).

15. Warren, "On the Moral and Legal Status of Abortion," 6.

16. See, for example, David Strauss, "Abortion, Toleration, and Moral Uncertainty," *The Supreme Court Review* (1992); see also Barbara Billauer, "Abortion, Moral Law, and the First Amendment: The Conflict Between Fetal Rights & Freedom of Religion," *William & Mary Journal of Women and the Law* 23, no. 2 (2017).

17. Ronald Dworkin, *Life's Dominion: An Argument about Abortion, Euthanasia, and Individual Freedom* (New York: Vintage, 1994), 26.

18. Linda Greenhouse, "Let's Not Forget the Establishment Clause," *New York Times*, May 23, 2019, https://www.nytimes.com/2019/05/23/opinion/abortion-supreme-court-religion.html.

19. Judith Jarvis Thomson, "A Defense of Abortion," *Philosophy & Public Affairs* 1 (1971).

20. For one of the first responses to Thomson's article, see John Finnis, "The Rights and Wrongs of Abortion: A Reply to Judith Thomson," *Philosophy & Public Affairs* 2, no. 2 (Winter 1973): 117–45, https://www.jstor.org/stable/2265137. For another response see Patrick Lee, *Abortion and Unborn Human Life*.

21. For instance, the Royal College of Obstetricians and Gynaecologists in the United Kingdom states that "in cases where the fetal abnormality is not lethal or the abortion is not for fetal abnormality and is being undertaken after 21 weeks and 6 days of gestation, failure to perform feticide could result in a live birth and survival, which contradicts the intention of the abortion." See Royal College of Obstetricians and Gynaecologists, "Termination of Pregnancy for Fetal Abnormality in England, Scotland and Wales," May 2010, 4, https://rcog.org.uk/media/21lfvl0e/terminationpregnancyreport18may2010.pdf.

22. To engage the philosophical debate further, in those situations where one could truly claim merely to want to detach from the unborn child—intending the child's death neither as a means nor an end—the procedure still would entail the use of unjustified lethal force. Foreseen but unintended killing still must be justified, as it is in the case of a cancerous uterus or ectopic pregnancy, or in the case of lethal force used in justified self-defense. But the lack of proportionality between nine months of pregnancy and letting your own child die render this removal unjustified.

23. Lawrence B. Finer et al., "Reasons U.S. Women Have Abortions: Quantitative and Qualitative," *Perspectives on Sexual and Reproductive Health* 37, no. 3 (2005): 113.

24. As a legal matter, exceptions for rape may be a political necessity to enact otherwise protective laws.

25. Alexandra DeSanctis, "Refuting the 'Forced Birth' Smear," *National Review*, December 2, 2021, https://www.nationalreview.com/2021/12/refuting-the-forced-birth-smear/.

26. See Transcript of Oral Argument, *Dobbs v. Jackson Women's Health Organization* (No. 19-1392), at 109–10.

27. The Editors, "An Appalling Attack on Adoption," *National Review*, December 7, 2021, https://www.nationalreview.com/2021/12/an-appalling-attack-on-adoption/.

Chapter Two: Abortion Harms Women and the Family

1. Nancy Mann, foreword in *Aborted Women, Silent No More*, by David Reardon (Chicago: Loyola University Press, 1987), xii–xiii.

2. Betsey Stevenson and Justin Wolfers, "The Paradox of Declining Female Happiness," *American Economic Journal: Economic Policy, American Economic Association* 1, no. 2 (2009): 27, https://www.nber.org/papers /w14969.

3. Sue Ellen Browder, *Sex and the Catholic Feminist* (San Francisco: Ignatius, 2020), 81–89.

4. Shulamith Firestone, *The Dialectic of Sex: The Case for Feminist Revolution* (New York: Farrar, Straus & Giroux, 2003), 11.

5. Ibid., 11.

6. Alexandra DeSanctis, "The True Goal of Feminism," *National Review*, May 5, 2017, https://www.nationalreview.com/2017/05/jill-filipovic-h-sp ot-feminism-hedonism-statism-sexual-revolution-abortion/.

7. See Alexandra DeSanctis, "Leave the Children Out of It," *National Review*, January 9, 2019, https://www.nationalreview.com/2019/01/sho ut-your-abortion-activist-group-video-children/.

8. Jill Filipovic, *The H-Spot: The Feminist Pursuit of Happiness* (New York: Nation Books, 2017), 87.

9. Ibid., 272.

10. See Erika Bachiochi, *The Rights of Women: Reclaiming a Lost Vision* (Notre Dame, Indiana: University of Notre Dame Press, 2021), 247–78; see also Bachiochi, "Women, Sexual Asymmetry, and Catholic Teaching," *Christian Bioethics* 19, no. 2 (2013), https://papers.ssrn.com/sol3/papers .cfm?abstract_id=2175332.

11. *Lawrence v. Texas*, 539 U.S. 558, 588 (2003) (Scalia, J., dissenting).

12. *Planned Parenthood v. Casey*, 505 U.S. 833, 856 (1992).

13. *Casey*, 505 U.S. 833, 928 (Blackmun, J., concurring in part, concurring in the judgment in part, and dissenting in part).

14. Brief for 240 Women Scholars and Professionals.

15. Melanie Israel, "A New Report Shows the U.S. Abortion Rate Is Declining. Here Are 4 Things You Need to Know," Heritage Foundation, September 19, 2019, https://www.heritage.org/life/commentary/new-report-shows -the-us-abortion-rate-declining-here-are-4-things-you-need-know.

16. "Women's Earnings: The Pay Gap (Quick Take)," Catalyst, March 23, 2021, https://www.catalyst.org/research/womens-earnings-the-pay-gap/.

17. Jessica Bryant, "Women Continue to Outnumber Men in College Completion," BestColleges.com, November 19, 2021, https://www.bestc olleges.com/news/analysis/2021/11/19/women-complete-college-more-th an-men/.

18. See Mark J. Perry, "Women Earned Majority of Doctoral Degrees in 2019 for 11th Straight Year and Outnumber Men in Grad School 141 to 100," American Enterprise Institute, October 15, 2020, https://www.aei.org/ca rpe-diem/women-earned-majority-of-doctoral-degrees-in-2019-for-11th -straight-year-and-outnumber-men-in-grad-school-141-to-100/.

19. Erika Bachiochi, "The Troubling Ideals at the Heart of Abortion Rights," *The Atlantic*, January 24, 2020, https://www.theatlantic.com/ideas/arch ive/2020/01/equality-autonomy-abortion/605356/.

20. Erika Bachiochi, "Reclaiming Feminism from the Logic of the Market," *Newsweek*, July 15, 2021, https://www.newsweek.com/reclaiming-femi nism-logic-market-opinion-1607303.

21. Catherine Glenn Foster, "I Was Pressured to Abort My Children. For My First Baby, I Gave In," *USA Today*, October 28, 2020, https://www.usat oday.com/story/opinion/voices/2020/10/28/abortion-amy-coney-barrett -genetic-testing-life-column/3745396001/.

22. Brief for 240 Women Scholars and Professionals, at 39.

23. George A. Akerlof and Janet L. Yellen, "New Mothers, Not Married: Technology Shock, the Demise of Shotgun Marriage, and the Increase in Out-of-Wedlock Births," Brookings Institution, September 1, 1996, https://www.brookings.edu/articles/new-mothers-not-married-technolo gy-shock-the-demise-of-shotgun-marriage-and-the-increase-in-out-of-we dlock-births.

24. Alexandra DeSanctis, "The Pro-Choice Movement Should Denounce Forced Abortion," *National Review*, August 31, 2017, https://www.nati onalreview.com/corner/abortion-choice-pro-abortion-left-should-denou nce-coercion/.

25. Anne Nordal Broen et al., "Reasons for Induced Abortion and Their Relation to Women's Emotional Distress," *General Hospital Psychiatry* 27, no. 1 (January–February 2005): 36–43, https://pubmed.ncbi.nlm.nih .gov/15694217/.

26. M. Antonio Biggs, Heather Gould, and Diana Foster, "Understanding Why Women Seek Abortions in the US," *BMC Women's Health* 13, no. 29 (2013), https://bmcwomenshealth.biomedcentral.com/articles/10.1186/1472-6874-13-29.

27. Robert Lerman, "The Impact of the Changing US Family Structure on Child Poverty and Income Inequality," *Economica* 63, no. 250 (1996): 119–39.

28. Recent studies have shown that women will have, on average, one child less than they want. See Lyman Stone, "American Women Are Having Fewer Children Than They'd Like," *New York Times*, February 13, 2018, https://www.nytimes.com/2018/02/13/upshot/american-fertility-is-falling-short-of-what-women-want.html.

29. See O. Carter Snead, *What It Means to Be Human: The Case for the Body in Public Bioethics* (Cambridge, Massachusetts: Harvard University Press, 2020), 70–74.

30. Conor Friedersdorf, "Why Dr. Kermit Gosnell's Trial Should Be a Front-Page Story," *The Atlantic*, April 12, 2013, https://www.theatlantic.com/national/archive/2013/04/why-dr-kermit-gosnells-trial-should-be-a-front-page-story/274944/.

31. Enjoli Francis and Terry Moran, "Abortion Doctor Kermit Gosnell Guilty of First Degree Murder," ABC News, May 13, 2013, https://abcnews.go.com/US/abortion-doctor-kermit-gosnell-guilty-degree-murder/story?id=19168967.

32. Alexandra DeSanctis, "Gosnell's Labyrinth of Terrors—a New Book Shines Light on His Practice and the Abortion Industry," *National Review*, February 3, 2017, https://www.nationalreview.com/2017/02/kermit-gosnell-untold-story-book-serial-killer-abortion/.

33. Ann McElhinney and Phelim McAleer, *Gosnell: The Untold Story of America's Most Prolific Serial Killer* (Washington, D.C.: Regnery, 2017), 15–16.

34. Ibid.

35. Ibid., 23.

36. See Grand Jury Report, *In re County Investigating Grand Jury XXIII*, No. 0009901-2008 (1st Jud. Dist. Pa. Jan. 14, 2011), https://cdn.cnsnews.com/documents/Gosnell,%20Grand%20Jury%20Report.pdf.

37. Americans United for Life (AUL), *Unsafe: America's Abortion Industry Endangers Women* (2021), 27, https://aul.org/wp-content/uploads/2021/02/AUL-Unsafe-2021.pdf.

38. Karima Sajadi-Ernazarova and Christopher L. Martinez, "Abortion Complications," National Center for Biotechnology Information, 2021, https://www.ncbi.nlm.nih.gov/books/NBK430793/.

39. See, for example, Lila Rose and Donna Harrison, "Abortion Is Never Medically Necessary," *Washington Examiner,* February 26, 2019, https://www.washingtonexaminer.com/opinion/op-eds/abortion-is-never-medically-necessary.

40. Suzanna Zane et al., "Abortion-Related Mortality in the United States: 1998–2010," Obstetrics & Gynecology 126, no. 2 (2015), https://doi.org/10.1097/AOG.0000000000000945.

41. AUL, *Unsafe.*

42. Alexis Shaw, "Chicago Woman's Family Lawyers Up after Abortion-Related Death," ABC News, July 24, 2012, https://abcnews.go.com/US/chicago-womans-family-lawyers-abortion-related-death/story?id=16845276.

43. Office of the Medical Examiner, "Report of Postmortem Examination for Tonya Reaves," Cook County Health Department (Chicago, Illinois), July 21, 2012, http://operationrescue.org/pdfs/Reaves%20Autopsy%20Report.pdf.

44. Amanda Marcotte, "The Death of Tonya Reaves Is Not an Argument for Banning Abortion," Slate, July 26, 2012, https://slate.com/human-interest/2012/07/tonya-reaves-her-death-is-not-an-argument-for-banning-abortion.html; see also Irin Carmon, "Tonya Reaves' Death: Right-Wing Abortion Exploitation," Salon, July 26, 2012, https://www.salon.com/2012/07/26/tonya_reaves_death_right_wing_abortion_exploitation/.

45. Shaw, "Chicago Woman's Family Lawyers Up."

46. Planned Parenthood, "The Abortion Pill," https://www.plannedparenthood.org/learn/abortion/the-abortion-pill.

47. Michael J. New, "Why Did the Abortion Rate Increase in 2018?," *National Review,* January 18, 2021, https://www.nationalreview.com/corner/why-did-the-abortion-rate-increase-in-2018/; see also Michael J. New, "New CDC Data Shows Slight Abortion Rate Increase in 2019," *National*

Review, November 29, 2021, https://www.nationalreview.com/corner/new-cdc-data-shows-slight-abortion-rate-increase-in-2019/.

48. Katherine Kortsmit et al., "Abortion Surveillance—United States, 2019," *Surveillance Summaries* 70, no. 9 (November 2021): 1–29, https://www.cdc.gov/mmwr/volumes/70/ss/ss7009a1.htm.

49. Rachel K. Jones et al., "Medication Abortion Now Accounts for More Than Half of All US Abortions," Guttmacher Institute, Febraury 24, 2022, https://www.guttmacher.org/article/2022/02/medication-abortion-now-accounts-more-half-all-us-abortions.

50. Planned Parenthood, "The Abortion Pill."

51. AUL, *Unsafe*, 49.

52. Ibid., 46.

53. World Health Organization, Safe Abortion: Technical and Policy Guidance for Health Systems, 2nd ed. (WHO: 2012): 35, http://apps.who.int/iris/bitstream/handle/10665/70914/9789241548434_eng.pdf?sequence=1.

54. Percuity Limited, "Hospital Treatments for Complications from Early Medical Abortion," February 22, 2021, https://percuity.files.wordpress.com/2021/02/complications-from-ema-kd210211.pdf.

55. "Parliament Votes to Make Telemedicine for Early Medical Abortion Permanent in England," Royal College of Obstetricians and Gynecologists, March 31, 2022, https://www.rcog.org.uk/news/parliament-votes-to-make-telemedicine-for-early-medical-abortion-permanent-in-england/.

56. Laura J. Lederer and Christopher A. Wetzel, "The Health Consequences of Sex Trafficking and Their Implications for Identifying Victims in Healthcare Facilities," *Annals of Health Law* 23 (2014): 77, https://www.icmec.org/wp-content/uploads/2015/10/Health-Consequences-of-Sex-Trafficking-and-Implications-for-Identifying-Victims-Lederer.pdf.

57. Alexandra DeSanctis, "Planned Parenthood's Continued Failure to Report Evidence of Child-Sex Trafficking," *National Review*, January 18, 2017, https://www.nationalreview.com/2017/01/planned-parenthood-child-sex-trafficking-crimes-still-unreported/.

58. Ibid.

59. Kathi Aultman et al., "Deaths and Severe Adverse Events after the Use of Mifepristone as an Abortifacient from September 2000 to February 2019," *Issues in Law & Medicine* 36, no. 1 (2021): 4, https://issuesinlawandme

dicine.com/wp-content/uploads/2021/01/Deaths-and-Severe-Adverse-Ev
ents-after-the-use-of-Mifepristone-as-an-Abortifacient-from-September
-2000-to-February-2019-copy5.pdf.

60. Patricia Anderson et. al., "Incidence of Emergency Department Visits and
Complications after Abortion," *Obsetrics and Gynecology* 125, no. 1
(2015): 175–83, https://journals.lww.com/greenjournal/Fulltext/2015/01
000/Incidence_of_Emergency_Department_Visits_and.29.aspx.

61. Ea Mulligan and Hayley Messenger, "Mifepristone in South Australia,"
Australian Family Physician 40, no. 5 (2011): 343, https://www.racgp.org
.au/download/documents/AFP/2011/May/201105mulligan.pdf.

62. Marie Stopes Australia, "Impact Report 2020," https://www.mariestop
es.org.au/wp-content/uploads/MSA-Impact-Report-2020.pdf.

63. Maarit Niinimäki et al., "Immediate Complications after Medical
Compared with Surgical Termination of Pregnancy," *Obstetrics &
Gynecology* 114, no. 4 (2009), http://www.ncbi.nlm.nih.gov/pubmed/19
888037.

64. James Studnicki et. al, "A Longitudinal Cohort Study of Emergency Room
Utilization following Mifepristone Chemical and Surgical Abortions,
1999–2015," *Health Services Research and Managerial Epidemiology* 8
(2021), https://journals.sagepub.com/doi/full/10.1177/2333392821105
3965.

65. Emphasis added. Baroness Stroud, "Women's Health Strategy—Statement,"
March 9, 2021, https://www.theyworkforyou.com/lords/?id=2021
-03-09a.1487.2.

66. Lord Bethell, "Women's Health Strategy—Statement," March 9, 2021,
https://www.theyworkforyou.com/lords/?id=2021-03-09a.1487.3

67. Abortion Data Reporting Bill, S. __ , 116th Congress (2019); see Tom
Cotton, "Cotton, Ernst Introduce Legislation to Hold States Accountable
for Botched Abortions," October 3, 2019, https://www.cotton.senate.gov
/news/press-releases/cotton-ernst-introduce-legislation-to-hold-states-acc
ountable-for-botched-abortions.

68. AUL, *Unsafe*, 44–50.

69. Laurie McGinley and Katie Sheperd, "FDA Eliminates Key Restriction
on Abortion Pill as Supreme Court Weighs Case That Challenges Roe v.
Wade," *Washington Post*, December 16, 2021, https://www.washington
post.com/health/2021/12/16/abortion-pill-fda/.

70. Alexandra DeSanctis, "Doctors Pioneer a Way to Halt Unwanted Chemical Abortions," *National Review*, April 13, 2021, https://www.na tionalreview.com/2021/04/doctors-pioneer-a-way-to-halt-unwanted-che mical-abortions/; see also Steven J. Condly et al., "A Case Series Detailing the Successful Reversal of the Effects of Mifepristone Using Progesterone," *Issues in Law and Medicine* 33, no. 1 (Spring 2018): 21–31, https://pubm ed.ncbi.nlm.nih.gov/30831017/.

71. American Association of Pro-Life Obstetricians and Gynecologists, "Committee Opinion 8: Abortion & Breast Cancer," January 5, 2020, https://aaplog.org/wp-content/uploads/2020/01/FINAL-CO-8-Abortion -Breast-Cancer-1.9.20.pdf.

72. Breast Cancer Prevention Institute, "Epidemiologic Studies: Induced Abortion and Breast Cancer Risk," April 2020, https://www.bcpinstitute .org/uploads/1/1/5/1/115111905/bcpi-factsheet-epidemiol-studies_2020 .pdf.

73. Clarke Forsythe, "The Medical Assumption at the Foundation of *Roe v. Wade* and Its Implications for Women's Health," *Washington & Lee Law Review* 71 (2014): 827, https://scholarlycommons.law.wlu.edu/wlulr/vol 71/iss2/8.

74. "Myths about Abortion and Breast Cancer," Planned Parenthood, 2013, https://www.plannedparenthood.org/uploads/filer_public/af/1a/af1ae95f -de81-43dd-91a3-470043b06dce/myths_about_abortion_and_breast_ca ncer.pdf.

75. Michael J. New and Donna Harrison, "New Report Misleads on the Health Risks of Abortion for Women," *National Review*, March 28, 2018, https://www.nationalreview.com/2018/03/abortion-safety-statisti cs-study-ignores-risks-women/.

76. American Association of Pro-Life Obstetricians and Gynecologists, "Committee Opinion 8: Abortion & Breast Cancer."

77. Email from Dr. Donna Harrison to authors.

78. Richard E. Behrman and Adrienne Butler, eds., *Preterm Birth: Causes, Consequences, and Prevention* (Washington, D.C.: National Academies Press, 2007), 625.

79. Jelle Schaaf et al., "Ethnic and Racial Disparities in the Risk of Preterm Birth: a Systematic Review and Meta-Analysis," *American Journal of*

Perinatology 30, no. 6 (2013), https://pubmed.ncbi.nlm.nih.gov/23059
494/.

80. Prakesh S. Shah and J. Zao, "Induced Termination of Pregnancy and Low
Birthweight and Preterm Birth: A Systematic Review and Meta-Analyses,"
International Journal of Obstetrics & Gynaecology, 116, no. 11 (2009):
1425–42, https://obgyn.onlinelibrary.wiley.com/doi/10.1111/j.1471-0528
.2009.02278.x.

81. American Association of Pro-Life Obstetricians and Gynecologists,
"APPLOG Policy Statement: The Women's Health Protection Act of
2021," December 30, 2019, https://aaplog.org/PB7.

82. American Association of Pro-Life Obstetricians and Gynecologists,
"Abortion and Risks of Preterm Birth," Practice Bulletin No. 5, November
2019, https://aaplog.org/wp-content/uploads/2019/12/FINAL-PRACTI
CE-BULLETIN-5-Abortion-Preterm-Birth.pdf.

83. Tracy Manuck, "Racial and Ethnic Differences in Preterm Birth: A
complex, Multifactorial Problem," *Seminars in Perinatology*, 41, no. 8
(2017): 511–18, doi:10.1053/j.semperi.2017.08.010.

84. Rebecca J. Rosen, "Consider the Coat Hanger," *The Atlantic*, August 23,
2012, https://www.theatlantic.com/technology/archive/2012/08/consider
-the-coat-hanger/261413/.

85. Carli Pierson, "My Great-Grandmother Died from an Illegal Abortion.
Her Story Could Be One You Know Soon," *USA Today*, November 1,
2021, https://www.usatoday.com/story/opinion/voices/2021/11/01/supre
me-court-texas-abortion-endanger-women/6235379001/.

86. Michael J. New, "How the Legal Status of Abortion Impacts Abortion
Rates," Charlotte Lozier Institute, May 23, 2018, https://lozierinstitute
.org/how-the-legal-status-of-abortion-impacts-abortion-rates/; Diana
Greene Foster, "Stop Saying That Making Abortion Illegal Won't Stop
People from Having Them," Rewire News Group, October 4, 2018,
https://rewirenewsgroup.com/article/2018/10/04/stop-saying-that-maki
ng-abortion-illegal-doesnt-stop-them/.

87. Caroline Kitchener, "With Most Abortions Illegal in Texas, Crisis
Pregnancy Centers See an Opportunity," The Lily, September 4, 2021,
https://www.thelily.com/with-most-abortions-illegal-in-texas-crisis-preg
nancy-centers-see-an-opportunity/.

88. Kim Roberts, "Pregnancy Centers See Increase in Call Volume, Client Appointments after Texas' Heartbeat Act Passage," *The Texan*, September 23, 2021, https://thetexan.news/pregnancy-centers-see-increase-in-call-vo lume-client-appointments-after-texas-heartbeat-act-passage/.

89. Casey Parks, "What Happens When People in Texas Can't Get Abortions: 'Diapers Save a Lot More Babies than Ultrasounds,'" *Washington Post*, November 13, 2021, https://www.washingtonpost.com/dc-md-va/2021 /11/13/san-antonio-pregnancy-center-texas-abortion-ban/.

90. Carrie Baker and Carly Thomsen, "Crisis Pregnancy Centers Endanger Women's Health—with Taxpayer Dollars and without Oversight," *Ms. Magazine*, October 29, 2021, https://msmagazine.com/2021/10/29/crisis -pregnancy-centers-cpc-fake-abortion-clinic-report/.

91. Clarke Forsythe, *Abuse of Discretion: The Inside Story of Roe v. Wade* (New York: Encounter, 2013).

92. Glenn Kessler, "Planned Parenthood's False Stat: 'Thousands' of Women Died Every Year before Roe," *Washington Post*, May 29, 2019, https:// www.washingtonpost.com/politics/2019/05/29/planned-parenthoods-fa lse-stat-thousands-women-died-every-year-before-roe/.

93. Louis M. Hellman and Jack A. Pritchard, eds., *Williams Obstetrics*, 520.

94. Forsythe, *Abuse of Discretion*, 63.

95. Elard Koch et al., "Abortion Legislation, Maternal Healthcare, Fertility, Female Literacy, Sanitation, Violence against Women and Maternal Deaths: A Natural Experiment in 32 Mexican States," *The BMJ* 23, no. 5 (2015), https://pubmed.ncbi.nlm.nih.gov/25712817/.

96. Margaret Hogan et al., "Maternal Mortality for 181 Countries, 1980– 2008: A Systematic Analysis of Progress towards Millennium Development Goal 5," *Lancet* 375, no. 9726 (2010), https://pubmed.ncbi.nlm.nih.gov /20382417/.

97. Calum Miller, "Backstreet Abortion Deaths: Not as Common or Preventable as Thought," *Journal of Medical Ethics* blog, November 1, 2021, https://blogs.bmj.com/medical-ethics/2021/11/01/backstreet-abor tion-deaths-not-as-common-or-preventable-as-thought/.

98. *June Medical Services LLC v. Russo*, 591 U.S. __ (2020).

99. *June Medical*, 591 U.S. slip op. at 7 (Alito, J., dissenting).

100. Steven Aden, "Justices Will Decide If Abortionists Can Sue on Patients' Behalf to Overturn Patient-Protection Rules," *Washington Examiner*,

March 3, 2020, https://www.washingtonexaminer.com/opinion/op-eds /justices-will-decide-if-abortionists-can-sue-on-patients-behalf-to-overtu rn-patient-protection-rules.

101. Alexandra DeSanctis, "Planned Parenthood Sues Montana over Four Pro-Life Laws," *National Review*, August 20, 2021, https://www.nation alreview.com/corner/planned-parenthood-sues-montana-over-four-pro-li fe-laws/.

102. Lindy West, "I Set up #ShoutYourAbortion because I am Not Sorry, and I Will Not Whisper," *The Guardian*, September 22, 2015, https://www .theguardian.com/commentisfree/2015/sep/22/i-set-up-shoutyouraborti on-because-i-am-not-sorry-and-i-will-not-whisper.

103. "I Took the Abortion Pill," Heartbeats, February 20, 2020, https://heart beats.org/2020/02/20/i-took-the-abortion-pill/.

104. Vincent Rue et al., "Induced Abortion and Traumatic Stress: A Preliminary Comparison of American and Russian Women," *Medical Science Monitor* 10, no. 10 (2004): SR9, https://www.medscimonit.com/abstract/index/id Art/11784.

105. Emphasis added. Declaration of Aaron Kheriaty, M.D., at 2, *Jackson v. Women's Health Organization v. Dobbs*, No. 3:18-CV-171 (S.D.MI. 2019).

106. Ibid., at 3.

107. As a result of non-responses and drop-outs, the final survey included only a small percentage of the women who began the study, which increased the possibility of self-selection bias toward women who were less affected by having an abortion. Women who dropped out of the study were probably more likely to have encountered later psychological problems than women who continued to participate. The cohort also excluded demographic factors known to increase the risk of adverse mental-health outcomes, such as the stage of pregnancy at which a woman obtained an abortion. There is a clear correlation, for instance, between abortions later in pregnancy and a higher rate of adverse mental-health outcomes. See David C. Reardon, "The Embrace of the Proabortion Turnaway Study: Wishful Thinking? or Willful Deception?" *Linacre Quarterly* 85, no. 3 (2018): 204–12.

108. Priscilla K. Coleman, "Abortion and Mental Health: Quantitative Synthesis and Analysis of Research Published 1995–2009," *British Journal*

of Psychiatry 199, no. 3 (2011): 180–86, https://pubmed.ncbi.nlm.nih.gov /21881096/.

109. See American Association of Pro-Life Obstetricians and Gynecologists, "Abortion and Mental Health," Practice Bulletin No. 7, December 2019, https://aaplog.org/wp-content/uploads/2019/12/FINAL-Abortion-Ment al-Health-PB7.pdf.

110. David M. Fergusson, L. John Horwood, and Joseph M. Boden, "Does Abortion Reduce the Mental Health Risks of Unwanted or Unintended Pregnancy? A Re-Appraisal of the Evidence," *Australian & New Zealand Journal of Psychiatry* 47, no. 9 (2013): 819–27.

Chapter Three: Abortion Harms Equality and Choice

1.   Catherine Glenn Foster, "I Was Pressured to Abort My Children. For My First Baby, I Gave In," *USA Today*, October 28, 2020, https:// www.usatoday.com/story/opinion/voices/2020/10/28/abortion-amy-coney-barrett-genetic-testing-life-column/3745396001/.

2.   Ibid.

3.   Ibid.

4.   "Our History," Planned Parenthood, https://www.plannedparenthood .org/about-us/who-we-are/our-history.

5.   New York University's Margaret Sanger Papers Project, "Margaret Sanger Answers Questions on Abortion—an MSPP Exclusive," Newsletter no. 60, Spring 2012, https://sanger.hosting.nyu.edu/articles/ms_abortion/.

6.   See generally G. E. Allen, "Eugenics and American Social History," *Genome* 31, no. 2 (1989): 885–89. https://pubmed.ncbi.nlm.nih.gov/269 8847/.

7.   Margaret Sanger, "Birth Control and Racial Betterment," *Birth Control Review* 3, no. 2 (1919): 11–12.

8.   Kevin Williamson, "Planned Parenthood's Century of Brutality," *National Review*, June 19, 2017, https://www.nationalreview.com/2017/06/plann ed-parenthoods-brutal-century/.

9.   Ibid.

10. Ibid.

11. Ibid.

12. *Buck v. Bell,* 274 U.S. 200, 205 (1927).

13. *Buck,* 274 U.S., at 207.

14. See Mark DeWolfe Howe, *Holmes-Laski Letters: The Correspondence of Mr. Justice Holmes and Harold J. Laski 1916–1935* (Cambridge, Massachusetts: Harvard University Press, 1953).

15. Emily Bazelon, "The Place of Women on Court," *New York Times Magazine*, July 7, 2009, https://www.nytimes.com/2009/07/12/magazine/12ginsburg-t.html.

16. Jessica Weisberg, "Remembering Ruth Bader Ginsburg in Her Own Words," *Elle*, September 21, 2020, https://www.elle.com/culture/career-politics/interviews/a14788/supreme-court-justice-ruth-bader-ginsburg/.

17. Jonathan Van Maren, "This Is the Alt-Right: Richard Spencer's Horrifying Abortion Rant," The Bridgehead, March 21, 2017, https://thebridgehead.ca/2017/03/21/this-is-the-alt-right-richard-spencers-horrifying-abortion-rant/.

18. Ibid.

19. Elliot Kaufman, "The Alt-Right Carries on Margaret Sanger's Legacy of Eugenics," *National Review*, August 22, 2017, https://www.nationalreview.com/2017/08/alt-right-abortion-richard-spencer-upholds-margaret-sanger-eugenicist-legacy/.

20. Alexis McGill Johnson, "I'm the Head of Planned Parenthood. We're Done Making Excuses for Our Founder," *New York Times*, April 17, 2021, https://www.nytimes.com/2021/04/17/opinion/planned-parenthood-margaret-sanger.html.

21. Nikita Stewart, "Planned Parenthood in N.Y. Disavows Margaret Sanger over Eugenics," *New York Times*, July 21, 2020, https://www.nytimes.com/2020/07/21/nyregion/planned-parenthood-margaret-sanger-eugenics.html.

22. "PPFA Margaret Sanger Award Winners: Recipients 1966–2015," Planned Parenthood, https://www.plannedparenthood.org/about-us/newsroom/campaigns/ppfa-margaret-sanger-award-winners.

23. Diana Chandler, "Benjamin Watson Calls on Planned Parenthood to End Sanger Legacy of Abortion," Baptist Press, April 20, 2021, https://www.baptistpress.com/resource-library/news/benjamin-watson-calls-on-planned-parenthood-to-end-sanger-legacy-of-abortion/.

24. Radiance Foundation, "Lack of Access," 2020, https://theradiancefoundation.org/wp-content/uploads/2014/04/lack-of-access-2020-copy.pdf.

25. Kortsmit et al., "Abortion Surveillance—United States, 2019," 6.

26. Susan A. Cohen, "Abortion and Women of Color: The Bigger Picture," *Guttmacher Policy Review* 11, no. 3 (2008): 2, https://www.guttmacher .org/gpr/2008/08/abortion-and-women-color-bigger-picture.

27. Radiance Foundation, "Lack of Access."

28. Jason L. Riley, "Let's Talk about the Black Abortion Rate," *Wall Street Journal*, July 10, 2018, https://www.wsj.com/articles/lets-talk-about-the -black-abortion-rate-1531263697.

29. Kortsmit et al., "Abortion Surveillance—United States, 2019," 6.

30. Cohen, "Abortion and Women of Color: The Bigger Picture," 3.

31. Alexandra DeSanctis, "The Pro-Life Movement You've Never Heard Of," *National Review*, April 6, 2020, https://www.nationalreview.com/maga zine/2020/04/06/the-pro-life-movement-youve-never-heard-of/.

32. Ibid.

33. Laura Bassett, "The Anti-Abortion Movement Was Always Built on Lies," *GQ*, May 20, 2020, https://www.gq.com/story/jane-roe-anti-abortion-lies.

34. Noah Smith, "OK, who's going to be the first to let conservatives know…," Twitter, December 1, 2021, 11:08 p.m., https://twitter.com/No ahpinion/status/1466258004865470464.

35. See P. R. Lockhart, "'Abortion as Black Genocide': Inside the Black Anti-Abortion Movement," Vox, January 19, 2018, https://www.vox.com/ide ntities/2018/1/19/16906928/black-anti-abortion-movement-yoruba-rich en-medical-racism; see also Issues4Life, https://issues4life.org/s4life.html.

36. Mark Joseph Stern, "Conservative Judges Are Manipulating the History of Eugenics to Overturn Roe v. Wade," Slate, April 15, 2021, https://slate .com/news-and-politics/2021/04/sixth-circuit-clarence-thomas-abortion -eugenics.html.

37. Fengqing Chao et al., "Systematic Assessment of the Sex Ratio at Birth for All Countries and Estimation of National Imbalances and Regional Reference Levels," *Proceedings of the National Academy of Sciences* 116, no. 19 (2019): 9303–11.

38. Fengqing Chao et al., "Projecting Sex Imbalances at Birth at Global, Regional and National Levels from 2021 to 2100: Scenario-Based Bayesian Probabilistic Projections of the Sex Ratio at Birth and Missing Female Births Based on 3.26 Billion Birth Records," *BMJ Global Health* (2021).

39.   Nicholas Eberstadt, "The Global War against Baby Girls," *New Atlantis,* Fall 2011, https://www.thenewatlantis.com/publications/the-global-war -against-baby-girls.

40.   Julian Quinones and Arijeta Lajka, "'What Kind of Society Do You Want to Live in?': Inside the Country Where Down Syndrome Is Disappearing," CBS News, August 14, 2017, http://www.cbsnews.com/news/down-syn drome-iceland/?linkId=40953194.

41.   Ibid.

42.   "Down's Syndrome Births at an All-Time Low in Denmark," RightToLife News, September 11, 2020, https://righttolife.org.uk/news/downs-syndr ome-births-at-an-all-time-low-in-denmark.

43.   Alison Gee, "A World without Down's Syndrome?," BBC News, September 29, 2016, http://www.bbc.com/news/magazine-37500189.

44.   Jaime L. Natoli et al., "Prenatal Diagnosis of Down Syndrome: A Systematic Review of Termination Rates (1995–2011)," *Prenatal Diagnosis* 32 (2012): 150, https://obgyn.onlinelibrary.wiley.com/doi/pdf/10.1002/pd .2910.

45.   Ruth Marcus, "I Would've Aborted a Fetus with Down Syndrome. Women Need That Right," *Washington Post,* March 9, 2019, https:// www.washingtonpost.com/opinions/i-wouldve-aborted-a-fetus-with-do wn-syndrome-women-need-that-right/2018/03/09/3aaac364-23d6-11e8 -94da-ebf9d112159c_story.html.

46.   Andrew Kageleiry et al., "Out-of-Pocket Medical Costs for Parents with Children with Down Syndrome in the United States," paper presented at the ISPOR 20th Annual International Meeting, Philadelphia, Pennsylvania, May 16–20, 2015, http://scholar.harvard.edu/files/campbell/files/ispor_ds _poster_-_2015_05_04.pdf.

47.   Brian G. Skotko, Susan P. Levine, and Richard Goldstein, "Self-Perceptions from People with Down Syndrome," *American Journal of Medical Genetics* 155A, no. 10 (2011): 2360, https://pubmed.ncbi.nlm.nih.gov/21 910246/.

48.   George F. Will, "Jon Will, 40 Years and Going with Down Syndrome," *Washington Post,* May 2, 2012, https://www.washingtonpost.com/opin ions/jon-will-40-years-and-going-with-down-syndrome/2012/05/02/gIQ AdGiNxT_story.html.

49. Sarah Kliff and Aatish Bhatia, "When They Warn of Rare Disorders, These Prenatal Tests Are Usually Wrong," *New York Times*, January 1, 2022, https://www.nytimes.com/2022/01/01/upshot/pregnancy-birth-ge netic-testing.html.

50. Heidi Cope et al., "Pregnancy Continuation and Organizational Religious Activity following Prenatal Diagnosis of a Lethal Fetal Defect Are Associated with Improved Psychological Outcome," *Prenatal Diagnosis* 35, no. 8 (2015): 761–68, https://pubmed.ncbi.nlm.nih.gov/25872901/.

51. Charlotte Wool, Rana Limbo, and Erin M. Denny-Koelsch, "'I Would Do It All Over Again': Cherishing Time and the Absence of Regret in Continuing a Pregnancy after a Life-Limiting Diagnosis," *Journal of Clinical Ethics* 29, no. 3 (2018): 227–36, https://pubmed.ncbi.nlm.nih .gov/30226824/.

52. Samantha Kamman, "'We Are Going to Defend Her': Diagnosed with Anencephaly," Live Action, August 16, 2021, https://www.liveaction.org /news/defend-diagnosed-anencephaly-angela-parents-chose-life/.

53. S.B. 96, Sess. of 2017 (Missouri 2017), https://www.senate.mo.gov/17in fo/BTS_Web/Bill.aspx?SessionType=R&BillID=57095319.

54. "SB 96: Abortion Ban," Planned Parenthood, https://www.plannedpare nthoodaction.org/planned-parenthood-advocates-missouri/issues-legisla tion/past-session-archive/sb-96-fact-sheet.

55. Ibid.

56. Planned Parenthood Advocates of Ohio (@PPAOhio), "PPAO supporters stood up against the continued attacks on abortion…," Twitter, December 13, 2017, 2:56 p.m., https://twitter.com/PPAOhio/status/9410342171018 07616.

57. Center for Reproductive Rights (@ReproRights), "This bill in Ohio is a dangerous attempt by anti-choice…," Twitter, December 14, 2017, 6:05 p.m., https://twitter.com/ReproRights/status/941443937398427649.

58. The original link to this statement is no longer active. See Alexandra DeSanctis, "Ohio Is Right to Ban the Abortion of Babies with Down Syndrome," *National Review*, December 19, 2017, https://www.nationalr eview.com/2017/12/ohio-down-syndrome-abortion-ban-moral-necessity/.

59. NARAL (@NARAL), "Gov. John Kasich is by no means a moderate…," Twitter, December 14, 2017, 6:03 p.m., https://twitter.com/NARAL/sta tus/941443436720336896; see also Mary Kuhlman, "Ohio Lawmakers

Approve 20th Abortion Restriction under Kasich," Public News Services, December 14, 2017, http://publicnewsservice.org/2017-12-14/womens-issues/ohio-lawmakers-approve-20th-abortion-restriction-under-kasich/a60640-1.

60. Kathryn Jean Lopez, "'Let's Just Make This Work: The Radical Hospitality of Pro-Life Communities," *National Review*, November 29, 2021, https://www.nationalreview.com/magazine/2021/11/29/lets-just-make-this-work/.

61. Carrie Baker and Carly Thomsen, "Crisis Pregnancy Centers Endanger Women's Health—with Taxpayer Dollars and without Oversight," *Ms. Magazine*, October 29, 2021, https://msmagazine.com/2021/10/29/crisis-pregnancy-centers-cpc-fake-abortion-clinic-report/..

62. Alice F. Cartwright, Katherine Tumlinson, and Ushma D. Upadhyay, "Pregnancy Outcomes after Exposure to Crisis Pregnancy Centers among an Abortion-Seeking Sample Recruited Online," *PLOS One* 16, no. 7 (2021): 7–8, https://journals.plos.org/plosone/article?id=10.1371/journal.pone.0255152.

63. Ibid.

64. See Jenifer McKenna and Tara Murtha, "Designed to Deceive: A Study of the Crisis Pregnancy Center Industry in Nine States," *The Alliance*, October 2021, https://alliancestateadvocates.org/wp-content/uploads/sites/107/Alliance-CPC-Study-Designed-to-Deceive.pdf.

65. "Unmasking FAKE Clinics: An Investigation into California's Crisis Pregnancy Centers," NARAL Pro-Choice, 2015, http://www.prochoiceamerica.org/wp-content/uploads/2018/03/NARAL-Pro-Choice-CA-Unmasking-Fake-Clinics-2015.pdf.

66. The Editors, "A Welcome Blow for Free Speech," *National Review*, June 26, 2018, https://www.nationalreview.com/2018/06/supreme-court-nifla-becerra-ruling-free-speech/.

67. *National Institute of Family and Life Advocates v. Becerra*, 585 U.S. __ (2018).

68. See, for example, Ari Paul, "Bill Seeks More Disclosure by Anti-Abortion Pregnancy Centers," Gotham Gazette, January 5, 2011, https://www.gothamgazette.com/index.php/health/676-bill-seeks-more-disclosure-by-anti-abortion-pregnancy-centers.

69. Planned Parenthood, "Annual Report: 2019–2020," 35.

70. Live Action, Facebook post, February 7, 2017, https://www.facebook.com /liveaction/videos/10154959592988728/.

71. Ibid.

72. Ibid.

73. Ibid.

74. Vincent M. Rue et al., "Induced Abortion and Traumatic Stress: A Preliminary Comparison of American and Russian Women," *Medical Science Monitor* 10, no. 10 (2004): SR5–16.

75. DeSanctis, "The Pro-Choice Movement Should Denounce Forced Abortion," *National Review.*

76. Biggs, Gould, and Foster, "Understanding Why Women Seek Abortions in the US," *BMC Women's Health.*

77. DeSanctis, "The Pro-Life Movement You've Never Heard Of."

Chapter Four: Abortion Harms Medicine

1. Tanya Lewis, "5 Fascinating Facts about Fetal Ultrasounds," Live Science, May 16, 2013, https://www.livescience.com/32071-history-of-fetal-ultra sound.html.

2. Ryan T. Anderson, "Present at the Creation," *National Review*, January 24, 2011, https://www.nationalreview.com/magazine/2011/01/24/prese nt-creation/.

3. Children's Hospital of Philadelphia, "Fetal Surgery," https://www.chop .edu/treatments/fetal-surgery.

4. Jay Marks, ed., "Medical Definition of the Hippocratic Oath," Medicine Net, June 6, 2021, https://www.medicinenet.com/ script/main/art. asp?articlekey=20909.

5. Robert Shmerling, "The Myth of the Hippocratic Oath," Harvard Health blog, November 25, 2015, https://www.health.harvard.edu/blog/the-my th-of-the-hippocratic-oath-201511258447.

6. NR Symposium, "One Untrue Thing," *National Review*, August 1, 2007, https://www.nationalreview.com/2007/08/one-untrue-thing-nro-sympo sium/.

7. Brief of the American College of Obstetricians and Gynecologists et al. as Amicus Curiae for Petitioners, *Roe v. Wade*, 410 U.S., at 113.

8. Ibid.

9. *Roe*, 410 U.S. at 163.

10. Ibid. at 143–44, nn.38–39.

11. See Katie L. Gibson, "The Rhetoric of *Roe v. Wade*: When the (Male) Doctor Knows Best," *Southern Communication Journal* 73, no. 4 (2008): 312–31, https://www.tandfonline.com/doi/abs/10.1080/1041794080241 8825.

12. Robert Barnes, "The Forgotten History of Justice Ginsburg's Criticism of *Roe v. Wade*," *Washington Post*, March 2, 2016, https://www.washingt onpost.com/politics/courts_law/the-forgotten-history-of-justice-ginsbur gs-criticism-of-roe-v-wade/2016/03/01/9ba0ea2e-dfe8-11e5-9c36-e1902 f6b6571_story.html.

13. *Roe*, 410 U.S. at 165.

14. Robert P. George, "Bernard Nathanson: A Life Transformed by Truth," Public Discourse, February 27, 2011, https://www.thepublicdiscourse.com /2011/02/2806/.

15. Bernard Nathanson, *Aborting America* (Garden City, New York: Doubleday & Company, 1979), 193.

16. Louis M. Hellman and Jack A. Pritchard, eds., *Williams Obstetrics*, 520.

17. Clarke Forsythe, *Abuse of Discretion: The Inside Story of Roe v. Wade* (New York: Encounter, 2013), 64 (citing the National Center for Health Statistics).

18. Nancy Aries, "The American College of Obstetricians and Gynecologists and the Evolution of Abortion Policy, 1951–1973: The Politics of Science," *American Journal of Public Health* 93, no. 11 (2003): 1812.

19. American College of Obstetricians and Gynecologists, Item 6.39, *Report of the Committee to Study Liberalization of the Laws Governing Therapeutic Abortion: Transcript of Executive Board Meeting* (May 9, 1968), 4.

20. *Doe*, 410 U.S. at 192.

21. Aries, "The American College of Obstetricians and Gynecologists and the Evolution of Abortion Policy," 1817.

22. Ibid.

23. Brief of the American College of Obstetricians and Gynecologists for Petitioners, *Roe*, at 113.

24. See Brief of American Association of Pro-Life Obstetricians and Gynecologists as Amicus Curiae for Petitioners, *Dobbs v. Jackson Women's Health Organization* (2021).

25. Committee on Patient Safety and Quality Improvement, "Communication Strategies for Patient Handoffs," *Obstetrics & Gynecology* 119, no. 2 (2012): 408, https://journals.lww.com/greenjournal/Citation/2012/02000 /Committee_Opinion_No__517___Communication.50.aspx.

26. Senator Dianne Feinstein (CA), "Partial Birth Abortion Ban-Act of 1999," *Congressional Record* 145 (1999): 26371, https://www.govinfo.gov/cont ent/pkg/CRECB-1999-pt18/html/CRECB-1999-pt18-Pg26366-8.htm.

27. Yuval Levin, "The War on Science," *National Review*, June 29, 2010, https://www.nationalreview.com/corner/war-science-yuval-levin/.

28. *Stenberg v. Carhart*, 530 U.S. 914, 932–35 (2000).

29. See ACOG Committee on Ethics, "The Limits of Conscientious Refusal in Reproductive Medicine," ACOG Committee Opinion no. 385 (2007), https://www.acog.org/clinical/clinical-guidance/committee-opinion/artic les/2007/11/the-limits-of-conscientious-refusal-in-reproductive-medicine.

30. Christina Francis, "The OB-GYNs Who Play Politics with Women's Lives," *Wall Street Journal*, March 3, 2020, https://www.wsj.com/articl es/the-ob-gyns-who-play-politics-with-womens-lives-11583279360.

31. See "Medical News," *Journal of the American Medical Association* 20, no. 2 (1967): 27, 38.

32. Gerald Harmon, "AMA Statement on Texas SB8," American Medical Association, September 1, 2021, https://www.ama-assn.org/press-center /press-releases/ama-statement-texas-sb8.

33. "American Medical Association v. Stenehjem," Alliance Defending Freedom, January 11, 2022, https://adflegal.org/case/american-medical -association-v-stenehjem.

34. Alexandra DeSanctis, "Planned Parenthood's Annual Report Proves It's an Abortion Group," *National Review*, February 24, 2021, https://www .nationalreview.com/2021/02/planned-parenthoods-annual-report-prov es-its-an-abortion-group/.

35. See Planned Parenthood, "Annual Report 2019–2020," 38, https://www .plannedparenthood.org/uploads/filer_public/67/30/67305ea1-8da2-4c ee-9191-19228c1d6f70/210219-annual-report-2019-2020-web-final.pdf.

36. *Rust v. Sullivan*, 500 U.S. 173 (1991).

37. Ryan T. Anderson and Robert P. George, "Government Should Not Fund Organizations That Kill Innocent Human Beings," Harvard Health Policy Review, May 21, 2016, http://www.hhpronline.org/articles/2016/10/21

/government-should-not-fund-organizations-that-kill-innocent-human-be ings?rq=ryan%20anderson.

38. Ibid.

39. Pam Belluck, "Planned Parenthood Refuses Federal Funds over Abortion Restrictions," *New York Times*, August 19, 2019, https://www.nytimes .com/2019/08/19/health/planned-parenthood-title-x.html.

40. See Joseph Biden, "Memorandum on Protecting Women's Health at Home and Abroad," White House, January 28, 2021, https://www.whitehouse .gov/briefing-room/presidential-actions/2021/01/28/memorandum-on-pr otecting-womens-health-at-home-and-abroad/.

41. Alexandra DeSanctis, "Planned Parenthood Jumps into the Hormone-Therapy Game," *National Review*, August 24, 2021, https://www.natio nalreview.com/2021/08/planned-parenthood-jumps-into-the-hormone-th erapy-game/.

42. See Planned Parenthood, *Annual Report: 2019–2020*, 35.

43. Amanda Marcotte, "Republicans Say 'Money Is Fungible' When It Comes to Planned Parenthood. It Is Not," Slate, September 11, 2015, https://slate .com/human-interest/2015/09/money-is-fungible-at-planned-parenthood -not-actually-true.html.

44. Alexandra DeSanctis, "Big Abortion v. David Daleiden," *Human Life Review* XLVII, no. 2 (Spring 2021): 21–22.

45. See Alex Dobuzinskis, " DOJ Moves to Investigate Planned Parenthood over Fetal Tissue Practices," HuffPost, December 8, 2017, https://www .huffpost.com/entry/doj-planed-parenthood-fetal-tissue-probe_n_5a2a3 026e4b069ec48ac39c7; Linley Sanders, "Trump's Justice Department Moves Ahead on Planned Parenthood Fetal Tissue Inquiry," *Newsweek*, December 8, 2017, https://www.newsweek.com/trumps-justice-departm ent-planned-parenthood-742204; E. A. Crunden, "Discredited Sting Videos Haunt Planned Parenthood as DOJ Opens Investigation," ThinkProgress, December 8, 2017, https://thinkprogress.org/pp-sting-vi deos-doj-3063c59b3761/.

46. See John Bowden, "Justice Dept. Moving to Probe Planned Parenthood over Fetal Tissue Practices," *The Hill*, December 7, 2017, https://thehill .com/homenews/administration/363892-justice-department-moving-to -probe-planned-parenthood-over-fetal; Alexa Lardieri, "Justice Department to Investigate Planned Parenthood," *U.S. News & World*

Report, December 8, 2017, https://www.usnews.com/news/national-ne ws/articles/2017-12-08/justice-department-to-investigate-planned-paren thood.

47. Ian Tuttle, "Planned Parenthood's Commissioned Video Review Proves the Authenticity of Its Employees' Ghoulish Statements," *National Review*, August 28, 2015, www.nationalreview.com/2015/08/planned-pa renthoods-fusion-inc-videos-review/.

48. "ADF Senior Counsel Discusses Forensic Report on Planned Parenthood Videos," *National Review*, October 12, 2015, www.nationalreview.com /2015/10/planned-parenthood-videos-forensic-analysis/.

49. See *Planned Parenthood v. Charles Smith*, No. 17-50282 (5th Cir. 2019).

50. American Association of Pro-Life Obstetricians and Gynecologists, "Fact Checking the Fact Checkers: Abortionists Misrepresent the Facts," AAPLOG website, https://aaplog.org/fact-checking-the-fact-checkers-ab ortionists-misrepresent-the-facts/.

51. Brief of American Association of Pro-Life Obstetricians and Gynecologists as Amicus Curiae for Respondents, *June Medical Services, L.L.C. v. Gee*, 586 U.S. __ (2019), https://www.supremecourt.gov/DocketPDF/18/18-13 23/126927/20191227154424488_AAPLOG%20Amicus%20Brief.pdf.

52. "Fetal Surgery for Spina Bifida," Children's Hospital of Philadelphia, https://www.chop.edu/conditions-diseases/spina-bifida/volumes-outc omes; see also Marla Ferschl et al., "Anesthesia for *in Utero* Repair of Myelomeningocele," *Anesthesiology* 118, no. 5 (2013): 1211–23, https:// www.ncbi.nlm.nih.gov/pmc/articles/PMC3755883/.

53. H. Olsson, T. R. Möller, and J. Ranstam, "Early Oral Contraceptive Use and Breast Cancer among Premenopausal Women: Final Report from a Study in Southern Sweden," *Journal of the National Cancer Institute* 81, no. 13 (1989): 1000–1004, https://pubmed.ncbi.nlm.nih.gov/2733043/#.

54. Victor Moreno et al., "Effect of Oral Contraceptives on Risk of Cervical Cancer in Women with Human Papillomavirus Infection: The IARC Multicentric Case-Control Study," *Lancet* 359, no. 9312 (2002): 1085–92, https://pubmed.ncbi.nlm.nih.gov/11943255/.

55. Rebecca Peck and Charles Norris, "Significant Risks of Oral Contraceptives (OCPs): Why This Drug Class Should Not Be Included in a Preventive Care Mandate," *The Linacre Quarterly* 79, no. 1 (2012): 41–56, https://doi.org/10.1179/002436312803571447.

56. "Male Birth Control Study Killed after Men Report Side Effects," NPR, November 3, 2016, https://www.npr.org/sections/health-shots/2016/11 /03/500549503/male-birth-control-study-killed-after-men-complain-abo ut-side-effects.

57. John T. Littell, "Why I Think Doctors Are Overprescribing the Pill," *Verily*, July 20, 2016, https://verilymag.com/2016/07/side-effects-of-the -pill-hormonal-contraceptives-birth-control-womens-health-fertility-awa reness.

58. See, for example, "Fertility Awareness Methods," Natural Womanhood, https://naturalwomanhood.org/topic/fertility-awareness-methods/.

59. Joseph Bottum and Ryan T. Anderson, "Stem Cells: A Political History," *First Things*, November 2008, https://www.firstthings.com/article/2008 /11/stem-cells-a-political-history.

60. "States with Legal Physician-Assisted Suicide," ProCon.org, December 14, 2021, https://euthanasia.procon.org/states-with-legal-physician-assis ted-suicide/.

61. Ryan T. Anderson, "Always Care, Never Kill: How Physician-Assisted Suicide Endangers the Weak, Corrupts Medicine, Compromises the Family, and Violates Human Dignity and Equality," Heritage Foundation Backgrounder no. 3004, March 24, 2015, https://ssrn.com/abstract=3113681.

62. See ACOG Committee on Ethics, "The Limits of Conscientious Refusal in Reproductive Medicine."

63. See Equality Act, H.R.5, 117th Congress (2021), congress.gov/bill/117th -congress/house-bill/5; see also Ryan T. Anderson, "Biden's Equality Act Is a Danger to Women's and Conscience rights," *New York Post*, February 21, 2021, https://nypost.com/2021/02/21/bidens-equality-act-is-a-danger -to-womens-and-conscience-rights/.

64. Alexandra DeSanctis, "The Equality Act Would Require Government-Funded Abortion," *National Review*, February 25, 2021, https://www.na tionalreview.com/2021/02/the-equality-act-would-require-government-fu nded-abortion/.

65. Richard Doerflinger, "The 'Equality Act': Threatening Life and Equality," *On Point* 54 (2021), https://lozierinstitute.org/the-equality-act-threateni ng-life-and-equality/.

66. Katelyn Burns, "New Congress Opens Door for Renewed Push for LGBTQ Equality Act," Rewire News, December 5, 2018, https://rewire .news/article/2018/12/05/new-congress-opens-door-lgbtq-equality-act/.

67. Sarah Kramer, "Why the 'Equality Act' Is Bad News for Unborn Babies and Those Who Defend Them," Alliance Defending Freedom, February 23, 2021, https://adflegal.org/blog/why-equality-act-bad-news-unborn-ba bies-and-those-who-defend-them.

68. Anna Maria Barry-Jester and Amelia Thomson-DeVeaux, "How Catholic Bishops Are Shaping Health Care in Rural America," FiveThirtyEight, July 25, 2018, https://fivethirtyeight.com/features/how-catholic-bishops -are-shaping-health-care-in-rural-america/.

69. Katie Hafner, "As Catholic Hospitals Expand, So Do Limits on Some Procedures," *New York Times*, August 10, 2018, https://www.nytimes .com/2018/08/10/health/catholic-hospitals-procedures.html.

Chapter Five: Abortion Harms the Rule of Law

1. *Memphis Center for Reproductive Health v. Slatery*, 14 F.4th 409, 437 (6th Cir. 2021) (Thapar, C.J., concurring in judgment in part and dissenting in part).

2. *Thornburgh v. American College of Obstetricians and Gynecologists*, 476 U.S. 747, 879 (1985) (O'Connor, J., dissenting).

3. *Thornburgh*, 476 U.S. at 132 (O'Connor, J., dissenting).

4. *June Medical*, 591 U.S. slip op. at 2 (Thomas, J., dissenting).

5. For a thorough treatment of *Roe* criticism, see Clarke D. Forsythe, "A Survey of Judicial and Scholarly Criticism of *Roe v. Wade* Since 1973: Legal Criticism and Unsettled Precedent," SSRN, January 20, 2022, https://papers.ssrn.com/sol3/papers.cfm?abstract_id=4016524.

6. John Hart Ely, "The Wages of Crying Wolf: A Commentary on *Roe v. Wade*," *Yale Law Journal* 82 (1973): 947.

7. Laurence H. Tribe, "Foreword: Toward a Model of Roles in the Due Process of Life and Law," *Harvard Law Review* 87 (1973), 1.

8. See Timothy P. Carney, "The Pervading Dishonesty of *Roe v. Wade*," *Washington Examiner*, January 23, 2012, https://www.washingtonexam iner.com/the-pervading-dishonesty-of-roe-v-wade.

9. See Brief for Scholars of Jurisprudence John M. Finnis and Robert P. George as Amicus Curiae Supporting Petitioners, *Dobbs v. Jackson*

Women's Health Organization, Docket No. 19-1392 (U.S. Dec. 1, 2021), https://www.supremecourt.gov/DocketPDF/19/19-1392/185196/202107 29093557582_210169a%20Amicus%20Brief%20for%20efiling%207 %2029%2021.pdf; see also Charles Rice, "The Dred Scott Case of the Twentieth Century," *Houston Law Review* 10 (1973): 1067–77, https:// scholarship.law.nd.edu/cgi/viewcontent.cgi?article=1809&context=law _faculty_scholarship.

10. *Roe v. Wade*, 410 U.S. 113, 157 n.54 (1973).

11. Woodrow Wilson, "What is Progress?," Teaching American History, https://teachingamericanhistory.org/document/what-is-progress/.

12. *Doe v. Bolton*, 410 U.S. 179, 192 (1973).

13. *Griswold v. Connecticut*, 381 U.S. 479, 484 (1965).

14. *Roe*, 410 U.S. at 152–54.

15. *Griswold*, 381 U.S. at 484–86.

16. *Eisenstadt v. Baird*, 405 U.S. 438, 453 (1972).

17. William J. Brennan, "Memorandum re: Abortion Cases," December 30, 1971, in William J. Brennan Papers, Library of Congress, Box I: 285, Folder 9. See also Forsythe, *Abuse of Discretion*, 34. A former Brennan clerk reflected, "We all saw that sentence, and we all smiled about it. Everyone understood what that sentence was doing. It was papering over holes in the doctrine."

18. Clarke Forsythe, *Abuse of Discretion: The Inside Story of Roe v. Wade* (New York: Encounter, 2013), 34.

19. Brennan, "Memorandum re: Abortion Cases," December 30, 1971.

20. *Roe*, 410 U.S. at 152.

21. *Pierce v. Society of Sisters*, 268 U.S. 510, 535 (1925).

22. Forsythe, *Abuse of Discretion*, 50. Blackmun began writing *Roe* based on a first-trimester limit on abortion but later jettisoned it, admitting to Justice Powell: "I could go along with viability if it could command a court."

23. Forsythe, *Abuse of Discretion*, 17–20.

24. See *Mitchum v. Foster*, 407 U.S. 225, 242–43 (1972).

25. James F. Simon, *The Center Holds: The Power Struggle Inside the Rehnquist Court* (New York: Touchstone, 1999), 85–86.

26. Forsythe, *Abuse of Discretion*, 41–43.

27. Ibid., 46–47.

28. Simon, *The Center Holds*, 104.

29. Ibid.

30. *Roe,* 410 U.S. at 221 (White, J., dissenting).

31. Ibid., at 172 (Rehnquist, J., dissenting).

32. Ibid., at 174 (Rehnquist, J., dissenting).

33. See, for Rehnquist's continued influence, Richard W. Garnett, "Rehnquist's Reservations and the Future of Roe," Law & Liberty, August 6, 2021, https://lawliberty.org/rehnquists-reservations-and-the-future-of-roe/.

34. *Casey,* 505 U.S. at 874.

35. Mary Ann Glendon and O. Carter Snead, "The Case for Overturning *Roe*," *National Affairs* (Fall 2021), https://nationalaffairs.com/publicatio ns/detail/the-case-for-overturning-roe.

36. *Casey,* 505 U.S. at 877.

37. Michael Stokes Paulsen, "The Worst Constitutional Decision of All Time," *Notre Dame Law Review* 78 (2003): 1040, https://scholarship.law.nd.edu /ndlr/vol78/iss4/2.

38. *June Medical*, 591 U.S. slip op. at 3.

39. *June Medical*, 591 U.S. slip op. at 11 (Roberts, C. J., concurring in judgment).

40. O. Carter Snead, "The Way Forward after *June Medical*," *First Things*, July 4, 2020, https://www.firstthings.com/web-exclusives/2020/07/the -way-forward-after-june-medical.

41. See Philip D. Williamson, "The Gordian Knot of Abortion Jurisprudence," *Federalist Society Review*, November 4, 2021, https://fedsoc.org/comme ntary/publications/the-gordian-knot-of-abortion-jurisprudence. As Williamson sharply summarizes, the Seventh and Eleventh Circuits have argued that the section of Roberts's concurrence arguing that *stare decisis* compelled him to enjoin the law in Louisiana is the Court's controlling opinion, such that the *Hellerstedt* standard remains in place. The Fifth and Sixth Circuits think that the controlling opinion is the *second* section of Roberts's opinion, in which he disputes *Hellerstedt*'s interpretation of *Casey* and argues that, under *Casey*, courts could invalidate only laws that created a "substantial obstacle" to abortion access, regardless of benefit. Finally, the Eighth Circuit agrees that the second section of Roberts's opinion is controlling, but it has urged the Court to review *Casey*'s viability standard,

arguing that it is insufficient for ruling on anti-discrimination laws that prevent, for example, sex-selective abortions.

42. See John Finnis "Abortion is Unconstitutional," *First Things*, April 2021, https://www.firstthings.com/article/2021/04/abortion-is-unconstitutional; and see John Finnis and Robert George, "An Enhanced Amicus Brief in *Dobbs*," SSRN, November 3, 2021, https://ssrn.com/abstract=3955231, (arguing that the unborn are entitled to Fourteenth Amendment protection as constitutional persons).

Chapter Six: Abortion Harms Politics and the Democratic Process

1. Kevin Sack, "Under the Big Top—the Candidate; Protestor Thrusts Fetus at a Surprised Clinton," *New York Times,* July 15, 1992, https://www.ny times.com/1992/07/15/news/under-the-big-top-the-candidate-protester -thrusts-fetus-at-a-surprised-clinton.html.

2. Alexandra DeSanctis, "How Democrats Purged 'Safe, Legal, Rare' from the Party," *Washington Post*, November 15, 2019, https://www.washing tonpost.com/outlook/how-democrats-purged-safe-legal-rare-from-the-pa rty/2019/11/15/369af73c-01a4-11ea-8bab-0fc209e065a8_story.html.

3. "1996 Democratic Party Platform," American Presidency Project, August 26, 1996, https://www.presidency.ucsb.edu/documents/1996-democratic -party-platform.

4. Eleanor Clift, "Democrats Push Envelope on Abortion, Drop Insistence That It Be Rare," The Daily Beast, September 15, 2012, https://www.the dailybeast.com/democrats-push-envelope-on-abortion-drop-insistence-th at-it-be-rare; see also "2004 Democratic Party Platform," American Presidency Project, July 27, 2004, https://www.presidency.ucsb.edu/docu ments/2004-democratic-party-platform; and "2008 Democratic Party Platform," American Presidency Project, August 25, 2008, https://www .presidency.ucsb.edu/documents/2008-democratic-party-platform.

5. Fernanda Crescente, "Anti-Abortion Dems Outraged by Platform Change," *USA Today*, July 17, 2016, https://www.usatoday.com/story/ne ws/politics/elections/2016/07/17/anti-abortion-democrats-outraged-platf orm-change/87220420/.

6. Aris Folley, "Senate Democrats Ditch Hyde Amendment for First Time in Decades," *The Hill*, October 18, 2021, https://thehill.com/policy/finance

/budget/577281-senate-democrats-release-spending-bill-without-decades
-old-abortion.

7.   Sarah Kliff, "Charts: How Roe v. Wade Changed Abortion Rights,"
      Washington Post, January 22, 2013, https://www.washingtonpost.com
      /news/wonk/wp/2013/01/22/charts-how-roe-v-wade-changed-abortion
      -rights/.

8.   Chief Justice Roberts observed this relationship in oral arguments for
      Dobbs. See Transcript for Oral Argument, *Dobbs v. Jackson Women's
      Health Organization* (No. 19-1392), at 54–55. See also Angelina Baglini,
      "Gestational Limits on Abortion in the United States Compared to
      International Norms," *American Report Series* 6 (2014), 3, https://s275
      89.pcdn.co/wp-content/uploads/2014/02/American-Reports-Series-INT
      ERNATIONAL-ABORTION-NORMS.pdf.

9.   Both the pro-life Charlotte Lozier Institute and the pro-abortion
      Guttmacher Institute agree on this point. See Baglini, "Gestational Limits
      on Abortion in the United States Compared to International Norms," 5–7;
      and Susheela Singh et al., "Abortion Worldwide 2017: Uneven Progress
      and Unequal Access," Guttmacher Institute, March 2018, https://www
      .guttmacher.org/report/abortion-worldwide-2017.

10.   "*Roe v. Wade* at 40: Most Oppose Overturning Abortion Decision," Pew
      Research Center, January 16, 2013, https://www.pewforum.org/2013/01
      /16/roe-v-wade-at-40/.

11.   See Kristen N. Jozkowski et al., "Knowledge and Sentiments of *Roe v.
      Wade* in the Wake of Justice Kavanaugh's Nomination to the U.S. Supreme
      Court," *Sexuality Research and Social Policy* 17 (2020): 285–300, https://
      link.springer.com/article/10.1007/s13178-019-00392-2.

12.   Victoria Balara, "Fox News Poll: A Record 65 Percent Favor Keeping *Roe
      v. Wade*," Fox News, September 23, 2021, https://www.foxnews.com/po
      litics/fox-news-poll-record-65-percent-favor-keeping-roe-v-wade. See full
      report at https://static.foxnews.com/foxnews.com/content/uploads/2021
      /09/Fox_September-12-15_Complete_National_Topline_September-23
      -Release.pdf.

13.   Lydia Saad, "Trimesters Still Key to U.S. Abortion Views," Gallup, June
      13, 2018, https://news.gallup.com/poll/235469/trimesters-key-abortion-vi
      ews.aspx.

14. Marist Poll, "Americans' Opinions on Abortion," Knights of Columbus, January 11, 2021, https://www.kofc.org/en/resources/news-room/polls /kofc-americans-opinions-on-abortion012021.pdf.

15. Ibid.

16. "Pro-Choice Americans Overwhelmingly Oppose Late-Term Abortion, Now Permitted in New York," Americans United for Life, February 12, 2019, https://aul.org/2019/02/12/pro-choice-americans-overwhelmingly -oppose-late-term-abortion-now-permitted-in-new-york/.

17. Saad, "Trimesters Still Key to U.S. Abortion Views."

18. John Murdock, "The Future of the Pro-Life Democrat," *National Affairs*, Winter 2020, https://www.nationalaffairs.com/publications/detail/the-fu ture-of-the-pro-life-democrat.

19. Valerie Nelson, "Ellen McCormack Dies at 84; Antiabortion Presidential Candidate," *Los Angeles Times*, April 2, 2011, https://www.latimes.com /local/obituaries/la-xpm-2011-apr-02-la-me-ellen-mccormack-20110402 -story.html.

20. Jennifer Haberkorn, "The Truth behind Bob Casey's 'Pro-Life' Stand," *Politico*, July 2, 2018, https://www.politico.com/story/2018/07/02/casey -abortion-pennsylvania-midterms-689505.

21. Robert P. George, "Remembering Robert Casey," *First Things*, August 2000, https://www.firstthings.com/article/2000/08/remembering-robert -casey.

22. William McGurn, "Bob Casey's Revenge," *First Things*, January 2005, https://www.firstthings.com/article/2005/01/bob-caseys-revenge.

23. Matthew Hay Brown, "Ted Kennedy, Abortion Opponent," *Baltimore Sun*, August 26, 2009, https://www.baltimoresun.com/bs-mtblog-2009 -08-kennedy_abortion_catholic-story.html; see also Donald R. McClarey, "Ted Kennedy and the 'A Word,'" The American Catholic, August 27, 2009, https://the-american-catholic.com/2009/08/27/11960/.

24. Edward Kennedy to Carolyn Gerster, October 5, 1979.

25. Lisa Lerer, "When Joe Biden Voted to Let States Overturn *Roe v. Wade*," *New York Times*, March 29, 2019, https://www.nytimes.com/2019/03 /29/us/politics/biden-abortion-rights.html.

26. Richard Durbin to Frank A. Tureskis, August 14, 1989.

27. Mario Cuomo, "Religious Belief and Public Morality: A Catholic Governor's Perspective" (speech, University of Notre Dame, September 13, 1984), http://archives.nd.edu/research/texts/cuomo.htm.

28. Ibid.

29. Christi Parsons, "Dick Durbin's Challenge," *Chicago Tribune,* December 2, 2007, https://www.chicagotribune.com/news/ct-xpm-2007-12-02-07 11270754-story.html.

30. Partial-Birth Abortion Ban Act of 2003 (Roll call vote), S.3, 108th Cong., 1st sess. (2003), https://www.senate.gov/legislative/LIS/roll_call_votes/vo te1081/vote_108_1_00402.htm.

31. Joseph R. Biden to Michael Gregg, April 7, 1997, https://www.documen tcloud.org/documents/6127592-biden94letter.html.

32. Alexandra DeSanctis, "Joe Biden Was Never Pro-Life," *National Review,* June 7, 2019, https://www.nationalreview.com/2019/06/joe-biden-was-ne ver-pro-life/.

33. Clift, "Democrats Push Envelope on Abortion"; Crescente, "Anti-Abortion Dems Outraged by Platform Change"; Folley, "Senate Democrats Ditch Hyde Amendment."

34. Barack Obama, "Commencement Address" (speech, University of Notre Dame, May 17, 2009), *Time,* https://time.com/4336922/obama-comme ncement-speech-transcript-notre-dame/.

35. Michael McGough, "Opinion: Does Hillary Still Think Abortion Should Be 'Safe, Legal and Rare'?," *Los Angeles Times,* July 27, 2015, https:// www.latimes.com/opinion/opinion-la/la-ol-hillaryclinton-abortion-plan nedparenthood-20150727-story.html; see also "Hillary Clinton Abortion," JPickD, YouTube, January 14, 2008, https://www.youtube .com/watch?v=N69e-hmmy14.

36. Alexandra DeSanctis, "Senate Democrats Fails to Pass Extreme Pro-Abortion Bill," *National Review,* February 28, 2022, https://www.natio nalreview.com/corner/senate-democrats-fail-to-pass-extreme-pro-aborti on-bill/.

37. Alice Miranda Ollstein, "How Kamala Harris Would Protect Abortion Rights," *Politico,* May 28, 2019, https://www.politico.com/story/2019/05 /28/how-sen-kamala-harris-would-protect-abortion-rights-1476696.

38. Alexandra DeSanctis, "Can One of the Last Pro-Life Democrats Survive?" *National Review,* September 26, 2019, https://www.nationalreview.com

/2019/09/dan-lipinski-pro-life-democrat-refuses-to-embrace-abortion-on
-demand/.

39. Sarah Jones, "Progressive Groups Back Marie Newman, despite DCCC
Blacklist," *New York*, Intelligencer, May 6, 2019, https://nymag.com/int
elligencer/2019/05/progressive-groups-back-marie-newman-despite-dccc
-blacklist.html.

40. Dan Lipinski, "No Compromise on Life," *Wall Street Journal*, March 25,
2020, https://www.wsj.com/articles/no-compromise-on-life-11585175034.

41. Ibid.

42. Alexandra DeSanctis, "Mayor Pete Dodges the Question, Again,"
National Review, January 28, 2020, https://www.nationalreview.com/co
rner/mayor-pete-dodges-the-question-again/.

43. Ibid.

44. Alexandra DeSanctis, "Bernie Sanders Reverses Course on Pro-Life
Democrats," *National Review*, February 10, 2020, https://www.national
review.com/corner/bernie-sanders-reverses-course-on-pro-life-democrats/.

45. Alexandra DeSanctis, "Farewell to the Pro-Life Democrats," *National
Review*, March 28, 2020, https://www.nationalreview.com/2020/03/farew
ell-to-the-pro-life-democrats/; and see Amée LaTour, "Fact Check: Heath
Mello's Voting Record on Abortion," Ballotpedia, May 1, 2017, https://bal
lotpedia.org/Fact_check/Heath_Mello%27s_voting_record_on_abortion.

46. Kristen Day and Xavier Bistis, "The Democrats Biden Doesn't Want,"
Wall Street Journal, August 6, 2020, https://www.wsj.com/articles/the-de
mocrats-biden-doesnt-want-11596755305.

47. Archbishop Salvatore Cordileone, "The Solution to Building a Culture of
Life is Being True Christians," *National Catholic Register*, January 24,
2022, https://www.ncregister.com/commentaries/archbishop-cordileone
-the-solution-to-building-a-culture-of-life-is-being-true-christians.

48. Alexandra DeSanctis, "'Catholics' for Choice Desecrates Basilica with
Pro-Abortion Display," *National Review*, January 21, 2022, https://www
.nationalreview.com/corner/catholics-for-choice-desecrates-basilica-with
-pro-abortion-display/.

49. Nicholas Kristof, "Meet Dr. Willie Parker, a Southern Christian Abortion
Provider," *New York Times*, May 6, 2017, https://www.nytimes.com/20
17/05/06/opinion/sunday/meet-dr-willie-parker-a-southern-christian-abo
rtion-provider.html.

50. Raphael Warnock (@ReverendWarnock), "As a pro-choice pastor, I've always believed…," Twitter, January 22, 2022, 12:55 p.m., https://twitt er.com/reverendwarnock/status/1484947902615146505.

51. See McGurn, "Bob Casey's Revenge."

52. Martin Luther King Jr., "Letter from Birmingham Jail," August 1963, https://www.csuchico.edu/iege/_assets/documents/susi-letter-from-birmi ngham-jail.pdf.

53. Andrew Prokop, "Did Democrats Blow It on *Roe v. Wade?*," *Vox*, December 7, 2021, https://www.vox.com/22814782/roe-v-wade-dobbs-de mocrats-republicans.

54. Ibid.

55. "How FDR Lost His Brief War on the Supreme Court," National Constitution Center, February 5, 2021, https://constitutioncenter.org/bl og/how-fdr-lost-his-brief-war-on-the-supreme-court-2.

56. Gerard V. Bradley, "'Dobbs' and the Conservative Legal Movement," *National Catholic Register*, December 7, 2021, https://www.ncregister .com/commentaries/dobbs-and-the-conservative-legal-movement.

57. Darla Cameron, "Confirmations for the Sitting Supreme Court Justices Were Not Nearly as Partisan as Judge Gorsuch's," *Washington Post*, April 7, 2017, https://www.washingtonpost.com/graphics/politics/scotus-confi rmation-votes/.

58. Nina Totenberg, "Robert Bork's Supreme Court Nomination 'Changed Everything, Maybe Forever'," NPR, December 19, 2012, https://www.npr .org/sections/itsallpolitics/2012/12/19/167645600/robert-borks-supreme -court-nomination-changed-everything-maybe-forever.

59. Alexandra DeSanctis, "Dianne Feinstein Attacks Judicial Nominee's Catholic Faith," *National Review*, September 6, 2017, https://www.nati onalreview.com/corner/dianne-feinstein-amy-coney-barrett-senator-atta cks-catholic-judicial-nominee/.

60. Alexandra DeSanctis, "The Kavanaugh Allegations Should Be Confronted, Not Ignored," *National Review*, September 20, 2018, https:// www.nationalreview.com/2018/09/brett-kavanaugh-allegations-dennis -prager-comments-wrong/.

61. See Mollie Hemingway and Carrie Severino, "21 Reasons Not To Believe Christine Blasey Ford's Claims about Justice Kavanaugh," The Federalist, December 2, 2019, https://thefederalist.com/2019/12/02/21-reasons-not

-to-believe-christine-blasey-fords-claims-about-justice-kavanaugh/; see also Margot Cleveland, "Christine Blasey Ford's Changing Kavanaugh Assault Story Leaves Her Short on Credibility," *USA Today*, October 3, 2018, https://www.usatoday.com/story/opinion/2018/10/03/christine-bla sey-ford-changing-memories-not-credible-kavanaugh-column/1497661 002/.

62. "In Rare Move, ACLU to Oppose Kavanaugh for Supreme Court," American Civil Liberties Union, September 29, 2018, https://www.aclu .org/press-releases/rare-move-aclu-oppose-kavanaugh-supreme-court-0.

63. "Senate Must Reject Supreme Court Nominee Brett Kavanaugh," Planned Parenthood, July 9, 2018, https://www.plannedparenthood.org/about-us /newsroom/press-releases/senate-must-reject-supreme-court-nominee-br ett-kavanaugh.

64. Natalie Delgadillo, "Update: Capitol Police Have Arrested More Than 200 Protesters at Kavanaugh Hearings," DCist, September 4, 2018, https://dcist.com/story/18/09/04/kavanaugh-hearing-arrests/.

65. Rita Beamish, "Abortion Rights Group Plans All-Out Attack on Bork Nomination," AP News, July 11, 1987, https://apnews.com/article/8b1f3 b8e4ff81ab2ec43ee213b4cc8e5.

66. Linda Greenhouse, "Washington Talk: The Bork Nomination; in No Time at All, Both Proponents and Opponents Are Ready for Battle; Foes on the Left Strive for Unity," *New York Times*, July 9, 1987, https://www .nytimes.com/1987/07/09/us/washington-talk-bork-nomination-no-time -all-both-proponents-opponents-are-ready.html.

67. Totenberg, "Robert Bork's Supreme Court Nomination."

68. Greg Neumayr, "Joe Biden, the Father of 'Borking,'" *The Hill,* September 23, 2020, https://thehill.com/opinion/campaign/517743-joe-biden-the-fa ther-of-borking; and see DeSanctis, "Joe Biden Was Never Pro-Life," *National Review.*

69. Mary Ellen Bork, "Joe Biden and the Borking of Supreme Court Nominees," *Wall Street Journal*, September 29, 2020, https://www.wsj .com/articles/joe-biden-and-the-borking-of-supreme-court-nominees-11 601319057.

70. See Adam White, "Justice Thomas, Undaunted," *Weekly Standard*, July 8, 2016, https://www.washingtonexaminer.com/tag/supreme-court?sour ce=%2Fweekly-standard%2Fjustice-thomas-undaunted; see also Stuart

Taylor Jr., "The Hollywood Hit-Job on Justice Clarence Thomas," *Wall Street Journal*, April 17, 2016, https://www.wsj.com/articles/the-hollywo od-hit-job-on-justice-clarence-thomas-1460930701; and see "'High-Tech Lynching': Thomas Denies Anita Hill Harassment Allegations," *Washington Post*, September 18, 2018, https://www.washingtonpost.com /video/politics/high-tech-lynching-thomas-denies-anita-hill-harassment -allegations/2018/09/18/370097aa-bbae-11e8-adb8-01125416c102_vid eo.html.

71. Sarah Pruitt, "How Anita Hill's Testimony Made America Cringe—and Change," History, February 9, 2021, https://www.history.com/news/ani ta-hill-confirmation-hearings-impact.

72. David Harsanyi, "Joe Biden Owes Clarence Thomas an Apology—and So Does the Entire Left," *New York Post*, March 13, 2020, https://nypo st.com/2020/03/13/joe-biden-owes-clarence-thomas-an-apology-and-so -does-the-entire-left/.

73. Ian Millhiser, "The Controversy over Chuck Schumer's Attack on Gorsuch and Kavanaugh, Explained," *Vox*, March 5, 2020, https://www.vox.com /2020/3/5/21165479/chuck-schumer-neil-gorsuch-brett-kavanaugh-supre me-court-whirlwind-threat.

Chapter Seven: Abortion Harms Media and Popular Culture

1. S.240, Sess. of 2019 (New York 2019), https://www.nysenate.gov/legisla tion/bills/2019/s240.

2. The official statement has been removed from the state's website since Governor Cuomo resigned, but see Grace Carr, "World Trade Center Lit Up in Pink to Celebrate Abortion Bill," The Daily Caller, January 23, 2019, https://dailycaller.com/2019/01/23/world-trade-center-lit-pink-abo rtion/.

3. See "Names on the 9/11 Memorial," 9/11 Memorial, https://www.911m emorial.org/visit/memorial/names-911-memorial.

4. "October Democratic Debate Transcript: 4th Debate in Ohio," Rev, October 16, 2019, https://www.rev.com/blog/transcripts/october-democ ratic-debate-transcript-4th-debate-from-ohio.

5. Ramesh Ponnuru, *The Party of Death: The Democrats, the Media, the Courts, and the Disregard for Human Life* (Washington, D.C.: Regnery, 2006), 43.

6. Rep. Charles T. Canady (FL), "H.R. 1833, The Partial-Birth Abortion Ban Act of 1995," *Congressional Record* 141, no. 169 (October 30, 1995): 11426, https://www.govinfo.gov/content/pkg/CREC-1995-10-30/html /CREC-1995-10-30-pt1-PgH11426-2.htm.

7. *Meet the Press*, NBC television broadcast, March 2, 1997.

8. Senator Dianne Feinstein (CA), "Partial Birth Abortion Ban-Act of 1999," *Congressional Record*.

9. Diane Gianelli, "Shock-Tactic Ads Target Late-Term Abortion Procedure," *American Medical News* (July 5, 1993), 21.

10. Planned Parenthood Federation of America, news release, November 1, 1995; see Hon. Robert Dornan, "A Closer Look at Partial-Birth Abortions," Congressional Record 142, no. 136 (September 27, 1996): E1744, https:// www.govinfo.gov/content/pkg/CREC-1996-09-27/html/CREC-1996-09- 27-pt1-PgE1743.htm; see also Marilyn Rauber, "Leading Doc Tells Congress Pro-Choicers 'Misinformed,'" New York Post, March 22, 1996.

11. See Sen. Barbara Boxer (CA), "Partial-Birth Abortion Ban Act," *Congressional Record* 141, no. 175 (November 7, 1995): S16742, https:// www.govinfo.gov/content/pkg/CREC-1995-11-07/html/CREC-1995-11 -07-pt1-PgS16730-3.htm.

12. Ronald Powers, "Moynihan, in Break with Clinton, Condemns Abortion Procedure," Associated Press, May 14, 1996, https://apnews.com/article /6e619434f53783d58df59a7f1331c8b0.

13. See Atul Gawande, "Partial Truths in the Partial-Birth-Abortion Debate," Slate, January 30, 1998, https://slate.com/technology/1998/01/partial-tru ths-in-the-partial-birth-abortion-debate.html; see also Will Saletan, "The 'Partial-Birth' Myth," Slate, October 22, 2003, https://slate.com/news-and -politics/2003/10/the-myth-of-partial-birth-abortions.html.

14. Jesse Holland, "House Approves Bill to Give Legal Protection to Some Fetuses after Abortion," Associated Press, March 13, 2002, https://www .nrlc.org/federal/bornaliveinfants/apmemo031302/.

15. Dahlia Lithwick, "Doctor, There's a Lawyer in My Womb," Slate, November 8, 2006, https://slate.com/news-and-politics/2006/11/doctor -there-s-a-lawyer-in-my-womb.html.

16. Ponnuru, *The Party of Death*, 45.

17. Matt Hadro, "HHS Secretary: 'There Is No Law' against 'Partial-Birth Abortion,'" Catholic News Agency, May 12, 2021, https://www.catholi

cnewsagency.com/news/247637/hhs-secretary-there-is-no-law-against-partial-birth-abortion.

18. Tony Marco, "New York Puts in Measures to Protect Access to Abortion Even If Roe v. Wade Is Overturned," CNN, January 23, 2019, https://www.cnn.com/2019/01/23/health/new-york-abortion-measures-trnd/index.html.

19. Vivian Wang, "As Supreme Court Shifts under Trump, Cuomo Vows to Expand Abortion Rights," *New York Times*, January 7, 2019, https://www.nytimes.com/2019/01/07/nyregion/cuomo-abortion-roe-vs-wade.html.

20. Sarah Jones, "New York Has Finally Updated Its Archaic Abortion Law," *New York*, Intelligencer, January 23, 2019, https://nymag.com/intelligencer/2019/01/new-york-has-finally-updated-its-archaic-abortion-law.html.

21. The Republican Standard, "Kathy Tran Presents Virginia Third Trimester Abortion Bill in Committee," YouTube, January 29, 2019, https://www.youtube.com/watch?v=OMFzZ5I30dg&t=234s.

22. Ibid.

23. Hannah Cortez, "VA Gov on Abortion: 'Infant Would Be Resuscitated If That's What the Mother and the Family Desired,'" YouTube, January 30, 2019, https://www.youtube.com/watch?v=SkTopSKo1xs&t=135s.

24. Irin Carmon, "The False Outrage over Kathy Tran's 'Infanticide' Bill," The Cut, February 1, 2019, https://www.thecut.com/2019/02/the-false-outrage-over-kathy-trans-infanticide-bill.html.

25. Michelle Goldberg, "Fake News about Abortion in Virginia," *New York Times*, https://www.nytimes.com/2019/02/01/opinion/abortion-virginia-kathy-tran.html.

26. Gregory S. Schneider and Laura Vozzella, "Abortion Bill Draws GOP Outrage against Va. Gov. Northam, Democratic Legislators," *Washington Post*, January 30, 2019, https://www.washingtonpost.com/local/virginia-politics/failed-abortion-bill-draws-gop-outrage-against-va-gov-northam-democratic-lawmakers/2019/01/30/4a18f022-24b2-11e9-ad53-824486280311_story.html; see also Daniel Moritz-Rabson, "Alex Jones, Joe Rogan War Leads to Conspiracy Theory Meltdown, InfoWars Host Says Babies Harvested for Organs," *Newsweek*, February 28, 2019, https://www.newsweek.com/alex-jones-joe-rogan-war-meltdown-conspiracy-theory-baby-organs-harvested-1347887.

27. "Fact Check: Virginia Governor's 2019 Comments about Abortion Bill Are Missing Context," Reuters, October 28, 2020, https://www.reuters .com/article/uk-factcheck-virginia-gov-abortion/fact-check-virginia-gove rnors-2019-comments-about-abortion-bill-are-missing-context-idUSKB N27D2HL.

28. Adam Rogers, "'Heartbeat' Bills Get the Science of Fetal Heartbeats All Wrong," *Wired*, May 14, 2019, https://www.wired.com/story/heartbeat -bills-get-the-science-of-fetal-heartbeats-all-wrong/.

29. Alyssa Milano (@Alyssa_Milano), "Dear Press, stop calling them 'heartbeat' bills…," Twitter, May 15, 2019, 7:45 a.m., https://twitter.com /Alyssa_Milano/status/1128627368023736320.

30. Madeleine Carlisle, "Federal Judge Blocks Georgia's Controversial Law Banning Most Abortions after 6 Weeks," *Time*, July 14, 2020, https://ti me.com/5866714/georgia-heartbeat-abortion-law-ban/.

31. Jessica Glenza, "Doctors' Organization: Calling Abortion Bans 'Fetal Heartbeat Bills' Is Misleading," *The Guardian*, June 5, 2019, https://www .theguardian.com/world/2019/jun/05/abortion-doctors-fetal-heartbeat-bi lls-language-misleading.

32. Robert Barnes et al., "Biden Blasts Supreme Court Refusal to Block Texas Abortion Ban; Pelosi Vows Vote on House Bill to Ensure Abortion Access," *Washington Post*, September 2, 2021, https://www.washington post.com/politics/courts_law/texas-six-week-abortion-ban/2021/09/01 /e53cf372-0a6b-11ec-a6dd-296ba7fb2dce_story.html.

33. Katie Heaney, "Embryos Don't Have Hearts," The Cut, May 24, 2019, https://www.thecut.com/2019/05/embryos-dont-have-hearts.html.

34. Alan Blinder, "Louisiana Moves to Ban Abortions after a Heartbeat Is Detected," *New York Times*, May 29, 2019, https://www.nytimes.com /2019/05/29/us/louisiana-abortion-heartbeat-bill.html.

35. J. David Goodman et al., "Confusion in Texas as 'Unprecedented' Abortion Law Takes Effect," *New York Times*, September 2, 2021, https://www.nytimes.com/2021/09/02/us/supreme-court-texas-abortion -law.html.

36. Anna Smith, "When Does a Fetus Have a Heartbeat?," MedicalNewsToday, June 9, 2020, https://www.medicalnewstoday.com /articles/ when-does-a-fetus-have-a-heartbeat.

37. Joe Simpson et al., "Low Fetal Loss Rates after Ultrasound-Proved Viability in Early Pregnancy," *Journal of the American Medical Association* 258, no. 18 (1987): 2555–57.

38. S. A. Brigham, C. Conlon, and R. G. Farquharson, "A Longitudinal Study of Pregnancy Outcomes following Idiopathic Recurrent Miscarriage," *Human Reproduction* 14, no. 11 (1999): 2869.

39. Selena Simmons-Duffin, "The Texas Abortion Ban Hinges on 'Fetal Heartbeat.' Doctors Call That Misleading," NPR, September 3, 2021, https://www.npr.org/sections/health-shots/2021/09/02/1033727679/fetal-heartbeat-isnt-a-medical-term-but-its-still-used-in-laws-on-abortion.

40. "What Happens in the Second Month of Pregnancy?," Planned Parenthood, https://www.plannedparenthood.org/learn/pregnancy/pregnancy-month-by-month/what-happens-second-month-pregnancy.

41. Born-Alive Abortion Survivors Protection Act, S.311, 116th Congress (2019), https://www.congress.gov/bill/116th-congress/senate-bill/311/text?q=%7B%22search%22%3A%22S.+311%22%7D&r=2&s=2.

42. Born-Alive Infants Protection Act, H.R.2175, 107th Congress (2002), https://www.congress.gov/bill/107th-congress/house-bill/2175/text.

43. See Hadley Arkes, *Natural Rights & The Right to Choose* (Cambridge: Cambridge University Press, 2004), 245; see also Hadley Arkes, "Revisit the Born-Alive Act," *Washington Examiner*, April 30, 2013, https://www.washingtonexaminer.com/weekly-standard/revisit-the-born-alive-act.

44. Alexandra DeSanctis, "Why a Ban on Infanticide Is Necessary," *National Review*, February 6, 2019, https://www.nationalreview.com/2019/02/born-alive-abortion-survivors-protection-act-infanticide-ban/.

45. David Harsanyi, "Mainstream Media Blacks Out the Democrats' Infanticide Vote," The Federalist, February 27, 2019, https://thefederalist.com/2019/02/27/mainstream-media-blacks-democrats-infanticide-vote/.

46. Vivian Wang, "Trump, Pence Lead G.O.P. Seizure of Late-Term Abortion as a Potent 2020 Issue," *New York Times*, January 31, 2019, https://www.nytimes.com/2019/01/31/nyregion/late-term-abortion-pence-trump-republicans.html.

47. Matt Viser, "Republicans Seize on Liberal Positions to Paint Democrats as Radical," *Washington Post*, January 31, 2019, https://www.washingtonpost.com/politics/republicans-seize-on-liberal-positions-to-paint-democrats-as-radical/2019/01/31/d705603e-24f2-11e9-ad53-824486280311_story.html; see also Eugene Scott, "Trump and Republicans Are Trying

to Paint Democrats as Radical on Abortion," *Washington Post*, February 26, 2019, https://www.washingtonpost.com/politics/2019/02/26/trump -republicans-are-trying-paint-democrats-radical-abortion/.

48. Kate Smith, "Senate Rejects 'Born-Alive' Bill as Anti-Abortion Advocates Reignite 'Late-Term' Abortion Debate," CBS News, February 27, 2019, https://www.cbsnews.com/news/born-alive-act-senate-rejects-born-alive-bill-anti-abortion-advocates-reignite-late-term-abortion-debate-2019-02-27/.

49. See, for example, *The Hill* (@thehill), "Just in: Senate Dems block anti-abortion bill...," Twitter, February 4, 2019, 7:52 p.m., https://twitter.com /thehill/status/1092586617758461952.

50. Alice Miranda Ollstein, "Senate Defeats Anti-Abortion Bill, as GOP Tries to Jam Dems," *Politico*, February 25, 2019, https://www.politico.com/st ory/2019/02/25/senate-defeats-anti-abortion-bill-1185531.

51. See Jonathan Abbamonte, "Why We Need the Born-Alive Abortion Survivors Protection Act," Population Research Institute, January 26, 2018, https://www.pop.org/need-born-alive-abortion-survivors-protecti on-act/; see also DeSanctis, "Why a Ban on Infanticide Is Necessary."

52. Alexandra DeSanctis, "'A Fetus That Was Born,'" *National Review*, February 25, 2020, https://www.nationalreview.com/corner/a-fetus-that -was-born/.

53. Timothy P. Carney, "The Awful Coverage of This Born-Alive Bill Shows the Media's Strongest Bias," *Washington Examiner*, February 26, 2020, https://www.washingtonexaminer.com/opinion/the-awful-coverage-of-th is-born-alive-bill-shows-the-medias-strongest-bias.

54. "Timeline: Censorship of Pro-life Speech by Big Tech," Susan B. Anthony List, https://www.sba-list.org/censorship.

55. Peter Hasson, *The Manipulators: Facebook, Google, Twitter, and Big Tech's War on Conservatives* (Washington, D.C.: Regnery, 2020), 119.

56. Ibid.

57. Samuel Chamberlain, "Facebook Apologizes after Blocking Pro-Life Group's Ads for GOP Senate Candidates," Fox News, November 1, 2018, https://www.foxnews.com/tech/facebook-apologizes-after-blocking-ads -for-gop-senate-candidates-from-pro-life-group.

58. Hasson, *The Manipulators*, 120.

59. "Timeline: Censorship of Pro-life Speech by Big Tech," SBA List.

60. April Glaser, "YouTube's Search Results for 'Abortion' Show Exactly What Anti-Abortion Activists Want Women to See," Slate, December 21, 2018, https://slate.com/technology/2018/12/youtube-search-abortion-res ults-pro-life.html.

61. Ibid.

62. Alexandra DeSanctis, "YouTube Changed 'Abortion' Search Results after a Slate Writer Complained," *National Review*, December 22, 2018, https://www.nationalreview.com/corner/youtube-changed-abortion-sear ch-results-after-a-slate-writer-complained/.

63. Lila Rose (@LilaGraceRose), "Breaking: At the request of abortion activists…," Twitter, September 14, 2021, 2:09 p.m., https://twitter.com /LilaGraceRose/status/1437840978610622465.

64. Alexandra DeSanctis, "Doctors Pioneer a Way to Halt Unwanted Chemical Abortions," *National Review*, April 13, 2021, https://www.na tionalreview.com/2021/04/doctors-pioneer-a-way-to-halt-unwanted-che mical-abortions/.

65. Alexandra DeSanctis, "Google Blocks Ad for Safe and Effective Abortion-Pill Reversal," *National Review*, September 14, 2021, https://www.natio nalreview.com/corner/google-blocks-ad-for-safe-and-effective-abortion -pill-reversal/; see also "Abortion Pill Rescue Network," Heartbeat International, https://www.heartbeatinternational.org/our-work/apr.

66. "Live Action Fights Youtube and Pinterest Censorship," Live Action, September 5, 2019, https://www.liveaction.org/youtubepinterest/.

67. Mairead McArdle, "Pro-Life Group Sends Cease-and-Desist Letters to YouTube, Pinterest Alleging Censorship," *National Review*, September 6, 2019, https://www.nationalreview.com/news/pro-life-group-alleges-ce nsorship-by-youtube-pinterest/.

68. Alexandra DeSanctis, "Four Republican Senators Write to Facebook over 'Censorship' of Pro-Life Content," *National Review*, September 11, 2019, https://www.nationalreview.com/corner/four-republican-senators-write -to-facebook-over-censorship-of-pro-life-content/.

69. "Lila Rose Claim That 'Abortion Is Never Medically Necessary' Is Inaccurate; It Is Necessary in Certain Cases to Preserve Mother's Life," Health Feedback, https://healthfeedback.org/claimreview/lila-rose-claim -that-abortion-is-never-medically-necessary-is-inaccurate-it-is-necessary -in-certain-cases-to-preserve-mothers-life-young-america-foundation/;

and see Lila Grace Rose, "Abortion Is NEVER Medically Necessary," Facebook post, August 8, 2019, https://www.facebook.com/lilagracerose /videos/508941603187665/.

70. Nora Caplan-Bricker, "'Planned Parenthood's Secret Weapon,'" *Washington Post* magazine, September 23, 2019, https://www.washingt onpost.com/news/magazine/wp/2019/09/23/feature/planned-parenthoo ds-woman-in-hollywood/.

71. Ibid.

72. See, for example, Danielle Campoamor, "We Need to See More Parents Having Abortions in Film and Television," *Marie Claire*, July 16, 2021, https://www.marieclaire.com/culture/a35802152/parents-having-aborti ons-on-tv-films/; see also Erika Smith, "It Took Almost 50 Years, but TV Is Finally Getting Abortion Stories (Mostly) Right," Refinery29, December 6, 2019, https://www.refinery29.com/en-us/abortion-on-tv-history.

73. Kathryn Jean Lopez, "No Silent Night," *National Review*, November 23, 2015, https://www.nationalreview.com/2015/11/no-silent-night-abortion -prime-time/; see also "Planned Parenthood Commemorates 100 Years of Care, Education, and Activism with the Celebration of a Century," Planned Parenthood, April 6, 2017, https://www.plannedparenthood.org /about-us/newsroom/press-releases/planned-parenthood-commemorates -100-years-of-care-education-and-activism-with-the-celebration-of-a- century.

74. Ariane Lange, "The Year Abortion Was Destigmatized On TV," BuzzFeed, December 19, 2016, https://www.buzzfeed.com/arianelange /abortions-on-tv-2016?utm_term=.by1RWmjmz#.qrGNr1w1p.

75. Stephanie Herold and Gretchen Sisson, "In 2020, TV and Film Still Couldn't Get Abortion Right," The Conversation, December 29, 2020, https://theconversation.com/in-2020-tv-and-film-still-couldnt-get-aborti on-right-152223.

76. Katharine Swindells, "Are We Making Progress in Depicting Abortion on Screen?," *New Statesman*, May 13, 2021, https://www.newstatesman .com/culture/tv-radio/2021/05/are-we-making-progress-depicting-aborti on-screen.

77. Ineye Komonibo, "Barbie Ferreira's Unpregnant Character Doesn't Exactly Fit In, but Neither Does She," Refinery29, September 10, 2020,

https://www.refinery29.com/en-us/2020/09/10016558/barbie-ferreira-un pregnant-teenage-angst-interview.

78. Ian Tuttle, "NARAL: Isn't Abortion Just Hilarious?," *National Review*, July 13, 2016, https://www.nationalreview.com/corner/naral-comedians -cars-getting-abortions/.

79. Saturday Night Live, "Weekend Update: Goober the Clown on Abortion—SNL," YouTube, November 7, 2021, https://www.youtube .com/watch?v=exSZQICbSb8.

80. Amber Heard (@realamberheard), "My body. My choice…," Twitter, August 20, 2019, 6:34 p.m., https://twitter.com/realamberheard/status/11 63942382242394112.

81. Hilary Weaver, "Dakota Johnson and Emma Stone Supported Planned Parenthood at the Oscars," *Vanity Fair*, February 26, 2017, https://www .vanityfair.com/style/2017/02/dakota-johnson-planned-parenthood-pin -oscars.

82. Alyssa Milano, Facebook post, November 29, 2018, https://www.facebo ok.com/AlyssaMilano/posts/planned-parenthood-is-health-care-thisishe althcare/2352003604871868/.

83. Cydney Henderson, "Alyssa Milano Reveals She Had Two Abortions in 1993 within Months: 'It Was My Choice,'" *USA Today*, August 19, 2019, https://www.usatoday.com/story/entertainment/celebrities/2019/08/19/al yssa-milano-reveals-she-had-two-abortions-within-months-1993/20578 29001/.

84. NBC, "Michelle Williams: Best Actress, Lim. Series, TV Movie—Golden Globes," YouTube, January 5, 2020, https://www.youtube.com/watch?v= Gj-r0tcvLh8.

85. Lynette Rice, "Golden Globes Viewership Hits Another Low," *Entertainment Weekly*, January 6, 2020, https://ew.com/golden-globes /2020/01/06/golden-globes-2020-ratings/; Chloe Melas, "Read Michelle Williams' Powerful Speech about Choice," CNN, January 8, 2020, https://www.cnn.com/2020/01/05/entertainment/michelle-williams-gol den-globes-2020-speech/index.html; Abby Gardner, "Michelle Williams Delivers Powerful Golden Globes Speech about a Woman's Right to Choose," *Glamour*, January 5, 2020, https://www.glamour.com/story /michelle-williams-speech-2020-golden-globes; Christina Cauterucci, "Michelle Williams' Surprisingly Personal Speech about Abortion Was

the Golden Globes' Most Powerful Moment," Slate, January 6, 2020, https://slate.com/culture/2020/01/michelle-williams-golden-globes-speech-video-abortion-choice.html.

86. Bill Chappell, "High School Valedictorian Swaps Speech to Speak Out against Texas' New Abortion Law," NPR, June 3, 2021, https://www.npr.org/2021/06/03/1002831545/high-school-valedictorian-swaps-speech-to-speak-out-against-texas-new-abortion-l.

87. Alexandra DeSanctis, "High-School Valedictorian Celebrates Abortion in Her Commencement Speech," *National Review*, June 4, 2021, https://www.nationalreview.com/corner/high-school-valedictorian-celebrates-abortion-in-her-commencement-speech/.

88. Chappell, "High School Valedictorian Swaps Speech."

89. The original video was removed and later reposted: Shout Your Abortion, "Abortion is for Everyone—Kids Episode," YouTube, October 7, 2020, https://www.youtube.com/watch?v=pgDVwHarxjY.

90. Alexandra DeSanctis, "Pro-Life States Should Disregard Corporate Support for Abortion," *National Review*, March 17, 2022, https://www.nationalreview.com/corner/pro-life-states-should-disregard-corporate-support-for-abortion/.

91. Julia Alexander, "Eight Hollywood Studios Threaten to Leave Georgia If an Abortion Ban Becomes Law," The Verge, May 30, 2019, https://www.theverge.com/2019/5/29/18645156/disney-production-georgia-abortion-ban-bob-iger-netflix-avengers.

92. Jackie Wattles, "The List of 180 Companies That Say Restricting Abortion Is Bad for Business," CNN, June 10, 2019, https://www.cnn.com/2019/06/10/business/ceo-letter-abortion-ad-new-york-times/index.html.

93. "Cotton Targets Corporate Attack on Pro-Life Americans," Tom Cotton, June 19, 2019, https://www.cotton.senate.gov/news/speeches/cotton-targets-corporate-attack-on-pro-life-americans.

94. Shannon Bond, "Lyft and Uber Will Pay Drivers' Legal Fees If They're Sued under Texas Abortion Law," NPR, September 3, 2021, https://www.npr.org/2021/09/03/1034140480/lyft-and-uber-will-pay-drivers-legal-fees-if-theyre-sued-under-texas-abortion-la.

95. Clare Duffy, "Lyft General Counsel: I Hope That More of Corporate America Takes a Stand on Texas Abortion Law," CNN, September 6,

2021, https://www.cnn.com/2021/09/06/tech/lyft-general-counsel-texas-abortion-law-response/index.html.

96. Anastasia Moloney, "Analysis: U.S. Abortion Curbs: Fearing Business Impact, Companies Speak Out," Reuters, November 9, 2021, https://www.reuters.com/legal/transactional/us-abortion-curbs-fearing-business-impact-companies-speak-out-2021-11-09/.

97. See "Don't Ban Equality," https://dontbanequality.com/.

98. Natalie Kitroeff and Jessica Silver-Greenberg, "Pregnancy Discrimination Is Rampant inside America's Biggest Companies," *New York Times*, February 8, 2019, https://www.nytimes.com/interactive/2018/06/15/business/pregnancy-discrimination.html.

99. Natalie Kitroeff and Jessica Silver-Greenberg, "Planned Parenthood Is Accused of Mistreating Pregnant Employees," *New York Times*, December 20, 2018, https://www.nytimes.com/2018/12/20/business/planned-parenthood-pregnant-employee-discrimination-women.html.

100. Ibid.

101. Ibid.

102. Lyman Stone, "American Women Are Having Fewer Children Than They'd Like," *New York Times*, February 13, 2018, https://www.nytimes.com/2018/02/13/upshot/american-fertility-is-falling-short-of-what-women-want.html.

Conclusion

1. Emphasis added. Frederica Mathewes-Green, *Real Choices: Listening to Women, Looking for Alternatives to Abortion* (Linthicum, Maryland: Felicity Press: 2013), 101.

2. Mikaela Kook and Shawnte Mallory, "Abortion Felt like an Excuse to Avoid Helping Us. Thankfully We Found Another Option," *USA Today*, January 15, 2022, https://www.usatoday.com/story/opinion/2022/01/15/alternatives-abortion-consider-maternity-home-shelter-programs/9131180002/?gnt-cfr=1.

3. Melanie Israel, "Defending Life: Recommendations for the 117th Congress," Heritage Foundation, March 22, 2021, https://www.heritage.org/life/report/defending-life-recommendations-the-117th-congress.

4. On this question, one of us agrees with these scholars and the other is undecided on the question. See Brief for Scholars of Jurisprudence John

M. Finnis and Robert P. George as Amicus Curiae Supporting Petitioners, *Dobbs v. Jackson Women's Health Organization*, Docket No. 19-1392 (2021), https://www.supremecourt.gov/DocketPDF/19/19-1392/185196/20210729093557582_210169a%20Amicus%20Brief%20for%20efiling%207%2029%2021.pdf; see also Charles Rice, "The Dred Scott Case of the Twentieth Century," *Houston Law Review* 10 (1973): 1067–77, https://scholarship.law.nd.edu/cgi/viewcontent.cgi?article=1809&context=law_faculty_scholarship.

5.   Virginia Allen, "Men Play Large Role in Women's Abortion Decision, Study Finds," The Daily Signal, January 31, 2022, https://www.dailysignal.com/2022/01/31/men-play-large-role-in-womens-abortion-decision-study-finds/.

6.   Lawrence B. Finer et al., "Reasons U.S. Women Have Abortions: Quantitative and Qualitative Perspectives," *Perspectives on Sexual and Reproductive Health* 37, no. 3 (2005): 110–18, https://www.guttmacher.org/sites/default/files/pdfs/pubs/psrh/full/3711005.pdf.

Index